MONETARY THEORY

ADVANCED TEXTBOOKS IN ECONOMICS

VOLUME 10

Editors:

C. J. BLISS

M. D. INTRILIGATOR

Advisory Editors:
S. M. GOLDFELD
L. JOHANSEN
D. W. JORGENSON
M. C. KEMP
J.-C. MILLERON

NORTH-HOLLAND PUBLISHING COMPANY
AMSTERDAM · NEW YORK · OXFORD

MONETARY THEORY

KEIZO NAGATANI

University of British Columbia

NORTH-HOLLAND PUBLISHING COMPANY
AMSTERDAM · NEW YORK · OXFORD

ISBN North-Holland for this volume   0 444 85032 5

Publishers

NORTH-HOLLAND PUBLISHING COMPANY
AMSTERDAM · NEW YORK · OXFORD

Sole distributors for the U.S.A. and Canada

ELSEVIER NORTH-HOLLAND, INC.
52 VANDERBILT AVENUE
NEW YORK, N.Y. 10017

Library of Congress Cataloging in Publication Data

Nagatani, Keizo.
Monetary theory.
(Advanced textbooks in economics; 10)
Translation of Kahei keizai no riron.
Includes bibliographies.
1. Money. I. Title.
HG221.N2513   332.4'01   77-23894
ISBN 0-444-85032-5

1st edition 1978
2nd printing 1980

PRINTED IN THE NETHERLANDS

Introduction to the Series

The aim of the series is to cover topics in economics, mathematical economics and econometrics, at a level suitable for graduate students or final year undergraduates specializing in economics. There is at any time much material that has become well established in journal papers and discussion series which still awaits a clear, self-contained treatment that can easily be mastered by students without considerable preparation or extra reading. Leading specialists will be invited to contribute volumes to fill such gaps. Primary emphasis will be placed on clarity, comprehensive coverage of sensibly defined areas, and insight into fundamentals, but original ideas will not be excluded. Certain volumes will therefore add to existing knowledge, while others will serve as a means of communicating both known and new ideas in a way that will inspire and attract students not already familiar with the subject matter concerned.

The Editors

Preface

This monograph is a revised version of the lecture notes I prepared for a graduate monetary theory course during years 1973–1975 at the University of British Columbia and the University of Tokyo. It consists of a total of thirteen chapters and can be covered adequately in one semester. These thirteen chapters are divided up into three parts. Part I studies individuals' demand for money. A special attention is paid to commercial banks as demanders of high-powered money. An emphasis is laid on the comparisons of various alternative formulations of demand for money. Part II is entitled "Markets". In this part we pursue some of the fundamental questions about money in a general equilibrium framework. What is a monetary economy? Why does money exist? How should we measure the benefit of money in a static exchange economy? In a dynamic economy? Other problems relevant to market organization are also discussed. Part III deals with various issues concerning money in a more conventional macroeconomic framework. The basic strategy employed in this part is to examine and compare the two opposing views on money-macro issues, namely, the Monetarism and the Keynesianism. We shall attempt to identify the two theories and assess the evidence in the light of the identified theories. Finally we draw implications of the two theories as to how money should be managed.

As lecture notes, this monograph has certain constraints in terms of the coverage of materials and objectivity. These constraints, I hope, are minimally satisfied. But the main theme of this monograph is money in general equilibrium theory. In my view, money has not been handled properly in general equilibrium analysis and this gap we must fill. A partial equilibrium model of money not only precludes the analysis of exact mechanisms through which money affects the rest of the system but also leaves many crucial variables undetermined. A case in point is price expectations. An increase in real cash balances can be interpreted as the result of an expansionary (inflationary) monetary policy if price expectations are assumed to be given and fixed. A decrease in real cash balances can also be interpreted as the result of an expansionary monetary policy if price expectations are assumed to be adjusting quickly to the actual price changes. Unless a theory as to how expectations are formed and the model is closed, any interpretation is possible. The conventional general equilibrium models, on the other hand, have largely ignored money and financial variables as well as the important problems of market adjustments. It is our hope that a workable temporary equilibrium theory which has all these essential ingredients will soon be developed. Such a theory will no doubt contribute significantly to our understanding of the problems in monetary theory and in macroeconomics in general.

In the course of preparation, I received help from many of my colleagues and graduate students in the above institutions. But my special thanks go to Erwin Diewert, John Helliwell, David Rose, Ronald Shearer and John Young, all of the University of British Columbia, and to Koichi Hamada and Takashi Negishi of the University of Tokyo. I am also grateful to Dr. Donal Donovan for his valuable editorial assistance. Needless to say, all the errors and shortcomings are solely mine. Efficient typing services were provided by Mrs. May McKee throughout my preparation. Finally, I acknowledge the kindness of the Sobunsha Publishing Company of Tokyo, from whom an earlier version of this book had been published in Japanese, to generously support the publication in the present form.

KEIZO NAGATANI
University of British Columbia

Contents

Part I

Individuals

One of the oldest unresolved problems of monetary theory
is to explain the use and holding of money.

K. Brunner and A. Meltzer (1971)

In this part we plan to survey theories of money with respect to the micro foundations of the demand for money. As Brunner and Meltzer noted, the existence of a positive demand for money is still an unresolved problem and has been made to depend on such diverse factors as the anticipation of price or interest rate changes, uncertainty, the embarrassment of default, legal restrictions, or some undefined set of services – such as "liquidity" – that money provides. Our survey inevitably reflects such diversity, but we shall try to be clear in assessing various alternative formulations.

The study of individuals' motives to hold money originates in Walras. Walras developed the notion of *encaisse désirée* (desired cash balance) on the basis of the *service d'approvisionnement* (service of storage or availability) of money. He then postulated the utility of such services and incorporated money into his system of general equilibrium in a logically consistent manner. However, Walras' utility analysis of money was defective in a few important respects and was to be remedied and refined by Schlesinger and more significantly by Patinkin. This development is described under the title The Direct Utility Approach (Chapter 1).

The portfolio theory of demand for money which constitutes the kernel of Keynes' theory is surveyed under The Risk–Return Approach (Chapter 2) and The Expected Utility Approach (Chapter 3). The main feature of these approaches is to confine attention to the asset market and study the allocation of wealth among various types of assets, money being one of them. This is in contrast to the traditional quantity theory which focused attention to the relationship between the stock of money and the flow of magnitude – the volume of transactions. The main virtue of this asset approach is that it provides a neat choice-theoretic basis for the demand for money, even though any theory of demand for money which has no bearing on the volume of expenditures must be deemed incomplete. In Chapter 2 we study the Markowitz–Tobin mean-variance model as a model of choice involving risk. We pay a particular attention to the applicability of this model to the demand for money. Chapter 3 describes the expected utility theory as a general theory of choice involving risk of which the mean-variance model can be thought of as an approximation. Again, the relevance of this theory as a theory of demand for money will be investigated.

Finally, the recent revival of interests in the exchange mechanisms and hence in the medium of exchange function of money is reflected in The Transactions Cost Approach (Chapter 4). After a very brief discussion of the classic models of Baumol–Tobin, we proceed to the precautionary demand by introducing uncertainty concerning cash needs which will be discussed using a few simple models. The study of this type of models again dates back to Edgeworth (1888). It will be found that the implications of the precautionary demand models are considerably different from those of the portfolio selection models discussed in Chapters 2 and 3. Chapter 4 (The Transactions Cost Approach) closes with a discussion of models of Commercial bank behaviour.

1

The Direct Utility Approach

(A) In the Preface to the 4th edition of the *Elements*, Walras (p. 38) wrote:[1]

> "Chiefly, however, it was my theory of money that underwent the most important changes as a result of my research on the subject from 1876 to 1899 .... In the first edition, this solution [of the problem of the value of money] was founded on a consideration of the 'circulation to be cleared', which I had borrowed from the economists. In the second and subsequent editions, however, I based the solution on the concept of a 'desired cash balance' (encaisse désirée).... Nevertheless, I continued in the second and third editions, as in the first, to write the equation of offer and demand for money apart from the other equations and as empirically given. In the present edition this equation is deduced rationally from the equations of exchange and maximum satisfaction as well as from the equations showing equality between the demand and offer of circulating capital goods. In this way, the theory of circulation and money, like the theories of exchange, production, capital formation and credit, not only posits, but solves the relevant system of equations."

[1]Page numbers are those of the English translation (1954).

According to Walras (Lesson 29), various commodities and raw materials in inventories render "services of availability" either in the larders and cupboards of consumers or in the storerooms and salerooms of producers, just as capital goods in use render productive services. Cash held by individuals can be looked upon as one such circulating capital good.

Let $A, B, C, \ldots$ be commodities, and $T, P, K, \ldots$ be productive fixed capital goods. Let $A', B', C', \ldots$ be the same commodities considered, however, as circulating capital goods, i.e., as goods rendering services of availability. If the prices of $A, B, C, \ldots$ are $1, p_b, p_c, \ldots$ in terms of the numéraire A, then the prices of the services $A', B', C', \ldots$ will be $p'_a = i$, $p'_b = ip_b$, $p'_c = ip_c, \ldots$, where i is the interest rate. Here Walras ignores the "depreciation and insurance" of circulating capital goods. Further, let U be money with its price (in terms of A), p_u. Then the price of its services U' will be $p'_u = ip_u$. Finally, let E be perpetuities whose price (in terms of A) is p_e, with the price of its services $p'_e = ip_e$.

Now consider an individual with certain initial endowments of productive capital goods as well as commodities and money. Denote the prices of the services of productive capital goods (in terms of A) by $p_t, p_p, p_k, \ldots$, his excess supplies of circulating capital goods including money by $o'_a, o'_b, o'_c, \ldots, o'_u$; and his excess demands for commodities including perpetuities by $d_a, d_b, d_c, \ldots, d_e$. Also denoting the amounts of capital goods offered by o_t, o_p, o_k, the equation of exchange can be written as

$$o_t p_t + o_p p_p + o_k p_k + \cdots + o'_a p'_a + o'_b p'_b + o'_c p'_c + \cdots + o'_u p'_u$$

$$= d_a + d_b p_b + d_c p_c + \cdots + d_e p_e. \tag{1.1}$$

For solutions for $o_t, o_p, o_k, \ldots$ and $d_a, d_b, d_c, \ldots, d_e$, we have the following conditions of maximum satisfaction (p. 278):

$$\begin{aligned}
\phi_i(q_i - o_i) &= p_i \phi_a(d_a), & i &= t, p, k, \ldots, \\
\phi_j(d_j) &= p_j \phi_a(d_a), & j &= b, c, \ldots, e,
\end{aligned} \tag{1.2}$$

where q are the amounts of initial holdings. As for $o'_a, o'_b, o'_c, \ldots$, we have (p. 320)

$$\phi'_j(q'_j - o'_j) = p'_j \phi_a(d_a), \qquad j = b, c, \ldots, \tag{1.3}$$

where q' are the initial holdings of the services of availability. Finally, as for money o_u, let his desired quantities of the services of availability of A', B', C', ... and perpetual net income E', *not in kind but in money*, be $\alpha, \beta, \gamma, \ldots, \varepsilon$. Then for these quantities, we have the following conditions of maximum satisfaction (p. 321):

$$\begin{aligned}
\phi_\alpha(\alpha) &= p'_a \phi_a(d_a), \\
\phi_\beta(\beta) &= p'_b \phi_a(d_a), \\
\phi_\varepsilon(\varepsilon) &= p'_a \phi_a(d_a).
\end{aligned} \tag{1.4}$$

Upon solving (1.1)–(1.4), $\alpha, \beta, \gamma, \ldots, \varepsilon$ will each be a function of $(p_t, p_p, p_k, \ldots; p_b, p_c, \ldots, p_e; p'_a, p'_b, \ldots, p'_u)$. The value of these quantities in terms of A will be

$$\alpha p'_a + \beta p'_b + \gamma p'_c + \cdots + \varepsilon p'_a.$$

So the excess supply of money will be

$$\begin{aligned}
o_u &= q_u - \frac{\alpha p'_a + \beta p'_b + \cdots + \varepsilon p'_a}{p'_u} \\
&= q_u - \left(\alpha \frac{p_a}{p_u} + \beta \frac{p_b}{p_u} + \cdots + \varepsilon \frac{p_a}{p_u} \right).
\end{aligned} \tag{1.5}$$

Thus, the optimum amount of cash holdings is determined in exactly the same way as those of other types of inventory goods through the notion of the services of availability.

Walras' theory of demand for money is unconvincing in two important respects. First, what are the reasons that individuals wish to hold stores of goods, i.e., what causes individuals to appreciate services of availability of circulating capital? Second, given that individuals wish to hold inventories, what determines the choice between money and other forms of circulating capital goods?

As for the first question, we note that Walras mentions

"uncertainty" in two places in Lesson 29 (pp. 317, 318), but these passages indicate that Walras tended to ignore it. For example, on p. 317:

> "In a real operating economy, every consumer, whether landowner, labourer or capitalist, has at every moment a fairly exact idea of (1) what stocks of [final] products he ought to have for his convenience, and (2) what cash balance he ought to have, not only in order to replenish these stocks and make current purchases of consumers' goods and services for daily consumption while waiting to receive rents, wages and interest payable at fixed future dates, but also in order to acquire new capital goods. There may be a small element of uncertainty which is due solely to the difficulty of foreseeing possible changes in the data of the problem. If, however, we suppose these data constant for a given period of time and if we suppose the prices of goods and services and also the dates of their purchase and sale to be known for the whole period, there will be no occasion for uncertainty."

The relevant passage on p. 318 makes the same point regarding entrepreneurs. With the amounts of payments and receipts along with their dates all known for certain, however, there would be no demand for money as the source of liquidity, i.e., as reserves against contingencies. Instead, Walras seems to depend on the lack of synchronization between payments and receipts for some reasons external to the individuals. While such lack of synchronization compels them to carry stores of goods, it hardly provides room for choice among different types of inventory goods. This leads us to the second question raised above.

If the institutional arrangements external to individuals are the only reason for individuals to carry inventories of goods, what explanation could we give to the choice among different types of goods to be stored? In particular, why would they wish to hold cash rather than some other goods? To explain such portfolio choice, we would have to postulate differential storage costs and transaction costs. But as his ignoring of the "depreciation and insurance" of circulating capital suggests, he does not consider these costs either. Walras merely postulates a utility function which is additive in different types of services of availability without any explanation. It is for these reasons that Patinkin argued that "Walras did not succeed in providing a conceptual framework which logically entitles him to introduce the service d'approvisionnement of money into the utility function" [Patinkin (1965, pp. 549–550)].

(B) Karl Schlesinger (1914), one of the important followers of Walras, develops a similar analytical framework but carefully distinguishes between the demand for money arising out of the known patterns of payments and receipts over time (the "transactions demand") and the demand for money due to uncertainty concerning the amounts and the dates of these transactions (the "precautionary demand").[2]

Schlesinger restricts the use of the utility concept to the latter case, i.e., the case where uncertainty and risk exists. [See, however, Patinkin (1965, p. 576, fn. 21).] Moving directly to this uncertainty case, we find in Schlesinger (p. 29):

> "Every economic unit reckons with the sudden appearance of consumption needs, as well as with unexpectedly favourable new business opportunities

[2]*Theorie der Geld- und Kreditwirtschaft* (1914). An English translation of Ch. iii of this book is in International Economic Papers (1959), pp. 20–38. Unfortunately, this translation is the only source available to me to date. The famous study by Howard Ellis (1934), *German Monetary Theory 1905–1933*, is totally helpless, for Ellis dismisses Schlesinger by simply saying that Schlesinger's mathematical exposition in a foreign tongue "prevents my utilizing" the book (footnote on p. 175).

or unexpected business expenditures. Similarly, account has to be taken of the possibility of an interruption in the sales – whether of labour, services or products – which provide the economic unit with an income. Unless these goods are traded on a stock or product exchange, individual receipts cannot be determined in advance at all, and the total amount of receipts can be so determined only approximately, according to the law of large numbers.

Let us suppose that chance deficits cannot be covered by credits. They can then be covered only by selling the firm or part of its assets negotiable in the form of shares, or else by cash reserves held against such contingencies. Depending on the intensity of frictions, . . . , the sale of a firm or its assets may become a very costly affair. If these frictions are considerable, it may well pay to forestall this risk by large cash reserves which, being usable for all kinds of needs, are in any case preferable to stocks of particular goods. The individual loss involved in not earning an interest on these cash reserves can be regarded as a risk premium.

. . . .

Cash reserves are increased to the point where the real value of the resulting annual loss of interest is less than the marginal utility of the premium determined by the sum of the two elements: (a) the product of the possibility that the losses forestalled by higher reserves will actually occur in the course of the year, times the real value of these losses; plus (b) the real value of the insurance quota in excess of mathematical equivalence which the individual is prepared to pay in these, as in any other, insurance transactions. We have to prove that there exists a point at which loss of interest equals marginal utility of [insurance] . . . ."

Now, let $f(r_v)$ be the marginal utility of the insurance service of a real reserve r_v, and let i be the annual interest rate. Then the equilibrium of the firm, says Schlesinger, is expressed by

$$i = f(r_v). \tag{1.6}$$

This expression is not quite right. Since the right-hand side measures the contribution of an extra dollar put in reserve and since i is the interest a dollar could earn per year, the left-hand side must be the marginal utility of the marginal i dollars. The minor error aside, Schlesinger improves on Walras by laying down the basis for the utility of money. From (1.6) or its corrected version, the cash reserve in terms of money can be written as

$$r_v p_u = \phi(i), \qquad \phi' < 0. \tag{1.7}$$

Recalling the dependence of the desired cash reserve on the (expected) volume of transactions, (1.7) may be written

$$r_v = \frac{\phi(i, v)}{p_u} \tag{1.8}$$

Adding the first source of demand (in the absence of uncertainty) which depends exclusively on the volume of trade, and aggregating over all units, the aggregate demand for money can be written as

$$Q_u = \frac{F_v(V) + \Phi_v(i, V)}{p_u}, \tag{1.9}$$

which shows a remarkable resemblance to our modern demand for money functions.

(C) So much for history. Let us proceed to Patinkin. In his book, *Money, Interest and Prices*, the utility analysis is presented in Chs. V–VII and Mathematical Appendix 2. We shall confine ourselves to Chs. V and VI.

Patinkin begins his analysis with the following remark (p. 79):

> "It is essential to make clear at the outset the sense in which 'utility of money' will be used in the present discussion. Clearly it does not represent Marshall's use of this term. Nor is it intended to denote the utility of money commodity; indeed, we continue to assume a fiat paper money precisely in order to avoid any ambiguities on this score. Nor, finally, is it intended to denote the 'marginal utility of the goods for which the money can be exchanged'. Instead, our concern is with the utility of *holding* money, not with that of *spending* it. This is the concept implicit in all cash-balance approaches to the quantity theory of money; and it is the one that will be followed explicitly here."

Patinkin employs the Hicksian notion of "weeks", and assumes that payments and receipts on commodity contracts occur randomly during the week. The redemption of bonds is assumed to take place at fixed dates. Thus if an individual runs out of cash during the week, he must either default temporarily on the payment which has fallen due or cash his bonds prior to maturity. In either case he incurs some embarrassment or extra bother. These embarrassments or bothers constitute the source of utility of money. Ch. V deals with the simplest case where commodity prices, interest rates on bonds, and non-property incomes are all known for certain over the entire horizon so that the only uncertainty is that associated with the timing of payments. To simplify analysis, he further assumes that relative commodity prices remain constant so that all commodities may be bundled into one composite commodity. His assumption of the constant absolute price of this composite commodity makes life even simpler.

Consider an individual who starts with the initial holding

of money and bonds, M_0, B_0, and has a two-week horizon. All bonds mature in one week. One unit of bonds is a promise to pay one dollar at the end of one week. Hence its price is $1/(1 + r)$ if r is the weekly interest rate. Besides these initial endowments, he earns (or inherits) $\bar{z}_1$, $\bar{z}_2$ in kind over the two weeks. Assume that the individual possesses a preference which we represent by

$$U = f\left(z_1, \frac{M_1}{p}, z_2, \frac{M_0}{p}\right), \tag{1.10}$$

where z_1, z_2 are the commodity consumption in week 1 and week 2, respectively, and M_1 is the amount of cash to be held during the second week. The f function may be taken to be a monotone increasing, quasi-concave function of all its arguments. The budget constraints are

$$z_1 + \frac{1}{1+r}\frac{B_1}{p} + \frac{M_1}{p} = \bar{z}_1 + \frac{B_0}{p} + \frac{M_0}{p}, \tag{1.11}$$

$$z_2 = \bar{z}_2 + \frac{B_1}{p} + \frac{M_1}{p}, \tag{1.12}$$

where B_1 is the number of one-dollar bonds carried over to the second week. The choice variables are of course z_1, z_2, M_1 and B_1. Maximizing U with respect to these choice variables, we would obtain the demand functions of the form

$$z_1 = z_1\left(\bar{z}_1, \bar{z}_2, r, \frac{B_0 + M_0}{p}\right),$$

$$z_2 = z_2\left(\bar{z}_1, \bar{z}_2, r, \frac{B_0 + M_0}{p}\right),$$

$$\frac{B_1}{p} = b_1\left(\bar{z}_1, \bar{z}_2, r, \frac{B_0 + M_0}{p}\right), \tag{1.13}$$

$$\frac{M_1}{p} = m_1\left(\bar{z}_1, \bar{z}_2, r, \frac{B_0 + M_0}{p}\right).$$

These demand functions have the following properties. Given the values of "real" variables, $\bar{z}_1, \bar{z}_2, r$, an equi-pro-

portional change in (M_0, B_0, p) leaves the "real" demands
undisturbed. That is, z_1, z_2 are homogeneous of degree zero
in (M_0, B_0, p), while M_1, B_1 are homogeneous of degree one
in the same variables. On the other hand, a change in M_0
and/or B_0 alone, or a change in p alone, would generally
affect the quantities demanded of commodities, bonds and
money. For example, a fall in p alone would probably
increase these demands. This fact, i.e., the dependence of
real demands on the absolute price level, provides the microeconomic rationale of Patinkin's real balance effect.
Another way of putting it is that the demand for money M_1
will not be unitary elastic with respect to its price $(1/p)$, but
the elasticity will be somewhat less than unity, providing
$1 > \partial m_1 / \partial (M_0 + B_0)/p > 0$. This property of the demand for
money function contains the essence of Patinkin's work. It
shows that the demand for money will not be identically
equal to the supply. The demand and supply will be different
in general, which effectively invalidates Say's Identity.

As is well known, Patinkin's major purpose was to correct
a logical error contained in the classical quantity theory of
money as part of the general equilibrium system. According
to Patinkin, the point of departure was the quantity equation
of the form

$$M = kPy,$$

where M is the nominal amount of money, P is the absolute
level of money prices, y is the real volume of transactions,
and k is an (institutional) parameter relating M to Py, the
nominal volume of transactions. This equation had traditionally been interpreted as the equation for the money
market whose role was to determine the absolute price level
P. Namely, given k and y, once M was specified, a specific
level of P would follow. This equation was then used to
deduce a proportionate *causal* relation from M to P, i.e., a
doubling of M will entail a doubling of P. In order for this
proposition to be true, it was thought necessary that the real
variable y be independent of the absolute price level,

depending only on relative money prices (the "homogeneity postulate"). But if so, how should we explain the causal relation from M to P? Imagine an economy which was originally in general equilibrium at $M = M_0$ and $P = P_0$, and at some specific relative prices. Let M be increased from M_0 to M_1 in a manner which does not disturb relative prices. This should create a *pari passu* increase in P from P_0 to P_1. But by assumption, the markets for real goods have not been disturbed by the initial monetary increase and hence are still in equilibrium. By Walras' Law, the market for the remaining good, money, must also still be in equilibrium at now $M = M_1$ which must mean $P = P_1$. But nowhere in this argument have we explained the rise in the price level. There is no market force that can create the requisite price increase. On these grounds, Patinkin argued that such a dichotomy was invalid and arrived at a conclusion that the general dependence of various excess demand functions on the absolute price level (via the real balance effect) was the essence of a money economy. We shall see below how his system with the real balance effect resolves the above difficulty.

We have so far been concerned with what Patinkin called the "individual experiment". But the quantity theory concerns the "market experiment" whereby the nominal quantity of money is increased for the economy. To do such a market experiment, let us suppose that the previous individual demand functions are aggregated into the following functions:

$$z = z\left(\bar{y}, r, \frac{M}{P}\right) \quad \text{demand for commodities,} \qquad (1.14)$$

$$\frac{B}{P} = b\left(\bar{y}, r, \frac{M}{P}\right) \quad \text{demand for bonds,} \qquad (1.15)$$

$$\frac{M}{P} = m\left(\bar{y}, r, \frac{M}{P}\right) \quad \text{demand for money.} \qquad (1.16)$$

Here $\bar{y}$ represents the aggregate supply of commodities. If we imagine an economy consisting of a group of young generation whose demand is z_1 and a group of old generation whose demand is z_2, then the aggregate demand z is a weighted sum of these z_1's and z_2's. Since we assume that these goods are all perishables, we can similarly aggregate $\bar{z}_1$ and $\bar{z}_2$ into $\bar{y}$. We also assume that bonds are all private bonds so that the total net value of bonds is zero. Hence bonds do not appear as part of wealth. Money, on the other hand, is assumed to be purely "outside" money.[3] The equilibrium of this system may be written

$$z\left(\bar{y}, r, \frac{\bar{M}}{P}\right) = \bar{y}, \tag{1.17}$$

$$b\left(\bar{y}, r, \frac{\bar{M}}{P}\right) = 0, \tag{1.18}$$

$$m\left(\bar{y}, r, \frac{\bar{M}}{P}\right) = \frac{\bar{M}}{P}. \tag{1.19}$$

Suppose the economy was originally in equilibrium at $y = y_0$, $r = r_0$, $M = M_0$ and $P = P_0$. Suppose M was increased to M_1 once and for all. From the nature of the demand functions (1.14)–(1.16), we know that *if* the price level rose equiproportionately to $P_1 = P_0 \times (M_1/M_0)$, with y and r unchanged, then the equilibrium would have been restored. But a complete analysis cannot stop here; it must explain the dynamics of adjustments that restore the equilibrium. Patinkin devotes the main portion of Part Two of his book to this analysis. In essence, his analysis rests on the following dynamic model:

$$DP = \alpha\left\{z\left(\bar{y}, r, \frac{M}{P}\right) - \bar{y}\right\}, \tag{1.20}$$

$$Dr = -\beta b\left(\bar{y}, r, \frac{M}{P}\right), \tag{1.21}$$

[3]When money consists of a mix of outside and inside money, the money that appears as the third argument of these demand functions is the outside money, whereas the money on the left-hand side of (1.16) or the right-hand side of (1.19) is the total of the two monies.

where D denotes the derivative with respect to time, and where α and β are some positive coefficients of adjustments. Equation (1.20) states that the excess demand for commodities pushes up prices. Similarly, (1.21) states that the excess demand for bonds pushes down the interest rate.

To fix ideas, let us assume with Patinkin that the real balance effect is positive in every market, i.e., $z_3 > 0$, $b_3 > 0$. Let us also assume that a rise in the interest rate increases the demand for bonds, but reduces (if anything) the demand for commodities, i.e., $z_2 \leq 0$, $b_2 > 0$. On the basis of these assumptions, we can study the dynamics of this system using a diagram. In Figure 1.1, we plot P on the horizontal axis and r on the vertical axis. In view of the above assumptions, the curve representing the commodity market equilibrium (1.17) may be shown by a downward-sloping curve for given values of $\bar{y}$, $\bar{M}$. Similarly, the bond market equilibrium (1.18) becomes an upward-sloping curve in the same space. The curves C_0 and B_0 in Figure 1.1 are these equilibrium relations for the commodity market and the bond market, respectively, at $M = M_0$, $y = y_0$. The intersection E_0 of these two curves determines $P = P_0$ and $r = r_0$. This was the situation before the monetary change. An increase in M from M_0 to M_1 causes an outward shift in both these curves. Thus the C_1 curve now represents the (P, r) combination that equilibrates

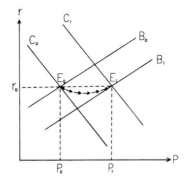

Figure 1.1

the commodity market. Similarly, the B_1 curve is now the new bond market equilibrium relation. At the new intersection E_1, it is shown that $P = P_1$ and $r = r_0$. That this must be so can be seen quite simply. Suppose, to the contrary, that the new intersection is at P_2 (not shown in Figure 1.1) such that $P_0 < P_2 < P_1$. Then at $P = P_2$, $M_1/P_2 > M_0/P_0$. The commodity market equilibrium would then require $r > r_0$, while the bond market equilibrium would need $r < r_0$, an impossibility. Likewise, the case where $P_2 > P_1$ can be refuted. Hence the new intersection must be at $P = P_1$ and $r = r_0$.

Having identified the new equilibrium position, the adjustment path from E_0 to E_1 can be studied from (1.20) and (1.21), which indicates a path as shown by the arrow in Figure 1.1. Thus, according to the above model à la Patinkin, a once-and-for-all monetary increase generates a temporary decline in the interest rate, but as time lapses, the interest rate turns upward again. In the meantime, the price level keeps rising. This dynamic adjustment process comes to a halt when the interest rate has returned to the original level and the price level has undergone the same proportionate increase as the nominal money supply. To summarize, the initial increase in M creates excess demands in all the markets via the real balance effect, and it is exactly such excess demands that cause P to rise. But when all these dynamic adjustments have been completed, all the real variables, including r, have returned to their old levels, with only P capturing the permanent effect in full. For a more complete analysis, see Chs. IX–XII in Patinkin (1965).

Patinkin (1965, p. 21) maintained that the existence of a real balance effect is the "*sine qua non*" of monetary theory, and that its role "depends not on the strength of this effect but only on its existence". But in what sense is it the *sine qua non* of monetary theory? What is the real balance effect? Was Patinkin's charge against classical and neoclassical monetary theory really valid? We shall look at these issues from two related but different angles. The first is the nature of equilibria with reference to which the effect of monetary changes is being studied. This is the well-known distinction between Temporary Equilibrium and Full Equilibrium due to Hicks (1939, 1946). The second concerns the validity of the conventional non-monetary demand theory and its comparative static propositions.

(D) Let us begin with the first. Consider an economy which extends over time in the sense that the agents' time horizon contains multiple periods. This means that the agents' decisions in any period have the nature of intertemporal resource allocation. This fact that the agents possess a horizon of multiple periods is a necessary condition for a dynamic economy. However, it is not a sufficient condition. To make an economy dynamic, we must provide these agents with an instrument by means of which to effect intertemporal resource allocation. Namely, there must exist in the system a good which serves as a store of value. We call such a good a capital good. Note that money is one such capital good. Another important source of dynamics is the dynamics of expectations. Expectations are said to be endogenous if the agents form their future prospects on the basis of the actual developments of the economy.[4] When all these conditions are satisfied, the current decisions of the agents, and hence, of the economy as a whole depends on the past (by the amount of capital goods) and also on the future (by the future prospects). The temporary equilibrium is a state in which all the markets operated in the current period have cleared *relative to given states of legacy and expectations.* Under the assumption of flexible prices, the economy may be taken to be always in (temporary) equilibrium. In con-

---

[4]A special case in which all the futures markets exist has been studied by Arrow (1952, 1964) and Debreu (1959). See Chapter 8 below. In this case, all the (discounted) future prices are quoted by the market in the current period and hence all contracts for the entire horizon will be concluded in the current period. But we shall assume throughout that the futures markets are scarce.

trast, the full or statical equilibrium is a state in which the stock of capital goods is of the optimal size and expectations are consistent so that the agents repeat identical decisions period after period. It is important, therefore, to make clear which equilibrium we are referring to when we speak of the real balance effect.

Archibald and Lipsey (1958) challenged Patinkin emphasizing the distinction between the two equilibria. They concluded that "the real balance effect is a transitory phenomenon, which is operative only in some disequilibrium situations", and hence, that "if we are interested in those well-known propositions of the quantity theory which are propositions in comparative statics, the real balance effect is irrelevant". Putting it differently, disturb an individual in his personal equilibrium by giving him any large amount of cash. Throughout the adjustment process, his consumption will be larger than in his original equilibrium. But when the adjustments have been completed, the individual will be exactly in his original equilibrium position with the same amounts of consumption and real balances as he had enjoyed before the disturbance. This fact came to be known as the Invariance Principle. To illustrate their point, Archibald and Lipsey presented a simple graphical analysis of a consumer. But since their graphical analysis is a little short for our purpose, let us formulate an explicit dynamic programming model of a consumer and prove their proposition.

Let us assume the consumer has a T-period horizon over which he expects a constant stream of money income Y. Besides, he owns a certain amount of cash at the very start. His objective is to maximize the utility sum

$$\sum_{t=1}^{T} U(x^t, m^t), \tag{1.22}$$

where x is an n-vector of consumption of non-money goods, m are real balances, and the U function is assumed to be non-decreasing, concave and twice continuously differentiable in its arguments. The side constraints are

$$p_m m^{t-1} + Y - px^t - p_m m^t = 0, \qquad t = 1, 2, \ldots, T, \quad (1.23)$$

$$m^0 \text{ and } m^{T+1} \text{ given,} \quad (1.24)$$

where p is the n-vector of money prices of the non-money goods, and p_m is the money price of real balances.

Define the Lagrangian

$$L(x, m, \lambda) \equiv \sum_{t=1}^{T} [U(x^t, m^t)$$
$$+ \lambda^t (p_m m^{t-1} + Y - px^t - p_m m^t)]. \quad (1.25)$$

Maximizing L with respect to the triplet (x, m, λ), we get

$$p_m m^{t-1} + Y - px^t - p_m m^t = 0,$$

$$U_x^t - \lambda^t p = 0, \quad (1.26)$$

$$U_m^t - p_m(\lambda^t - \lambda^{t+1}) = 0.$$

This dynamic programming problem can be solved as follows. First, solve the second set of equations for x^t as $x^t = x(p, m^t, \lambda^t)$. Then substitute these solutions into the first and the third equations. These equations become a pair of difference equations in (m, λ), which, given m^0 and m^{T+1}, will determine a unique path of (m^t, λ^t) for all $t = 1, 2, \ldots, T$. Finally, substituting these values of (m^t, λ^t) into the solution functions for x, we get the path of x^t.

Suppose the individual starts with an arbitrary m^0. Then he will generally adjust both x and m from one period to the next. This generates a sequence of temporary equilibrium solutions which depends not only on p but also on m^{t-1}, namely, the real balance effect is in operation. But now let the time horizon extend indefinitely and consider the full equilibrium in which both m and λ have settled down to stationary values. Denoting the full-equilibrium values by asterisks, we get from (1.26)

$$Y - px^* = 0,$$

$$U_x^* - \lambda^* p = 0, \quad (1.27)$$

$$U_m^* = 0.$$

The first two equations of (1.27) are the familiar equations in the usual non-monetary consumer theory. The only difference is that U_x^* contains m^*. The last equation means that the individual is sated with the services of cash in hand.

What can we say about the effects of money on the full equilibrium solution (x^*, m^*)? Specifically, what will be the effect of a change in the initial balance m_0? It is evident that the system of equation (1.27) is free from m_0, which implies that (x^*, m^*) is independent of m_0. Also, an equi-proportionate change in (P, Y) leaves (x^*, m^*) unchanged. Hence the Invariance Principle is valid.

Many economists found the Invariance Principle puzzling and conjectured that it must be due to the absence of any income-earning assets in the Archibald–Lipsey model. Clower and Burstein (1960), however, subsequently showed that the principle remained valid in a more general model with income-earning assets. The essence of the Clower–Burstein argument can be captured in a model similar to the above but which has a productive capital good. We assume that the individual can hold this capital k which reproduces itself following the production function $f(k)$. The individual is assumed to freely sell this capital at a given price P_k. Also we introduce a positive time preference parameter δ for generality. His problem now becomes maximizing

$$\sum_{t=1}^{T} (1 + \delta)^{-t} U(x^t, m^t),$$

subject to

$$p_m m^{t-1} + p_k f(k^{t-1}) + Y - px^t - p_m m^t - p_k k^t = 0,$$
$$t = 1, 2, \ldots, T, \quad (1.28)$$

$$m^0, m^{T+1}, k^0, k^{T+1} \text{ given.} \quad (1.29)$$

The first-order conditions for this maximization problem are given as follows:

$$p_m m^{t-1} + p_k f(k^{t-1}) + Y - px^t - p_m m^t - p_k k^t = 0,$$

$$U_x^t - \lambda^t p = 0,$$

$$U_m^t - p_m \left[\lambda^t - \frac{\lambda^{t+1}}{1+\delta} \right] = 0,$$

$$\lambda^{t+1} \frac{f'(k^t)}{1+\delta} - \lambda^t = 0.$$

(1.30)

Suppose a full-equilibrium exists. In such a state, (1.30) becomes

$$p_k [f(k^*) - k^*] + Y - px^* = 0,$$

$$U_x^* - \lambda^* p = 0,$$

$$U_m^* - \frac{\delta}{1+\delta} p_m \lambda^* = 0,$$

$$f'(k^*) - (1+\delta) = 0.$$

(1.31)

The last equation in (1.31) is a well-known condition for a steady state. If δ is a given constant and if the production function $f(k^*)$ satisfies this last equation at some finitely positive k^*, then the full-equilibrium capital stock follows immediately from this equation. Apart from this complication, the system (1.31) is the same as the system (1.27) in that the solution (x^*, m^*, k^*) is independent of m^0 and homogeneous of degree zero in (P, Y, P_k). In other words, the Invariance Principle remains valid.

But is this principle really general? Liviatan (1965) contended that it was not. He argued that there was no assurance that the dynamic systems described above should always reach a stationary equilibrium. If not, a secular growth of wealth or a secular shrinkage of wealth would be the consequence of a monetary disturbance. And such possibilities were open whenever there were income-earning assets. In terms of our second model, this possibility becomes reality whenever the rate of return on the income-earning capital is bounded away from δ. Another contention may be put against the Invariance Principle with regard to the static nature of the behaviour underlying these dynamic models. In these models, the monetary change was a once-and-for-all change and the individual's expectations about the future prices were completely static. But what if the monetary change were of continuous nature, i.e., what if there were a continuous injection of money into the system? Such a continuous injection of money into the system would generate a continuous change in the money prices. If individuals took such a change in the money prices into account, their decisions could be affected permanently by the monetary change. It is exactly this type of problem that the modern monetary growth theory is concerned with, and we shall see in Chapter 12 that the Invariance Principle need not hold in such a case.

(E) The Real Balance Effect and the Slutsky Equation: While there is obviously no reason why real balances should be in the utility function, it is true that this is a way of recognizing the satisfaction a consumer derives from holding cash. If real balances were an argument of the utility function, the conventional demand theory might be regarded as a special case and the validity of such a theory must be investigated. This was the problem Lloyd (1964) addressed himself to. The complexity which arises from the inclusion of real balances in the utility function derives from the fact that the money price of real balances, p_m, is not just another money price independent of the rest of the money prices p, but is actually a function of p. In terms of our first model (which is what Lloyd has), the temporary equilibrium solution can be written as

$$x^t = x(p, p_m, Y + M^{t-1}),$$

or, using the homogeneity property,

$$x^t = x\left(\frac{p}{p_m}, \ \frac{Y + M^{t-1}}{p_m}\right).$$

Now the real balance effect may be defined as $(\partial x^t/\partial M^{t-1})|p = \text{constant}$. This is the "defined" real balance effect, to use the term of Lloyd. But obviously, there is another source of real balance effect, namely, the effect on x^t of a change in one of the components of p, say, p_j, since it affects p_m. Lloyd called it the "derived" real balance effect. Performing the analysis and evaluating $\partial x_i/\partial p_j$, Lloyd arrived at a conclusion that the existence of the real balance effect has a grave effect on the demand theory because it deprives the Slutsky equation of all its empirical implications. He further argued that not only the temporary equilibrium solution, but also the full equilibrium solution, suffered from this effect.

Lloyd considers the problem of maximizing $U(x, m)$ subject to $\bar{M} + Y - px - p_m m = 0$, and writes the first-order conditions for this maximization problem as

$$\bar{M} + Y - px - p_m m = 0,$$

$$U_x - \lambda p = 0, \tag{1.32}$$

$$U_m - \lambda p_m = 0.$$

From this he gets for a change in p_j,

$$\frac{\partial x_i}{\partial p_j} = \frac{1}{A}\left(x_j A_{0i} + \lambda A_{ji} + m\frac{\partial p_m}{\partial p_j}A_{0i} + \lambda\frac{\partial p_m}{\partial p_j}A_{mi}\right), \tag{1.33}$$

where

$$A = \begin{bmatrix} 0 & -p_1 & \cdots & -p_n & -p_m \\ -p_1 & U_{11} & \cdots & U_{1n} & U_{1m} \\ \vdots & \vdots & & & \\ -p_n & U_{n1} & \cdots & U_{nn} & U_{nm} \\ -p_m & U_{m1} & & U_{mn} & U_{mm} \end{bmatrix}, \tag{1.34}$$

and A_{pq} is the p, qth cofactor of A. Of the four terms on the right-hand side of (1.33), the first two terms are familiar. The last two terms represent the latter type of real balance effect. This derived real balance effect is itself a sum of an income effect and a substitution effect (between the ith good and real balances), each weighted by $\partial p_m/\partial p_j$. While $A_{0i}/A = -\partial x_i/\partial Y = \partial x_i/\partial \bar{M}$ and $\partial p_m/\partial p_i$ are capable of economic interpretations and measurement, the term A_{mi}/A is not. Thus the sign or the magnitude of the derived real balance effect is ambiguous. Furthermore, from (1.33) the substitution effect or the income-compensated change in x_i becomes

$$\left.\frac{\partial x_i}{\partial p_j}\right|_{u=\text{constant}} = \frac{\lambda}{A}\left(A_{ji} + \frac{\partial p_m}{\partial p_j}A_{mi}\right). \tag{1.35}$$

In the conventional analysis, the second term on the right-hand side of (1.35) is absent. From the symmetry of $[A]$ and the negative semi-definiteness of the inverse $[A]^{-1}$, the usual properties of the demand functions follow. But in the presence of real balances, none of these properties seems to follow. First, the symmetry property does not follow, since it would require the equality between $(\partial p_m/\partial p_j)A_{mi}$ and $(\partial p_m/\partial p_i)A_{mj}$. Second, let $j = i$ in (1.35) and we get

$$\left.\frac{\partial x_i}{\partial p_i}\right|_{u=\text{constant}} = \frac{\lambda}{A}\left(A_{ii} + \frac{\partial p_m}{\partial p_i}A_{mi}\right),$$

whose negativity cannot be established on a priori grounds. Lloyd (1971) later offered a partial consolation by showing that the traditional Slutsky results are retained if the utility function satisfies the condition of weak separability between goods and real balances.

Lloyd then turned to the full equilibrium and argued that the derived real balance effect persisted in the full equilibrium and hence all these troubles. Lloyd wrote the first-order conditions for the full equilibrium as

$$Y - px^* = 0,$$

$$U_x^* - \lambda^* p = 0, \tag{1.36}$$

$$U_m^* - \lambda^* p_m = 0.$$

The persistence of p_m in (1.36) gave rise to his conclusion. But this formulation is not right; p_m is *not* the price of the services of real balances, but the price of real balances as an asset. What is relevant here is of course the former, which should measure the opportunity cost of holding cash. In the absence of a positive interest rate, such an opportunity cost is zero, and hence the price of the services of real balances is zero. In other words, the third equation becomes $U_m^* = 0$. Recall equation (1.27). When correctly formulated, there should be no derived real balance effect in the full equilibrium in an economy where money is the only asset. Archibald and Lipsey were perfectly right.

This suggests two things. First, in order to deal squarely with money, which is a capital good, one needs an appropriate capital-theoretic framework. The analysis of Lloyd, even of the temporary equilibrium solution, is quite questionable. Second, in the presence of income-earning assets, p_m will not disappear even in the full equilibrium. See equation (1.31). In such a case, Lloyd's concern is wholly justified, although we must admit that he is right for wrong reasons.[5]

Let us come back, by way of conclusion, to the central theme of the present chapter. Patinkin elaborated on Walras' notion of *service d'approvisionnement* of money, incorporated money into the utility analysis, and arrived at an "integration" of monetary and value theories. The implied real balance effect on the commodity market has provided a theory as to how monetary disturbances are to be eliminated through adjustments in many inter-related markets. The temporary real balance effect is consistent with the "final neutrality" of money, as we saw above. The reader is referred to an excellent survey on this matter by Johnson (1962).

---

[5]The fact that the individual holds real balances only to a point where the marginal utility of real balances is equal to a positive opportunity cost in the presence of income-earning assets has been pointed out and labelled the "non-optimality of laissez faire" by Samuelson (1969). For more on this matter, see Chapter 13. If $U_m^* = 0$ corresponds to a social optimum, then one can say that the real balance effect is absent in a socially optimal full-equilibrium.

Also see Samuelson (1968).

But what is the utility of money in the first place? Why does the Patinkinesque individual feel "embarrassed" when presented with a bill within a week? Why does he incur an "extra bother" cashing bonds before maturity? Why does he not simply issue bonds, especially since there is no uncertainty between weeks? It is plain that it is not just uncertainty concerning payments but the existence of various market imperfections that causes him to hold cash. Throwing cash into the utility function obscures this peculiar nature of the utility of money, and precludes further analysis of these market imperfections. Secondly, there is no explanation as to what the nature of the debts is that the individual is carrying. Are these debts related to his current spending plans? If so, the utility of money can be determined only in relation to the spending plan. If not, there is not much operational meaning to the utility of money.

References

Archibald, G. C. and R. G. Lipsey, "Monetary and value theory: A critique of Lange and Patinkin", *Review of Economic Studies* (1958); also in: R. W. Clower, ed., *Monetary theory* (Harmondsworth, 1969).

Arrow, K. J., "The role of securities in the optimal allocation of risk-bearing", *Review of Economic Studies* (1964). This is a translation of a French original (1952).

Brunner, K. and A. L. Meltzer, "The use of money: Money in the theory of an exchange economy", *American Economic Review* (1971).

Clower, R. W. and M. L. Burstein, "On the invariance of demand for cash and other assets", *Review of Economic Studies* (1960).

Debreu, G., *Theory of value* (New York, 1959) ch. 7.

Edgeworth, F. Y., "Mathematical theory of banking", *Journal of the Royal Statistical Society* (1888).

Hicks, J. R., *Value and capital* (Oxford, 1939, 1946) parts III and IV.

Johnson, H. G., "Monetary theory and policy", *American Economic Review* (1962); also in his *Essays in Monetary Economics* (Chicago, Ill., 1967).

Liviatan, N., "On the long-run theory of consumption and real balances", *Oxford Economic Papers* (1965).

Lloyd, C., "The real balance effect and the Slutsky equation", *Journal of Political Economy* (1964).

Lloyd, C., "Preferences, separability and the Patinkin model", *Journal of Political Economy* (1971).

Patinkin, D., *Money, interest and prices* (New York, 1965).

Samuelson, P. A., "What classical and neo-classical monetary theory really was", *Canadian Journal of Economics* (1968); also in: R. W. Clower, ed., *Monetary theory* (Harmondsworth, 1969).

Samuelson, P. A., "Non-optimality of money holding under laissez faire", *Canadian Journal of Economics* (1969).

Schlesinger, K., "Basic principles of the money economy", in *International Economic Papers* (1959) pp. 20–38.

Walras, L., *Elements of pure economics* (Paris, 1926; Homewood, Ill., 1954).

2

The Risk–Return Approach

> In value theory, we take a private individual's income and expenditure account; we ask which of the items in that account are under the individual's own control, and then how he will adjust these items in order to reach a most preferred position. On the production side, we make a similar analysis of the profit and loss account of the firm. My suggestion is that monetary theory needs to be based again upon a similar analysis, but this time, *not of an income account, but of a capital account,* a balance sheet.
>
> J. R. Hicks (1935)

(A) Hick's paper cited above is a basic paper pointing clearly to the move from the previous income theory of demand for money to the asset theory of demand for money, or more concisely, the portfolio theory of money. The decision to hold money belongs to a "point of time", i.e., it is a decision on stocks, and therefore, the connection between demand for money and income, which is a flow concept, must always be indirect. Any attempt to establish a close relation between the two is "superficially natural" but "highly inconvenient" and "ought only to be hoped for at a late stage of investigation". Hicks regarded the portfolio theory of money as "the most important part of Keynes' theoretical contribution". As we all know, this approach has been the predominant approach since Keynes. In fact, it has become so predominant that even the Quantity Theory as restated by Friedman (1956) had a drastically different appearance from its previous forms; see also Chapter 10 below.

By the risk–return approach is meant the class of model formulations which postulates a performance criterion explicitly in terms of two characteristics, an expected rate of return on a portfolio and a measure of the portfolio risk, and which attempts to determine, as a set of derived demands, the amounts held of various assets that maximize the above performance criterion. Needless to say, this is not the only approach to the problem of choice involving risk. Historically, the economics of uncertainty began with D. Bernoulli's expected utility theory which was later (and much later) axiomatized by von Neumann and Morgenstern (1944). Since the utility functions employed in the expected utility approach are assumed concave, the expected utility associated with a random variable is lower than the utility of the expected value of the random variable. In this way, the concavity of the utility function captures the idea of risk and people's aversion of it. Thus the distinction between them is one of formality but not of substance. If an appropriate measure of risk were adopted in the risk–return approach, the two approaches might become equivalent. However, as we shall see shortly, such a risk measure will not be so simple as variance. Indeed the mean-variance analysis was proposed, because of its operationality, as an approximation to the analysis in terms of the general expected utility theory. In assessing the mean-variance analysis, therefore, the questions of crucial importance are: (1) Is it a "good" approximation to the expected utility theory? and (2) Particularly for our purpose, is it capable of explaining the speculative demand for money? In the rest of this chapter, we attempt to provide an assessment of the mean-variance analysis along these lines.

(B) The first formal presentation of the risk–return approach appears to be that of Markowitz (1952). Markowitz assumes (1) that investors possess knowledge about probability distributions of the rates of return on a set of securi-

ties, (2) that these distributions have finite means and variances, (3) that an individual's preferences are a function of
the mean portfolio return and the portfolio variance alone,
(4) that there are decreasing returns to risk bearing beyond
some point, and (5) that for any given mean return on a
portfolio, the portfolio with the smallest variance is preferred to all others.

Let us assume there are n assets, and let the *gross* rate of
return per dollar on the jth asset be R_j and its expected value
be r_j $(j = 1, 2, \ldots, n)$. Let us also assume that the joint
probability distribution of the R_j's is characterized by the
mean vector $(r_1, \ldots, r_n)$ and the variance–covariance matrix
S which are independent of individuals' decisions. Consider
an individual who has an initial fund equalling A dollars. If
we let x_j denote the number of dollars invested in the jth
asset, then

$$A = \sum_{j=1}^{n} x_j \equiv v^T x, \tag{2.1}$$

where $v \equiv (1, 1, \ldots, 1)$, $x \equiv (x_1, \ldots, x_n)$, and T stands for
transposition. For a portfolio x, we have the mean return M
and the variance V as follows:

$$M = \sum_{j=1}^{n} r_j x_j = r^T x, \tag{2.2}$$

$$V = x_1^2 \sigma_{11} + \cdots + x_n^2 \sigma_{nn} + 2\sigma_{12} x_1 x_2 + \cdots + 2\sigma_{n-1n} x_{n-1} x_n$$
$$= x^T S x. \tag{2.3}$$

Markowitz' procedure, given r and S, is first find an *efficient
frontier* which is defined as the set of portfolios that has a
minimum variance for any given portfolio return M.
Mathematically, solve the quadratic programming problem of
minimizing V with respect to x subject to (2.1) and (2.2) with
prescribed M. Since V is a continuous and convex function
of x (the convexity comes from the positive semi-definiteness of S), the problem yields a solution for a proper range
of M in terms of x. Substituting such x in (2.3) yields a

solution for V as a function of M and A. For given A, this will be a continuous function of M, and can be depicted in the (M, V) space. Once the efficient frontier is given this way, the second step is to maximize a utility function of the form $u(M, V)$ over the efficient frontier. If such a maximum point exists, the problem of optimal portfolio selection has been solved.

To see how this works, consider first the case where there are no added restraints on the values of x_j's (due to the possibility of short sales). Then to obtain the efficient frontier, set up a Lagrangian function,

$$L(x, \lambda, \mu) = \tfrac{1}{2}V + \lambda(M - r^T x) + \mu(A - V^T x),$$

and minimize it with respect to (x, λ, μ). This would yield, in addition to (2.1) and (2.2), the following system of equations:

$$\sigma_{j1}x_1 + \sigma_{j2}x_2 + \cdots + \sigma_{jn}x_n = \lambda r_j + \mu, \qquad j = 1, 2, \ldots, n.$$
$$\text{(2.4)}$$

Solving these n equations for $x = (x_1, \ldots, x_n)$, we would obtain solutions for x_j as linear functions of λ and μ. On the other hand, multiplying the jth equation of (2.4) by x_j and adding all the n equations yields

$$V = \lambda M + \mu A. \tag{2.5}$$

Substituting the above solutions for the x_j's into (2.1) and (2.2) yields a solution for λ and μ in terms of M and A. Finally, substituting these solutions into (2.5), we would get

$$V = \phi(M, A)$$

as an expression for the efficient frontier. The shape of the efficiency frontier is known to depend critically on the existence or non-existence of a riskless asset. If a riskless asset exists and can be held in any amount, the efficiency frontier will be a straight line in the $(V^{1/2}, M)$ space; otherwise, the frontier will be a curve concave from below in the same space. So, if the indifference curves are convex, an optimal portfolio will normally be characterized by a diversification.

When short sales are not freely allowed, it would be

reasonable to add a non-negativity constraint on x. The problem of finding an efficient portfolio would then be: minimize $x^T S x$ subject to (2.1) and (2.2) and $x \geq 0$. This brings back a set of Kuhn–Tucker inequalities at zero values of x_j's. The student is referred to Ch. 7 of Hadley (1964).

It may be worthwhile to investigate the nature of an efficient frontier a bit more closely. Let us first assume that S is positive definite, and let S_{ij} be its ijth cofactor. Then solving the equations (2.4) for x_j's, we get

$$
\begin{aligned}
x_i &= \frac{\lambda \sum_j r_j S_{ij} + \mu \sum_j S_{ij}}{|S|} \\
&= \lambda \sum_j r_j s_{ij}^{-1} + \mu \sum_j s_{ij}^{-1},
\end{aligned}
\tag{2.6}
$$

where s_{ij}^{-1} is the ijth element of the inverse of S. Substituting these solutions in the two constraint equations, we get the following pair of equations for λ and μ:

$$
\begin{aligned}
M &= \lambda \sum_i \sum_j r_i r_j s_{ij}^{-1} + \mu \sum_i \sum_j r_i s_{ij}^{-1}, \\
A &= \lambda \sum_i \sum_j r_j s_{ij}^{-1} + \mu \sum_i \sum_j s_{ij}^{-1}.
\end{aligned}
\tag{2.7}
$$

The Jacobian determinant of this system,

$$
|J| = (r^T S^{-1} r)(v^T S^{-1} r) - (v^T S^{-1} r)(v^T S^{-1} r),
$$

is non-negative under our assumption on S by the Cauchy–Schwartz Inequality, zero possibly occurring only when r is proportional to Sv.[1] So we can take $|J| > 0$. Solving (2.7) for λ and μ, and substituting the solutions in (2.5), we finally obtain the following parabolic equation:

$$
\begin{aligned}
V &= \frac{(v^T S^{-1} v) M^2 - 2AM(r^T S^{-1} v) + A^2 (r^T S^{-1} r)}{|J|} \\
&= \frac{v^T S^{-1} v}{|J|} \left(M - \frac{r^T S^{-1} v}{v^T S^{-1} v} A \right)^2 + \frac{A^2}{v^T S^{-1} v},
\end{aligned}
\tag{2.8}
$$

[1]See, e.g., Rao (1965, p. 43).

as the expression for an efficient frontier. Alternatively, if we represent this equation in (σ, M) space, where $\sigma = V^{1/2}$, the efficient frontier becomes a hyperbola with asymptotes

$$M = \frac{r^T S^{-1} v}{v^T S^{-1} v} A \pm \left(\frac{|J|}{v^T S^{-1} v} \right)^{1/2} \sigma.$$

Since $|J| > 0$ and $v^T S^{-1} v > 0$, the coefficient on the quadratic term is positive, and so is the constant term. The constant term is the minimum possible variance associated with the investment of A dollars. Alternatively, $(v^T S^{-1} v)^{-1}$ is the minimum possible variance per dollar of investment. The quantity $A(r^T S^{-1} v)/(v^T S^{-1} v)$ may be interpreted as the minimum expected yield required to make the mean-variance choice meaningful, given S.

Let us now assume that the nth asset is a riskless asset, i.e., $\text{Prob}(R_n = r_n) = 1$. In this case $\sigma_{nj} = 0$ for all j and hence S is singular. Define

$$\hat{S} = \begin{bmatrix} \sigma_{11} & \cdots & \sigma_{1, n-1} \\ \vdots & & \vdots \\ \sigma_{n-11} & \cdots & \sigma_{n-1, n-1} \end{bmatrix},$$

and assume it is positive definite. Letting $\hat{x} = (x_1, \ldots, x_{n-1})$, $V = \hat{x}^T \hat{S} \hat{x}$. Since $\lambda r_n + \mu = 0$ from the last equation of (2.4), $\mu = -\lambda r_n$. Substituting this in (2.5), the equation becomes

$$V = \lambda (M - r_n A). \tag{2.9}$$

The equations corresponding to (2.7) are

$$M = \lambda \left(\sum_i^{n-1} \sum_i^{n-1} r_i r_j \hat{s}_{ij}^{-1} - \sum_i^{n-1} \sum_j^{n-1} r_i r_n \hat{s}_{ij}^{-1} \right) + r_n x_n,$$

$$A = \lambda \left(\sum_i^{n-1} \sum_j^{n-1} r_j \hat{s}_{ij}^{-1} - \sum_i^{n-1} \sum_j^{n-1} r_n \hat{s}_{ij}^{-1} \right) + x_n. \tag{2.10}$$

Hence

$$\lambda = \frac{M - r_n A}{D}. \tag{2.11}$$

Substituting this in (2.9), we get

$$V = \frac{1}{D}(M - r_n A)^2 \quad \text{or} \quad M = r_n A + D^{1/2}\sigma, \qquad (2.12)$$

whenever $M > r_n A$.

In these equations,

$$D = [(r_1 - r_n), \ldots, (r_{n-1} - r_n)]^T \hat{S}^{-1}$$
$$\times [(r_1 - r_n), \ldots, (r_{n-1} - r_n)],$$

which is positive by assumption. Thus the efficient frontier with a riskless asset becomes a positively sloped straight line in the (σ, M) space. The slope relative to the σ axis, $D^{1/2}$, measures the "price of risk aversion" in the sense that it shows how much less mean return one must accept to reduce the risk (σ) by one unit. If there are non-negativity constraints on x, then the typical frontier looks like BCD in Figure 2.1, where the line segment BC represents the range of portfolios in which the riskless asset is held in positive amounts and the curve CD represents the range of portfolios in which the riskless asset no longer exists. Once the efficient frontier is given as BCD, and given the individual's preferences by a well-behaved utility function $U = U(M, \sigma)$, $U_M > 0$, $U_\sigma < 0$, an asset equilibrium can be established in a straightforward manner (except for the case of a "plunger").

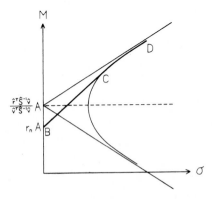

Figure 2.1

For an illuminating discussion on the mean-variance analysis, the reader is referred to Tobin (1958). Hicks (1962) may also be useful.

One remark about the construction of the efficient frontier. In the above figure, we assumed that $r_n < (\hat{r}^T \hat{S}^{-1} \hat{v})/(\hat{v}^T \hat{S}^{-1} \hat{v})$, the rate of return corresponding to the minimum variance in the absence of the riskless asset. In fact we can show that the investor will not otherwise invest in positive amounts in risky assets. To see this, we first note that the above inequality is equivalent to $\hat{v}^T \hat{S}^{-1} \hat{m} > 0$, where $\hat{m} = (r_1 - r_n, \ldots, r_{n-1} - r_n)$. Now fix M at some level higher than $r_n A$, and for this M, solve for the optimal $\hat{x}$. If this $\hat{x}$ coexists with the riskless asset in a portfolio, it is given by

$$\hat{x} = \frac{M - r_n A}{\hat{m}^T \hat{S}^{-1} \hat{m}} \hat{S}^{-1} \hat{m}.$$

Hence for $\hat{x} \geq 0$, it must be true that $\hat{S}^{-1} \hat{m} \geq 0$. But if $\hat{S}^{-1} \hat{m} \geq 0$, then $\hat{v}^T \hat{S}^{-1} \hat{m} > 0$, i.e., $r_n < (\hat{r}^T \hat{S}^{-1} \hat{v})/(\hat{v}^T \hat{S}^{-1} \hat{v})$. If this last inequality is reversed, then, not only must some of the risky assets be held in negative amounts, but also the total number of dollars invested in risky assets, $\hat{v}^T \hat{x}$, must be negative since $\text{sign}(\hat{v}^T \hat{x}) = \text{sign}(\hat{v}^T \hat{S}^{-1} \hat{m}) < 0$.

(C) The Comparative Statics of the Mean-Variance Model: Confining ourselves to the case in which all the risky and the riskless assets are held in positive amounts in a portfolio, we have found that the solution for x is given by

$$\hat{x} = \frac{M - r_n A}{\hat{m}^T \hat{S}^{-1} \hat{m}} \hat{S}^{-1} \hat{m}, \tag{2.13}$$

$$x_n = A - (M - r_n A) \frac{\hat{v}^T \hat{S}^{-1} \hat{m}}{\hat{m}^T \hat{S}^{-1} \hat{m}}. \tag{2.14}$$

Though M is yet to be determined by utility maximization, (2.13) shows an interesting property of the solution $\hat{x}$, namely, that the *composition* of the risky assets held in an optimal portfolio depends only on the investor's probabilities $(r, \hat{S})$ and not on the form of the utility function, a fact known as the Separation Theorem. Now to determine M, we must use the utility function $U(M, \sigma)$, which can be written, in view of (2.12),

$$U\left(M, \frac{M - r_n A}{D^{1/2}}\right). \tag{2.15}$$

Assuming the concavity of this function (as a function of M), the solution can be written as

$$M^* = M^*(r, \hat{S}, A). \tag{2.16}$$

Substituting (2.16) into (2.13) and (2.14), we finally obtain

$$x^* = x^*(r, \hat{S}, A). \tag{2.17}$$

But it turns out that there is not much we can say about the properties of the solution (2.17), despite Tobin's remark to the contrary (1969, p. 14). So we shall give just a brief sketch of what can be done.

From (2.13) and (2.14), it is evident that if we know enough about the properties of the solution M^* in (2.16), we should be able to say something about the optimal portfolio x^*. Suppose an interior maximum of the U function in (2.15) exists at some value of M, M^*, so that at $M = M^*$

$$U_M + D^{-1/2} U_\sigma = 0. \tag{2.18}$$

From this we get

$$
\begin{aligned}
dM ={} & \frac{r_n(D^{-1/2} U_{M\sigma} + D^{-1} U_{\sigma\sigma})}{B} \, dA \\
&+ \frac{A(D^{-1/2} U_{M\sigma} + D^{-1} U_{\sigma\sigma})}{B} \, dr \\
&+ \frac{D^{-1}(M - r_n A)(U_{M\sigma} + D^{-1/2} U_{\sigma\sigma}) + D^{-1} U_\sigma}{B} \, dD^{1/2},
\end{aligned}
\tag{2.19}
$$

where $B \equiv U_{MM} + 2D^{-1/2} U_{M\sigma} + D^{-1} U_{\sigma\sigma} < 0$ is the Jacobian of the equation (2.18). In (2.19), we are considering the three sources of changes: (1) the change in the wealth size A, (2) the parallel and equal change in *all* the mean returns r, and (3) the change in the slope of the efficient frontier or the price of risk aversion $D^{1/2}$ due to change in $\hat{S}$. First, the effect of an increase in A. From (2.19),

$$\text{sign}\left(\frac{\partial M}{\partial A}\right) = (-1) \times \text{sign}(D^{-1/2}U_{M\sigma} + D^{-1}U_{\sigma\sigma}).$$

The latter sign is the same as the sign of the term $d(U_\sigma/U_M)/d\sigma$. If the two "commodities", the mean portfolio return (M) and the aversion of risk $(-\sigma)$ are "normal" goods, then

$$d(-U_\sigma/U_M)/d(-\sigma) = d(U_\sigma/U_M)/d\sigma < 0,$$

$$d(-U_M/U_\sigma)/dM = -d(U_M/U_\sigma)/dM < 0.$$

The first inequality implies that $\partial M/\partial A > 0$. This also means, in view of (2.19) that $\partial M/\partial r > 0$. This is not enough to sign $\partial \hat{x}/\partial A$, however. To find out what $\partial \hat{x}/\partial A$ is, we must go back to (2.13). After a little manipulation, we find that

$$\text{sign}\left(\frac{\partial \hat{x}}{\partial A}\right) = \text{sign}\left(\frac{\partial M}{\partial A} - 1\right)\hat{S}^{-1}m.$$

Calculating the crucial term $(\partial M/\partial A - 1)$, we get

$$\text{sign}\left(\frac{\partial M}{\partial A} - 1\right) = (-1) \times \text{sign}\left(\frac{U_{MM} + D^{-1/2}U_{M\sigma}}{B}\right)$$

$$= \text{sign}[d(U_M/U_\sigma)/dM] > 0,$$

under the normality assumption. This means that if all the risky assets were held in positive amounts at the beginning and if both M and $-\sigma$ are normal goods, then, an increase in A increases the amounts of all the risky assets in an optimal portfolio. Second, an inspection of (2.13) and (2.19) shows that the effect of a parallel increase in r on $\hat{x}$ will be qualitatively the same as that of an increase in A. Finally, the effect of an increase in the price of risk aversion, $D^{1/2}$. From the last line of (2.19), we see that under the normality assumption, the two terms $D^{-1}U_\sigma/B$ and $D^{-1}(M -$

$r_n A)(U_{M\sigma} + D^{-1/2} U_{\sigma\sigma})/B$ are both positive. The first term corresponds to the substitution effect, and the second to the income effect, in the usual consumer theory. The situation is depicted in Figure 2.2.

In this figure, the line BD is the original efficient frontier and E is the original equilibrium. The line BD' is the new efficient frontier showing an increase in the price of risk aversion. This increase in the price of risk aversion induces the investor to substitute M for $-\sigma$, as shown by the northeastern movement from E to F. There is also an income effect. The normality assumption means that as you move up vertically holding σ constant, the slope of the indifference curves gets flatter. Therefore, the new equilibrium E', which is tangent to the now steeper frontier must lie further to the northeast of F. Thus, we have $\partial M/\partial D^{1/2} > 0$. From (2.13) we get

$$\partial(\hat{m}^T \hat{x})/\partial D^{1/2} = \partial M/\partial D^{1/2} > 0.$$

This means that in an aggregate sense, the investment in the risky assets increases with an increase in the price of risk aversion. But this seems to be all we can say, for the amounts of individual risky assets depend on the particular ways in which $\hat{S}$ has changed.

Interestingly enough, it is not this type of comparative statics analysis of a personal equilibrium, but that of a

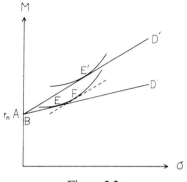

Figure 2.2

market equilibrium, that is better known in the literature. This may at first seem rather strange, since the comparative statics analysis of a market equilibrium is usually much harder than that of a personal equilibrium. But on second thought the riddle disappears. All the general equilibrium models, e.g., Sharpe (1966), Lintner (1965a, 1965b) and Mossin (1966), make, among others, the assumptions: (1) that there is a complete agreement about security parameters, i.e., r and S are the same for all investors, and (2) that there is a riskless asset which is held by everyone. Under these assumptions, all the investors face the same price of risk aversion to which they equate their marginal rates of substitution of σ for M, irrespective of the forms of their utility functions. This fact drives risk out of the model, formally speaking. Then there is the fact, peculiar to the mean-variance analysis, that the variance is a quadratic function of $\hat{x}$, so that the differentiation of the variance with respect to any component of $\hat{x}$ yields a linear function of $\hat{x}$, which paves the way for a simple aggregation.

To illustrate using our model, suppose we maximize $U(r^T x, (\hat{x}^T \hat{S} \hat{x})^{1/2})$ subject to $A - v^T x = 0$.

The first-order conditions may be written under the above assumptions,

$$A - v^T x = 0,$$

$$m_i - D^{1/2} \frac{\sum_{j=1}^{n-1} \sigma_{ij} x_j}{\sigma} = 0, \qquad i = 1, 2, \ldots, n-1.$$

The second equations can be written as

$$m_i \sigma = D^{1/2} \sum_{j=1}^{n-1} \sigma_{ij} x_j, \qquad i = 1, 2, \ldots, n-1,$$

from which follows the set of equations

$$\frac{\sum_{k=1}^{n-1} \sigma_{ik} x_k}{m_i} = \frac{\sum_{k=1}^{n-1} \sigma_{jk} x_k}{m_j}, \qquad i, j = 1, 2, \ldots, n-1. \tag{2.20}$$

Under the given assumptions, we can aggregate these equations over all the investors and obtain

$$\frac{\sum\limits_{k=1}^{n-1} \sigma_{ik}\bar{X}_k}{m_i} = \frac{\sum\limits_{k=1}^{n-1} \sigma_{jk}\bar{X}_k}{m_j}, \qquad i, j = 1, 2, \ldots, n-1, \qquad (2.21)$$

where $\bar{X}_k$ is the market demand for asset k which is also equal to the market supply of the same asset. All the results reported in the above literature are the direct consequences of these two sets of equations. Mossin (1966), for instance, rewrites these equations as

$$\frac{\sum\limits_{k=1}^{n-1} \sigma_{ik}x_k}{\sum\limits_{k=1}^{n-1} \sigma_{ik}\bar{X}_k} = \frac{\sum\limits_{k=1}^{n-1} \sigma_{jk}x_k}{\sum\limits_{k=1}^{n-1} \sigma_{jk}\bar{X}_k}, \qquad i, j = 1, 2, \ldots, n-1,$$

and derives a proposition that in market equilibrium every investor holds the same percentage of the total outstanding stock of all *risky* assets.[2] The reader interested in this kind of exercise is referred to the literature cited above.

(D) The portfolio variance (or the portfolio standard deviation) has been the predominant measure of risk employed in the risk–return approach. A few other measures of risk, e.g., loss functions, chance constraints, and confidence limits, have failed to gain popularity. Although the utility analysis of risk and return made a great contribution to the theory of portfolio selection, the validity of variance as a risk measure has long been questioned in relation to the more fundamental

---

[2]To handle market equilibrium, it is convenient, as these authors did, to introduce a vector of asset prices and write the individual budget constraint as $p^T(\bar{x} - x) = 0$, while making the end-of-period asset prices the random variables of the system. But this is of course not a change in substance.

theory of expected utility. To be precise, the mean-variance analysis is justifiable only if either the utility function is quadratic or the asset yields are distributed according to a two-parameter probability distribution with the property of finite additivity, or both. The only useful distribution that possesses these properties is the normal distribution. To give generality to the risk–return approach, it is therefore highly desirable to free it from such restrictions on the form of either the utility function or the probability distribution. To achieve this, we would need a more general risk measure than the variance.

It is quite easy to find a risk measure such that it is free from any such restrictions and makes the risk–return approach in terms of it equivalent to the expected utility theory. According to Stone (1970), such a generalized risk measure (GRM) can be defined as

$$\Phi \equiv U(M) - E(U(W)), \tag{2.22}$$

where W is the random wealth size, M is its expected value, U is the von Neumann–Morgenstern utility function, and Φ is the GRM. Equation (2.22) can be rewritten in the form

$$E(U(W)) = U(M) - \Phi \equiv \Psi(M, \Phi), \tag{2.23}$$

meaning that the expected utility is written exactly as a function of the mean M and the risk measure Φ. If a Taylor's expansion about $\bar{W}$ exists for $U(W)$ in a neighbourhood of M sufficiently large to include all W for which there is a non-zero probability of occurrence, and if the probability distribution for W is such that all central moments exist, then Φ is given by

$$\Phi = -\sum_{k=2}^{\infty} \frac{U^{(k)}(M)}{k!} M_k, \tag{2.24}$$

where M_k is the kth central moment of the probability

distribution and $U^{(k)}(M)$ is the kth derivative of $U(W)$ evaluated at $W = M.$[3]

Equation (2.24) above makes it clear that the mean-variance analysis is at best an approximation to the general theory of expected utility. The question is: Is it a good approximation? At the theoretical level, some writers have noted certain absurdities of the mean-variance formulation. Borch (1969) argues that it is generally impossible to draw indifference curves in the (σ, M) space without violating a basic axiom of the expected utility theory. He illustrates this point using the following example: Let (σ_1, M_1), (σ_2, M_2), $M_1 > M_2$, be on the same indifference curve. Then consider the following gambles:

gain x with probability $1 - p$,

or

gain y_i $(i = 1, 2)$ with probability p.

Comparing the two gambles, if $y_1 > y_2$, the first gamble dominates the second, and hence, according to the expected utility theory, the two gambles cannot be indifferent. But now let

$$x = \frac{\sigma_1 M_1 - \sigma_2 M_2}{\sigma_1 - \sigma_2},$$

$$p = \frac{(M_1 - M_2)^2}{(\sigma_1 - \sigma_2)^2 + (M_1 - M_2)^2},$$

$$y_1 = M_1 + \sigma_1 \frac{\sigma_1 - \sigma_2}{M_1 - M_2},$$

$$y_2 = M_2 + \sigma_2 \frac{\sigma_1 - \sigma_2}{M_1 - M_2},$$

[3]For a quadratic utility function ϕ becomes proportional to the variance. For a normal distribution,

$$\phi = -\sum_{k=1}^{\infty} \frac{U^{(2k)}(M)}{2^k k!} (\sigma^2)^k,$$

where σ^2 is the variance.

so that the first gamble has mean M_1 and variance σ_1^2, and the second gamble has mean M_2 and variance σ_2^2. By hypothesis, the two gambles are indifferent. But this is impossible since $y_1 > y_2$ according to the dominance axiom. Feldstein (1969) casts a doubt on the proper curvature of the indifference curves of the mean-variance analysis. Using a logarithmic utility function and a lognormal distribution, he has shown that the indifference curve has the desired convex curvature only if $M > (2\sigma)^{1/2}$.

Against these charges, Tsiang (1972) has offered a justification for the mean-variance analysis. He argues that the mean-variance analysis being an approximation, it is not surprising that the degree of approximation may become rather poor. But if its main use is in the problem of portfolio selection, and if the degree of approximation can be shown to be good for the situation encountered by the typical investor, the use of the mean-variance analysis is justified. In demonstrating this last point, Tsiang imposes restrictions on both the form of the utility function and the shape of the probability distribution.

First, he imposes the following restrictions on the utility function:

(a) $U'(W) > 0$ (non-satiation),
(b) $U''(W) < 0$ (risk aversion),
(c) $d[-U''(W)/U'(W)]/dW \leq 0$ (decreasing absolute risk aversion),
(d) $d[-U''(W)/U'(W)]/dW \geq 0$ (increasing relative risk aversion).

For the meaning of the last two terms, see Chapter 3, Section C, below. The conditions (c) and (d) together imply that the investor would hold an absolutely larger amount, but a smaller proportion, of risky assets when his wealth increases. The negative exponential function,

$$U(W) = B(1 - e^{-bW}), \qquad B, b > 0,$$

satisfies all these inequalities, with equality in (c). The family of constant elasticity utility functions,

$$U(W) = \frac{1}{1-a} W^{1-a}, \qquad a > 0 \quad \text{and} \quad U(W) = \ln W,$$

satisfies all these inequalities, with equality in (d). Hence these two families of functions set bounds on the class of utility functions Tsiang considers interesting. A justification for the conditions (c) and (d) comes from the general property of the empirical demand for money functions.

Second, as for the probability distribution of W, Tsiang argues that the size of the risk faced by the typical investor is rather small *relative to* the expected wealth size M, where W includes all the non-human assets as well as the human capital owned by the investor. Let us say that the standard deviation is at most one-tenth of the expected wealth, i.e., $\sigma/M < 1/10$.

Now take the negative exponential utility function. For this utility function, ϕ can be written [see (2.24)]

$$\phi = B\, e^{-bM} \left[\frac{b^2 \sigma^2}{2!} - \frac{b^3 M_3}{3!} + \cdots \right]$$

$$= B\, e^{-bM} \left[\frac{b^2 \sigma^2}{2!} - \frac{b^3 \sigma^3}{3!} \mu_3 + \cdots \right], \qquad (2.25)$$

where $\mu_k \equiv M_k/\sigma^k$ is the normalized kth central moment. Assume further that a ten-fold increase in M still does not bring him to within, say, 0.1 percent of his ultimate bliss, $U(\infty) = B$, i.e.,

$$B(1 - e^{-10bM}) \leq B(1 - 0,001).$$

Solving this for b, we get $b \leq 0.69/M$. This, along with the inequality $\sigma/M < 1/10$, implies that $b\sigma \leq 0.069$, and the coefficient on μ_3 becomes less than $1/17500$. The coefficients on higher-order μ's are naturally much less than that. Similarly, for $U(W) = (1-a)^{-1} W^{1-a}$, we have

$$\phi = \frac{a\sigma^2}{2!(M)^{1+a}} - \frac{a(1+a)\sigma^3}{3!(M)^{2+a}} \mu_3 + \cdots \qquad (2.26)$$

If we set $a = 1$ for simplicity (which is the logarithmic case), the coefficient on μ_3 becomes less than 1/3000. It appears therefore that for the class of utility functions and the size of risk relevant to portfolio choice problems, the mean-variance analysis yields quite good approximations despite some known absurdities in more general cases.[4]

(E) The Usefulness of the Mean-Variance Model as a Theory of Demand for Money: As is well known, Tobin's intention was to use the mean-variance analysis to explain why people hold cash in their portfolio. For the mean-variance analysis to do this job, it must meet the two conditions: (1) that it maintain the goodness of approximation, and (2) that it ensures the tangency of the indifference curve and the efficient frontier at an interior point of the linear portion of the efficient frontier.

Suppose we approximate ϕ by the variance term alone and write

$$E[U(W)] = U(M) + \frac{U''(M)}{2!}\sigma^2,$$

from which we get

$$\left.\frac{dM}{d\sigma}\right|_{E[U(W)]=\text{const}} = \frac{-U''(M)\sigma}{U'(M) + U'''(M)\sigma^2/2}. \tag{2.27}$$

For the negative exponential utility function, this becomes

$$\left.\frac{dM}{d\sigma}\right|_{E[U(W)]=\text{const}} = b\sigma \bigg/ \left[1 + \frac{b^2\sigma^2}{2}\right], \tag{2.28}$$

and for the logarithmic utility function,

---

[4]Samuelson (1970) has noted that the goodness of approximations depends on the *absolute* size of risk, as against Tsiang's relative size. Tsiang also notes the potential significance of the third moment (the skewness) and he attributes the difficulties raised by Borch and Feldstein to it.

$$\left.\frac{\mathrm{d}M}{\mathrm{d}\sigma}\right|_{E[U(W)]=\mathrm{const}} = \frac{\sigma}{M}\bigg/\left[1+\frac{\sigma^2}{M^2}\right].$$ (2.29)

If we apply to these equations the restrictions, $\sigma/M < 1/10$ and $b\sigma \leq 0.069$, we see that the marginal rates of substitution of M for σ in (2.28) and (2.29) are far less than unity. But the very restriction $\sigma/M < 1/10$ means that the investor is likely to be able to move from any point on an indifference curve in a direction whose slope is greater than 45°, and hence, to a higher indifference curve. This means that under these restrictions, the equilibrium is bound to be at a point which lies far past the linear portion of the efficient frontier. Such would be the case even when we allowed the risk to grow ten times larger so that $\sigma < M$.

What this all means is that while the mean-variance analysis can be a good approximation to the expected utility theory when the risk is small relative to the mean return, and hence, can be applied to the portfolio choice problem among risky assets, the same condition serves to deny its applicability to the demand for money. We must therefore conclude with Tsiang that the relevance of the mean-variance analysis as a theory of demand for cash is, to say the least, in grave doubt and that we should perhaps pursue the alternative theory of demand for cash for transactions purposes more seriously. But does this mean, as Tsiang suggests, that the wealth approach to monetary theory should be buried altogether? We shall come back to this question in Chapter 3.

(F)   Even apart from the difficulty related to cash holdings, another unattractive feature of the mean-variance analysis as a theory of portfolio selection is the fact that the planning horizon is just one period and that the meaning of utility as a function of the terminal wealth is unclear. As a theory of household behaviour, one central reason households hold wealth is to optimally reallocate their incomes for consumption over multiple periods. It might be argued that consumption can be readily absorbed in the above mean-variance analysis by regarding consumption as an asset yielding a sure rate of return equalling minus one. But this is obviously unacceptable. A more natural and useful formulation is to define the objective criterion explicitly in terms of a flow of consumption which in turn defines a sequence of optimal portfolios in the sense of maximizing such a criterion. An attempt was made in Tobin (1965) to extend the mean-variance model in these directions. We shall study this problem more explicitly in this section.

The conventional single-period portfolio model takes the total wealth as given and concentrates on the allocation of a given wealth among various assets. It allows us to explain the peaceful coexistence of various assets. But it does not explain why people hold wealth, which was the main problem of Irving Fisher (1930). As we all know, Fisher explained wealth holdings as arising out of people's desire to optimally reallocate their lifetime earnings for consumption. Two parameters played a crucial role in determining the time profile of an optimal consumption stream. They were (1) people's "impatience" (thrift) and (2) the "opportunities to invest" (productivity). On the basis of such a model, Fisher was able to explain the rate of interest. The portfolio model is an extension of Fisher's analysis in that it deals with multiple assets as against Fisher's single asset. But the conventional portfolio theory can hardly be said to be a generalization of Fisher's analysis unless it can explain wealth and interest rates. In order to explain wealth, however, we cannot avoid consumption and its intertemporal allocation. In other words, we cannot be content with the cozy balance sheet framework. It is time we made a step forward to Hicks' "late stage of investigation". Tobin (1965) made a pioneering study in this direction. The model presented below is a formalization of Tobin's work (1965, 1968).

Consider an individual with an initial wealth $W_0 > 0$. In the first period he may consume part of W^0 for consumption. Denote it by C^1, $W^0 > C^1 > 0$. He then invests $W^0 - C^1$ in n

alternative assets whose returns per dollar are $R = \{R_1, \ldots, R_n\} \geq 0$. We assume this R to be random with mean r and covariances S. At the end of period one, the investments $x^1 (v^T x^1 = W^0 - C^1)$ will have grown to $R^{1T} x^1$, where R^1 is the vector of realized returns. With $R^{1T} x^1$ as the initial wealth, the individual repeats the same pattern of decisions in the second period, and so forth.

Let us assume for simplicity that the individual has a two-period horizon. If we ignore bequests, his second period consumption will be $C^2 = R^{1T} x^1$. We suppose that he derives satisfaction $U(C^2) = U(R^{1T} x^1)$ in the second period. Let us now go back one period and consider his decision problem. At the beginning of period one, he does not know R^1. Hence C^2 is not known for certain. To take account of this fact, let us assume that the utility of C^2, as viewed at the beginning of period one, is assessed in terms of its mean and variance. We shall write such an ex ante utility of C^2 as

$$f(\text{mean of } C^2, \text{ variance of } C^2) = f(r^T x^1, x^{1T} S x^1).$$

His problem then is to maximize

$$u(C^1) + (1 + \delta)^{-1} f(r^T x^1, x^{1T} S x^1)$$
$$\text{with respect to } C^1 \text{ and } x^1 \qquad (2.30)$$

subject to

$$0 \leq C^1 \leq W^0 \quad \text{and} \quad v^T x^1 = W^0 - C^1.$$

The parameter δ is a discount factor which is non-negative. This problem can be solved in two stages. First, for any prescribed value of C^1, f must be maximized with respect to x^1, for, otherwise, (2.30) can never be maximal. But this is a familiar problem. Let us denote the maximum of f by f^*, i.e.,

$$f^* = f[M^*, V(M^*)], \qquad (2.31)$$

where $V(M^*)$ is as given by (2.8). The second stage of the problem can now be handled readily. The problem is to maximize (2.30) with respect to C^1 using (2.31). Differentiating $u(C^1) + (1 + \delta)^{-1} f^*$ with respect to C^1 and setting the expression at zero,

$$0 = U'(C^1) + (1 + \delta)^{-1} \left[f_M^* \frac{\partial M^*}{\partial C^1} + 2f_V^* \frac{v^T S^{-1} v}{|J|} \right.$$
$$\left. \times \left(M^* - \frac{r^T S^{-1} v}{v^T S^{-1} v} (W^0 - C^1) \right) \left(\frac{\partial M^*}{\partial C^1} - \frac{r^T S^{-1} v}{v^T S^{-1} v} \right) \right]$$
$$= U'(C^1) - (1 + \delta)^{-1} f_M^* \frac{r^T S^{-1} v}{v^T S^{-1} v},$$

which is a straightforward generalization of Fisher's result.

It is worth emphasizing that this model is capable of explaining wealth and interest rates. The size and composition of wealth are chosen so as to secure the most desirable stream of consumption. In an uncertain world, one important element of desirability is stability. The portfolio choice consists in weighing high returns against such stability. Also, by adding up individuals' demands for consumer goods and assets and by equating them with social endowments, a vector of equilibrium interest rates would be determined.

References

Broch, K., "A note on uncertainty and indifference curves", *Review of Economic Studies* (1969).

Feldstein, M. S., "Mean-variance analysis in the theory of liquidity preference and portfolio selection", *Review of Economic Studies* (1969).

Fisher, I., *The theory of interest* (New York, 1930) chs. V, VI.

Friedman, M., "The quantity theory of money: A restatement", in: M. Friedman, ed., *Studies in the quantity theory of money* (Chicago, Ill., 1956); also in his *Optimum quantity of money and other essays* (Chicago, Ill., 1969).

Hadley, A., *Nonlinear and dynamic programming* (New York, 1964).

Hicks, J. R., "A suggestion for simplifying the theory of money", *Economica* (1935); also in: *Readings in monetary theory* (Homewood, Ill., 1952).

Hicks, J. R., "Liquidity", *Economic Journal* (1962).

Lintner, J., "The valuation of risk assets and the selection of risky investments in stock portfolio and capital budgets", *Review of Economics and Statistics* (1965a).

Lintner, J., "Security prices, risk and maximal gains from diver-
sifications", *Journal of Finance* (1965b).

Markowitz, H., "Portfolio selection", *Journal of Finance* (1952).

Mossin, J., "Equilibrium in a capital asset market", *Econometrica* (1966).

Rao, C., *Linear statistical inference and its applications* (New York, 1965).

Samuelson, P. A., "The fundamental approximation theorem of portfolio
analysis in terms of means, variances and higher moments", *Review of
Economic Studies* (1970).

Sharpe, W. F., "Capital asset prices: A theory of market equilibrium under
conditions of risk", *Journal of Finance* (1964).

Stone, B. K., *Risk, return and equilibrium* (Cambridge, Mass., 1970).

Tobin, J., "Liquidity preference as behavior towards risk", *Review of
Economic Studies* (1958).

Tobin, J., "Portfolio selection", in: F. H. Hahn and F. P. R. Brechling,
eds., *The theory of interest rates* (New York, 1965).

Tobin, J., "Notes on optimal monetary growth", *Journal of Political
Economy* (1968).

Tobin, J., "Comment on Borch and Feldstein", *Review of Economic
Studies* (1969).

Tsiang, S. C., "The rationale of the mean-standard deviation analysis,
skewness preference, and the demand for money", *American Economic
Review* (1972).

3

The Expected Utility Approach

(A)   Ever since the famous work by Daniel Bernoulli (1738), the expected utility approach has been the most popular method of dealing with the problems of choice under risk.

In this celebrated paper, Bernoulli postulates a logarithmic utility function, defines the expected utility ("moral expectation"), proposes it as the performance criterion, and applies it to a number of illustrative problems of choice involving risk. Among these problems is the famous St. Petersburg Paradox (§§ 17–19). The problem is stated as follows:

> "Peter tosses a coin and continues to do so until it should land 'heads' when it comes to the ground. He agrees to give Paul one ducat if he gets 'heads' on the very first throw, two ducats if he gets it on the second, four if on the third, eight if on the fourth, and so on, so that with each additional throw the number of ducats he must pay is doubled. Suppose we seek to determine the value of Paul's expectation . . . ."

Since the probability of getting "heads" on the nth throw for the first time is $1/2^n$, and the prize for that is 2^{n-1} ducats, the mathematical expectation of the prize is $\sum_{n=1}^{\infty} 2^{n-1}/2^n = 1/2 + 1/2 + \cdots = +\infty$. But, according to Nicolas Bernoulli, cousin of Daniel and the inventor of the problem, any fairly reasonable man would sell his chance, with great pleasure, for 20 ducats. Daniel Bernoulli applied his expected utility theory to this problem.

Assume that the utility function has the form

$$u = b \ln \frac{a + x}{a},$$

where b is a positive constant and a is a given positive initial wealth; x is, of course, the gain in the game. Then the expected utility of the game is

$$E(u) = \frac{b}{2} \ln \frac{a + 1}{a} + \frac{b}{2^2} \ln \frac{a + 2}{a} + \frac{b}{2^3} \ln \frac{a + 2^2}{a} + \cdots$$

$$+ \frac{b}{2^n} \ln \frac{a + 2^{n-1}}{a} + \cdots$$

For $a > 0$,[1] it can be shown that $E(u)$ converges, or has a finite limit. For example, let us apply the "Ratio Test" [see, e.g., Rudin (1964, Theorem 3.34, p. 57)] which states that the series $\Sigma\, a_n$ converges if $\lim_{n \to \infty} \sup |a_{n+1}/a_n| < 1$. In our problem,

$$\frac{a_{n+1}}{a_n} = \frac{(b/2^{n+1}) \ln (1 + 2^n/a)}{(b/2^n) \ln (1 + 2^{n-1}/a)} = \frac{\ln (1 + 2^n/a)}{2 \ln (1 + 2^{n-1}/a)}$$

$$= \frac{\ln (1 + 2^n/a)}{\ln (1 + 2^n/a + 2^{2(n-1)}/a^2)} < 1.$$

Furthermore, this ratio itself decreases as n increases. Hence, clearly $\lim_{n \to \infty} \sup |a_{n+1}/a_n| < 1$, and the proof is complete. Thus, in terms of the concave utility, the gain is finite. In fact, in order for an individual to purchase this chance for 20 ducats, his initial wealth would have to be quite substantial. This is how he provided a solution to the Paradox.[2] Bernoulli's solution left a basic question unanswered, however, Specifically, why should a decision be based on the expected value of these utilities? It was not until the monumental work by von Neumann and Morgenstern that this question was given a rigorous answer.

---

[1] Bernoulli takes a particular care to guarantee $a > 0$ by defining wealth including human capital so that $a = 0$ means starvation.

[2] For a comprehensive discussion of the Paradox, see Menger (1934).

(B) In their *Theory of Games and Economic Behavior* (1944, 1946, 1953), von Neumann and Morgenstern expounded the notion of utility in relation to uncertain prospects (pp. 17–27). Having accepted the basic notion of utility, they showed that a number of axioms on the preferences imply the existence of a function from utilities to real numbers $V: u \rightarrow p$, such that

$$u > v \quad \Rightarrow \quad V(u) > V(v), \tag{3.1}$$

$$V(au + (1 - a)v) = aV(u) + (1 - a)V(v), \tag{3.2}$$

If there are two functions V, V' satisfying these two conditions, one is a positive linear transformation of the other. (3.3)

Let U be a system of entities, $u, v, w, \ldots$. Then the axioms sufficient for the existence of such a V are stated as follows:

(A) $u > v$ is a complete ordering of U

   (A:a) For any two u, v, one and only one of the following three relations holds: $u = v$, $u > v$, $v > u$.

   (A:b) $u > v$, $v > w$ imply $u > w$.

(B) Ordering and combining

   (B:a) $u < v$ implies that $u < au + (1 - a)v$ for any $0 < a < 1$.

   (B:b) $u > v$ implies that $u > au + (1 - a)v$ for any $0 < a < 1$.

   (B:c) $u < w < v$ implies the existence of an a such that $au + (1 - a)v < w$.

   (B:d) $u > w > v$ implies the existence of an a such that $au + (1 - a)v > w$.

(C) Algebra of combining

   (C:a) $au + (1 - a)v = (1 - a)v + au$.

   (C:b) $a(bu + (1 - b)v) + (1 - a)v = cu + (1 - c)v$, where $c = ab$.

A rigorous proof that these axioms imply the existence of a function satisfying (3.1)–(3.3) is given in their appendix (pp. 618–628). While the proof is long, the idea can be sketched as follows:

First, they show that the so-called monotonicity or dominance relation,

$$u < v, 0 \leq a < b \leq 1 \;\Rightarrow\; (1 - a)u + av < (1 - b)u + bv,$$

follows from Axioms (B) and (C). But this qualitative information is not enough for the purpose.

Second, choose two utility levels u_0, v_0, $u_0 < v_0$, and consider the set of utilities w in the domain $[u_0, v_0]$. Any such w can be expressed as

$$w = (1 - a)u_0 + av_0,$$

for some $D \leq a \leq 1$. Using this relation, define $f(w)$ by

$$f(w) = \frac{w - u_0}{v_0 - u_0}.$$

Then, clearly, (i) $f(u_0) = 0$, (ii) $f(v_0) = 1$, (iii) f is monotone, (iv) $f((1 - b)u_0 + bw) = bf(w)$, (v) $f((1 - b)v_0 + bw) = 1 - b + bf(w)$, for $0 \leq b \leq 1$. It can be shown that a linear transformation of f,

$$g(w) = (b_0 - a_0)f(w) + a_0, \qquad b_0 > a_0,$$

has all these properties except for the obvious change in the value of the function.

Third, while the function f has the basic desirable properties one wishes V to have, it is defined on a fixed domain $[u_0, v_0]$. To remove this constraint, they choose two points u^*, v^* in this domain such that $u_0 \leq u^* < v^* \leq v_0$. Let $g(u^*) = 0$ and $g(v^*) = 1$. These equations can be solved uniquely for a_0 and b_0 to yield

$$g^*(w) = \frac{f(w) - f(u^*)}{f(v^*) - f(u^*)} = \frac{w - u^*}{v^* - u^*},$$

which is free from u_0 and v_0 and applicable to any w. That g^*

satisfies (3.1) and (3.2) is easy to see. As for (3.3), we note that the two points u^*, v^* are picked for the purpose of normalization. The fact that any positive linear transformation of g^* also satisfies (3.1) and (3.2) means that the particular way in which normalization is done is immaterial. Thus g^* is a general function. Finally, they show that only linear transformations will retain the properties (3.1) and (3.2), to establish (3.3).

It may be useful to illustrate the meaning of all this in terms of an example. Consider a variable W, say, the return from a given portfolio, defined on $[0, \bar{W}]$. Suppose that the preference ordering of W is complete and transitive, with a greater W always preferred to a smaller one [Axiom (A)]. Let us set the utility associated with $W = 0$ at zero and the utility associated with $W = \bar{W}$ at unity. Now to introduce risk, let us suppose that a sure prospect of earning $0.3\bar{W}$ is indifferent to a 50–50 chance (a simple lottery) of earning 0 and $\bar{W}$ [Axioms (B:c,d)]. Then we set the utility of the sure $0.3\bar{W}$ at $0.5 = 0.5(0) + 0.5(1)$. Write $U(0.3\bar{W}) = 0.5$. What can we say about the utility of W, say, $W = 0.7\bar{W}$? By the same axioms, the sure prospect of earning $0.7\bar{W}$ is indifferent to a certain chance of earning either $0.3\bar{W}$ or $\bar{W}$. Suppose that it is indifferent to a $(0.2, 0.8)$ chance of earning $0.3\bar{W}$ and $\bar{W}$. Then the utility of the sure $0.7\bar{W}$ becomes

$$U(0.7\bar{W}) = (0.2)(0.5) + (0.8)(1) = 0.9,$$

which is larger than $U(0.3\bar{W}) = 0.5$. To be precise, the lottery $(0.2$ of $0.3\bar{W}$, 0.8 of $\bar{W})$ can be considered as a compound lottery since $0.3\bar{W}$ itself can be regarded as a simple lottery $(0.5$ of 0, 0.5 of $\bar{W})$. By Axiom (C), a compound lottery can always be reduced to a simple lottery, and vice versa. The sure prospect of earning $0.7\bar{W}$, regarded as a simple lottery involving 0 and $\bar{W}$, can be written as $(0.1$ of 0, 0.9 of $\bar{W})$, where

$$0.1 = (0.2)(0.5),$$
$$0.9 = (0.2)(0.5) + 0.8.$$

In general, the sure prospect of earning any W, $0 < W <$ $\bar{W}$, can be represented by such a simple lottery involving only 0 and $\bar{W}$, and the corresponding $U(W)$ given by $U(W) = a$, where a is the appropriate probability assigned on $\bar{W}$ in the lottery. Thus, the axioms enable us to determine the utility function $U(W)$ over the whole domain $[0, \bar{W}]$. Axioms (B:a,b) imply that such a utility function is monotone. Furthermore, such a utility function is unique up to a positive linear transformation, namely, if $U(W)$ is the utility function derived above, then all other utility functions having the identical behavioural implications can be written as $V(W) = aU(W) + b$, $a > 0$. The force of the von Neumann–Morgenstern theorem is that if the individual acted on the criterion of maximum expected utility on the basis of the utility function U, he would be acting in a manner perfectly consistent with his preferences provided his preferences satisfy these axioms.[3]

(C) Arrow's Single-Period Model of Portfolio Selection:[4] As an application of the Expected Utility Theorem, Arrow considers the following simple problem. Consider an individual who is bound to hold his assets in either cash which has a secure return of zero, or risky investments that have a rate of return X which is random and independent of the amount invested. By virtue of limited liability, we assume $X \geq -1$. The individual with assets A can hold a in risky investments and $A - a$ in cash $(0 \leq a \leq A)$. If W is the future value of the investment,

$$W = a(1 + X) + (A - a) = A + aX. \qquad (3.4)$$

Let $U(W)$ be his utility function. Then according to the

---

[3]For a good exposition of the expected utility theory, see Arrow (1965, lecture 1).

[4]Based on Arrow's Lecture Notes at Stanford and on Arrow (1965, lecture 2).

Expected Utility Theorem, he attempts to maximize

$$M = E[U(W)], \tag{3.5}$$

subject to

$$0 \le a \le A.$$

We assume that the individual is a risk averter in the sense that the U function is concave. Under this assumption M is a concave function of the decision variable a as seen from

$$dM/da = E[U'(A + aX)X],$$
$$d^2M/da^2 = E[U''(A + aX)X^2] < 0.$$

Since M is concave, a unique maximum exists in the interval $0 \le a \le A$. Such a maximum occurs in exactly one of the three following ways:

Case (a):

$$a^* = 0 \quad \text{iff} \quad M'(0) = E[U'(A)X] \le 0.$$

Case (b):

$$a^* = A \quad \text{iff} \quad M'(A) = E[U'(A + AX)X] \ge 0.$$

Case (c):

$$0 < a^* < A \quad \text{with} \quad M'(a^*) = E[U'(A + a^*X)X] = 0.$$

Hereafter we shall concentrate on Case (c), the case of an interior maximum. Using the equilibrium condition

$$E[U'(A + a^*X)X] = 0,$$
$$da^*/dA = -E[U''(A + a^*X)X]/E[U''(A + a^*X)X^2], \tag{3.6}$$

or

$$\text{sign } da^*/dA = \text{sign } E[U''(A + a^*X)X]. \tag{3.7}$$

To study da^*/dA, Arrow first defines a measure of absolute risk aversion $R_A(W)$ as

$$R_A(W) \equiv -U''(W)/U'(W), \tag{3.8}$$

where $R_A(W)$ is assumed to be bounded and monotonic.

Using this definition,

$$U''(A + aX)X = -U'(A + aX) \cdot R_A(A + aX) \cdot X.$$

Suppose $R_A(W)$ is decreasing. Then for $X < 0$,

$$R_A(A) < R_A(A + aX),$$

and

$$-U'(A + aX)X \cdot R_A(A) \leq -U'(A + aX)X \cdot R_A(A + aX).$$

Similarly, for $X > 0$,

$$R_A(A + aX) \leq R_A(A),$$

and

$$-U'(A + aX)XR_A(A) \leq -U'(A + aX)XR_A(A + aX).$$

That is, for all values of X, this last inequality holds. Hence,

$$\begin{aligned}
E[-U'&(A + aX)XR_A(A + aX)] \\
&= E[U''(A + aX)X] \geq E[-U'(A + aX)XR_A(A)] \\
&= R_A(A)E[-U'(A + aX)X] = 0 \quad \text{at} \quad a = a^*.
\end{aligned} \quad (3.9)$$

So, $da^*/dA \geq 0$ if $R_A(W)$ is decreasing.

Next, proceeding to the analysis of demand for cash in terms of elasticities, let $b = A - a$ be the demand for cash and let Eb/EA be the elasticity of demand for cash with respect to assets A,

$$Eb/EA = (A/b)\, db/dA = \{A/(A - a)\}(1 - da/dA), \quad (3.10)$$

or

$$\begin{aligned}
Eb/EA - 1 &= (A/b)\{1 + E[U''(A + aX)X] \\
&\quad /E[U''(A + aX)X^2]\} - 1 \\
&= E[U''(A + aX)(A + aX)X] \\
&\quad /bE[U''(A + aX)X^2].
\end{aligned} \quad (3.11)$$

Thus

$$\text{sign}(Eb/EA - 1) = -\text{sign}\, E[U''(A + aX)(A + aX)X].$$
$$(3.12)$$

To study $Eb/EA - 1$, Arrow defines a measure of relative risk aversion $R_R(W)$ as

$$R_R(W) \equiv -RU''(W)/U'(W), \qquad (3.13)$$

where $R_R(W)$ is again assumed to be bounded and monotonic. Using $R_R(W)$,

$$U''(A + aX)(A + aX)X = -U'(A + aX)XR_R(A + aX).$$

By exactly the same argument, we can show that if $R_R(A + aX)$ is monotone increasing, then

$$-U'(A + aX)XR_R(A + aX) \leq -U'(A + aX)X \cdot R_R(A),$$

for all values of X.

So

$$\begin{aligned}
&E[-U'(A + aX)XR_R(A + aX)] \\
&= E[U''(A + aX)(A + aX)X] \\
&\leq R_R(A)E[-U'(A + aX)X] = 0 \quad \text{at} \quad a = a^*.
\end{aligned}$$

Therefore $Eb/EA - 1 \geq 0$ if $R_R(W)$ is increasing. Evidence suggests that this is the realistic case.[5]

Let us now turn to the interpretation of increasing $R_R(W)$. Let A be the initial amount, and consider a choice between R and an uncertain prospect $\{(1 + h)A$ with probability p and $(1 - h)A$ with probability $(1 - p)\}$. In particular, consider $p = p(A, h)$ such that the choice is indifferent.

Letting

$$P(A, h) = P(A, 0) + hP_h(A, 0), \qquad (3.14)$$

---

[5]See, however, Section D of Chapter 4. All the above results carry over to the case of many risky assets. Namely when $R_A(W)$ is constant, the amount of each risky asset is insensitive to the increase in A, and when $R_R(W)$ is constant, the amount of each risky asset increases in proportion to A. This can be seen by carrying out the problem of maximizing $E[U(R^T x)]$ subject to $A - v^T x = 0$, assuming as in Chapter 2 that the nth asset is riskless, and noting the special form the bordered Hessian matrix takes when either $R_A(W)$ or $R_R(W)$ is constant. Unfortunately, however, this nice property does not carry over to general concave U functions. See Cass and Stiglitz (1970).

for small enough h, and by definition of p,

$$U(A) = pU\{(1 + h)A\} + (1 - p)U\{(1 - h)A\}. \qquad (3.15)$$

Expanding with respect to h at $h = 0$,

$$U(A) = p\{U(A) + U'(A)Ah + U''(A)/2(Ah)^2 + 0(h^2)\}$$
$$+ (1 - p)\{U(A) - U'(A)Ah + U''(A)/2(Ah)^2 + 0(h^2)\}$$

where

$$0(h^2)/h^2 \to 0 \quad \text{as} \quad h^2 \to 0.$$

Rearranging terms,

$$0 = (2p - 1)U'(A)Ah + \tfrac{1}{2}U''(A)(Ah)^2 + 0(h^2). \qquad (3.16)$$

Divide by h and letting $h \to 0$,

$$(2p - 1)U'(A)A = 0, \qquad (3.17)$$

or

$$p(A, 0) = \tfrac{1}{2}. \qquad (3.18)$$

This states that when h is close to zero, the individual asks for a fair bet. Next divide (3.16) by h^2, and using

$$2p - 1 = 2((p - 1)/2) = 2\{P(A, h) - p(A, 0)\},$$

$$\{2\{p(A, h) - p(A, 0)\}/h\}U'(A)A$$
$$+ U''(A)A^2/2 + 0(h^2)/h^2 = 0,$$

Letting $h \to 0$,

$$2P_h(A, 0)U'(A)A + U''(A)A^2/2 = 0, \qquad (3.19)$$

or

$$P_h(A, 0) = -\tfrac{1}{4}U''(A)A/U'(A) = \tfrac{1}{4}R_R(A) > 0.$$

This means that as h gets larger, the individual asks for better and better odds. It also shows that if $R_R(A)$ is increasing, the willingness to take a risk proportional to one's wealth diminishes as wealth increases.

(D) Samuelson's Multi-Period Model of Portfolio Selection:[6] Samuelson's model differs from the ones discussed so far in two respects. Firstly, the time horizon of the agent contains multiple periods. The solution of the problem therefore takes the form of a sequence of decisions. Secondly, the objective criterion of the agent is the utility of consumption. The solution of the problem, therefore, includes both the consumption-saving and the portfolio decision. If we interpret one of the assets as money, the desirability of money rests on its contribution to a more stable and preferable stream of consumption. In this regard, the present formulation is superior also to the risk–return formulation which treats risk as parameters independently of the spending plans. See the Samuelson–Merton "util prob mean return" concept below.

Samuelson considers a consumer with a time horizon of $T + 1$ periods (from period 0 to period T). The individual starts with an initial wealth but has no other source of income over his lifetime. The possible bequest motive is ignored for simplicity. The lack of other sources of income means that the individual will be carrying some positive amount of wealth W_t throughout these periods. It is assumed that wealth must be carried either in the form of a safe asset which has a sure *net* rate of return r per dollar per period or in the form of a risky asset whose *gross* rate of return per dollar per period is Z_t, where Z_t is a random variable subject to the probability distribution

$$\text{Prob}(Z_t \leq z) = P(z), \qquad z \geq 0. \tag{3.20}$$

[6]Samuelson (1969). The same issue of the *Review of Economics and Statistics* contains the continuous version of the Samuelson model by R. Merton. Also see Mossin (1968).

Let w_t be the fraction of wealth put in the risky asset and $(1 - w_t)$ be the fraction of wealth put in the safe asset. Also let $U(C_t)$ be the utility function associated with consumption in period t. His problem is then (ignoring other constraints like $C_t \geq 0$, $0 \leq w_t \leq 1$)

$$\underset{\{C_t,\, w_t\}}{\text{Max.}} E \sum_{t=0}^{T} (1+\rho)^{-t} U(C_t), \tag{3.21}$$

subject to

$$C_t = W_t - W_{t+1}/[(1+r)(1-w_t) + w_t Z_t],$$
$$W_0 > 0 \text{ given}, \quad W_{T+1} = 0. \tag{3.22}$$

The problem would be quite simple if there were no uncertainty. For, in such a case, the choice of C_t, w_t, given W_t, would determine the value of W_{t+1} uniquely. But with uncertainty, this is no longer the case. It is not possible, looking forward in period 0, to solve for the complete sequence of optimal (C_t, w_t). The way to solve this type of problem is to decompose the solution in the form of a sequence $\{C_t, w_t\}$ into a sequence of single-period decisions and to do it backwards starting from the end of the planning horizon.

Suppose the individual is at the beginning of period $T - 1$. By then W_{T-1} is a known datum. He has two periods to go which involve a single set of decisions (C_{T-1}, w_{T-1}), since the final consumption is given by

$$C_T = W_T = (W_{T-1} - C_{T-1})\{(1 - w_{T-1})(1 + r) + w_{T-1} Z_{T-1}\}.$$

His problem is therefore to maximize with respect to (C_{T-1}, w_{T-1})

$$U(C_{T-1}) + (1+\rho)^{-1} E U[(W_{T-1} - C_{T-1})$$
$$\times \{(1 - w_{T-1})(1 + r) + w_{T-1} Z_{T-1}\}],$$

where the expectation operator E operates on the

random variable Z_{T-1} with its probability distribution $p(Z_{T-1}/Z_{T-2}, Z_{T-3}, \ldots, Z_0)$. Samuelson makes, throughout his paper, the assumption that $Z_0, Z_1, \ldots, Z_{T-1}$ are stochastically independent so that such conditional distributions are reduced to simple distributions. The first-order conditions for the above maximization problem are

$$0 = U'(C_{T-1}) - (1+\rho)^{-1}EU'(C_T)$$
$$\times \{(1 - w_{T-1})(1+r) + w_{T-1}Z_{T-1}\}, \qquad (3.23)$$
$$0 = (1+\rho)^{-1}EU'(C_T)(W_{T-1} - C_{T-1})(Z_{T-1} - 1 - r).$$

Under the assumption of a (strictly) concave utility function, the Jacobian matrix is negative definite and the existence of a unique set of optimal (C_{T-1}, w_{T-1}) is guaranteed. These optimal solutions are naturally a function of the initial wealth W_{T-1}, for a given probability distributions of the rates of return. We express this fact by

$$J_1(W_{T-1}) = \underset{\{C_{T-1}, w_{T-1}\}}{\text{Max.}} \ U(C_{T-1}) + (1+\rho)^{-1}EU[(W_{T-1} - C_{T-1})$$
$$\times \{(1 - w_{T-1})(1+r) + w_{T-1}Z_{T-1}\}]. \qquad (3.24)$$

Having solved this problem, we move back one period, and consider the problem of maximizing utility over three periods. The initial wealth is now W_{T-2}. For the immediate period $T-2$, he must decide on the optimal (C_{T-2}, w_{T-2}), which will determine, in turn, W_{T-1} subject to the randomness associated with Z_{T-2}. But no matter what the outcome of W_{T-1} is, we have already solved the maximization problem beyond that period. Hence, the present three-period maximization problem has been reduced to a single period problem. The problem is now to maximize with respect to (C_{T-2}, w_{T-2})

$$U(C_{T-2}) + (1+\rho)^{-1}EJ_1(W_{T-1})$$
$$= U(C_{T-2}) + (1+\rho)^{-1}EJ_1[(W_{T-2} + C_{T-2})$$
$$\times \{(1 - w_{T-2})(1+r) + w_{T-2}Z_{T-2}\}],$$

which yields an optimal set (C_{T-2}, w_{T-2}), and gives rise to

$$J_2(W_{T-2}) = \underset{\{C_{T-2},\, w_{T-2}\}}{\text{Max.}} U(C_{T-2}) + (1+\rho)^{-1} EJ_1[(W_{T-2} - C_{T-2})$$
$$\times \{(1 - w_{T-2})(1 + r) + w_{T-2}Z_{T-2}\}].$$

Moving back another period, the problem would be to maximize with respect to (C_{T-3}, w_{T-3})

$$U(C_{T-3}) + (1+\rho)^{-1} EJ_2(W_{T-2})$$
$$= U(C_{T-3}) + (1+\rho)^{-1} EJ_2 [(W_{T-3} - C_{T-3})$$
$$\times \{(1 - w_{T-3})(1 + r) + w_{T-3}Z_{T-3}\}],$$

which is but another single-period decision problem. Continuing recursively in this way, we would finally hit the period 0 and the solution would be complete.

The classic literature on dynamic programming is of course the book by Bellman (1957), where the term "dynamic programming" is used to describe the mathematical theory of multi-stage decision process. The particular framework in which the theory is developed is called the *Functional Equation Approach*.

To use Samuelson's above model without the risky asset as an example, define

$$J_{T-t}(W_t) = \underset{\{C_t,\dots,\, C_T\}}{\text{Max}} \sum_{\tau=t}^{T} (1+\rho)^{-(\tau-t)} U(C_\tau),$$

$$\text{given } W_t > 0, \quad W_{T+1} = 0.$$

The idea of the Approach is to decompose this single, multi-dimensional problem into T one-dimensional problems. The essential principle underlying the Approach is called the *Principle of Optimality*, which is stated as (p. 83):

> "Principle of Optimality: An optimal policy has the property that whatever the initial state and the initial decision are, the remaining decisions must constitute an optimal policy with regard to the state resulting from the first decision."

From this principle follows Bellman's *Functional Equation*:

$$J_{T-t}(W_t) = \underset{\{C_t\}}{\text{Max.}} [U(C_t) + (1+\rho)^{-1} J_{T-t-1}\{(W_t - C_t)(1 + r)\}].$$

Differentiating the right-hand side of this equation with respect to C_t and making use of the "envelope relation",

$$J'_{T-t}(W_t) = U'(C_t),$$

and setting it equal to zero,

$$U'(C_t) - (1 + \rho)^{-1}(1 + r)U'(C_{t+1}) = 0.$$

This is the discrete counterpart of Euler's equation in the calculus of variations. This equation, along with the state equation

$$C_t = W_t - W_{t+1}/(1 + r),$$

and the two endpoint conditions $W_0 > 0$, given and $W_{T+1} = 0$, determines the optimal sequence $\{C_0, C_1, \ldots, C_T\}$.

The remainder of Samuelson's paper discusses the special case in which the probability distributions of Z_t's are independent and the utility function U is of the constant-elasticity-of-marginal-utility variety (or of the constant-relative-risk-aversion variety). Formally this class of utility functions can be written as

$$U(C) = C^{1-a}/(1 - a), \qquad a > 0, \tag{3.25}$$

including

$$\lim_{a \to 1} C^{1-a}/(1 - a) = \ln C.$$

For this class of isoelastic utility functions, the optimal portfolio decision is independent of wealth at each stage and independent of all consumption-saving decisions. This can be readily seen by noting that $U(C_T)$ factors out into

$$(1/(1 - a))(W_{T-1} - C_{T-1})^{1-a}\{(1 - w_{T-1})(1 + r) + w_{T-1}Z_{T-1}\}^{1-a},$$

so that the objective functional is written

$$C_{T-1}^{1-a}/(1 - a) + (1 + \rho)^{-1}(W_{T-1} - C_{T-1})/(1 - a)$$
$$\cdot E\{(1 - w_{T-1})(1 + r) + w_{T-1}Z_{T-1}\}^{1-a}.$$

The optimal w_{T-1} is therefore determined by maximizing

$E\{(1 - w_{T-1})(1 + r) + w_{T-1}Z_{T-1}\}^{1-a}$ which does not contain W_{T-1} or C_{T-1}. The same reasoning applies to decisions at every other stage. This result is an extension of the result Arrow obtained for the single-period problem.

Before closing this section, let us take a brief look at other implications of the utility functions with constant elasticity of marginal utility. Using (3.25), (3.23) can be written

$$0 = C_{T-1}^{-a} - (1 + \rho)^{-1}(W_{T-1} - C_{T-1})^{-a}E_{T-1}\{\ \}^{1-a} = 0,$$
$$0 = (1 + \rho)^{-1}(W_{T-1} - C_{T-1})^{1-a}E_{T-1}\{\ \}^{-a}(Z_{T-1} - 1 - r),$$
(3.26)

where $E_{T-1}\{\ \}^{1-a}$ stands for

$$E\{(1 - w_{T-1})(1 + r) + w_{T-1}Z_{T-1}\}^{1-a}.$$

By the aforementioned dichotomy, the second equation of (3.26) determines an optimal portfolio allocation w_{T-1}^* independently of W_{T-1} and C_{T-1}. Substituting w_{T-1}^* into the first equation, we obtain an optimal consumption C_{T-1}^*. Samuelson writes $E_{T-1}\{\ \}^{1-a}|w_{T-1}^* = (1 + r_{T-1}^*)^{1-a}$, where r_{T-1}^* is the Samuelson–Merton "util-prob mean return" of the portfolio w_{T-1}^*. For convenience, we define $1 + g_{T-1}^* = (1 + r_{T-1}^*)^{1-a}$. Obviously, g_{T-1}^* depends both on the probability distribution of Z_{T-1} and the form of the utility function. Note that $a = 1$ (logarithmic utility) implies $g^* = 0$. Using g_{T-1}^*, the first equation of (3.26) can be solved for C_{T-1}^* as

$$C_{T-1}^* = a_{T-1}/(1 + a_{T-1}) \cdot W_{T-1} \equiv b_{T-1} \cdot W_{T-1}, \tag{3.27}$$

where

$$a_{T-1} \equiv [(1 + \rho)/(1 + g_{T-1}^*)]^{1/a}.$$

Equation (3.27) shows that the optimal consumption in period $T - 1$ is proportional to the initial wealth in that period W_{T-1}, with the marginal propensity to consume equalling $a_{T-1}/(1 + a_{T-1})$. Also, since the portfolio decision w_{T-1}^* was independent of W_{T-1} or C_{T-1}, the amounts held of various assets would similarly be proportional to wealth.

Moving back one period, we maximize

$$C_{T-2}^{1-a}/(1-a) + (1+\rho)^{-1}EJ_1(W_{T-1}),$$

$$W_{T-1} = (W_{T-2} - C_{T-2})\{(1 - w_{T-2})(1+r) + w_{T-2}Z_{T-2}\},$$

with respect to (C_{T-2}, w_{T-2}). It is useful to recall that

$$dJ_1/dW_{T-1} \equiv U'(C_{T-1}^*) = (b_{T-1}W_{T-1})^{-a}.$$

Using this envelope relation, the first-order conditions become

$$0 = C_{T-2}^{-a} - (1+\rho)^{-1}b_{T-1}^{-a}(W_{T-2} - C_{T-2})^{-a}E_{T-2}\{ \ \}^{1-a},$$

$$0 = E_{T-2}\{ \ \}^{-a}(Z_{T-2} - 1 - r). \tag{3.28}$$

The second equation determines w_{T-2}^* and using this w_{T-2}^*, the first equation becomes

$$0 = C_{T-2}^{-a} - (1+\rho)^{-1}(1 + g_{T-2}^*)b_{T-1}^{-a}(W_{T-2} - C_{T-2})^{-a},$$

which yields

$$C_{T-2}^* = b_{T-2}W_{T-2}, \tag{3.29}$$

where

$$b_{T-2} = b_{T-1}a_{T-2}/(1 + b_{T-1}a_{T-2}),$$

$$a_{T-2} \equiv [(1+\rho)/(1 + g_{T-2}^*)]^{1/a}. \tag{3.30}$$

Comparing (b_{T-2}, w_{T-2}^*) with (b_{T-1}, w_{T-1}^*), we note the following. First if the probability distributions of Z_{T-2} and Z_{T-1} are the same and if r is the same then $w_{T-2}^* = w_{T-1}^*$ since the second equation of (3.28) and the second equation of (3.26) would then be equivalent. This means $a_{T-2} = a_{T-1}$, $g_{T-2}^* = g_{T-1}^*$. Second, the marginal propensity to consume out of wealth changes systematically from period to period, even if the a's remain the same.

More generally, when we move back t periods, we face the following problem:

$$\operatorname*{Max.}_{\{C_{T-t}, w_{T-t}\}} C_{T-t}^{1-a}/(1-a) + (1+\rho)^{-1}EJ_{t-1}(W_{T-t+1}),$$

where

$$W_{T-t+1} = (W_{T-t} - C_{T-t})\{(1 - w_{T-t})(1+r) + w_{T-t}Z_{T-t}\},$$

and

$$\mathrm{d}J_{t-1}/\mathrm{d}W_{T-t+1} = C_{T-t+1}^{-a}.$$

This problem is formally identical to the one for the period $T-2$. Hence all the results obtained there apply to each period. Namely, with fixed probabilities, g^* will remain the same, and the marginal propensity to consume out of wealth follows the recursive relation

$$b_{T-t} = b_{T-t+1}a_{T-t}/(1 + b_{T-t+1}a_{T-t}), \qquad 2 \le t \le T.$$

So much for the mechanics. While the utility functions of the constant elasticity of marginal utility variety have been especially popular in empirically oriented studies, the implied independence of portfolio decisions from wealth size makes this class of functions rather unattractive. In fact, as Mossin (1968) showed, this class of utility functions makes multi-period analysis superfluous by rendering a multi-period portfolio solution to a sequence of single-period solutions. The reason is as follows. This class of utility functions has the property that the portfolio allocation decision is independent of the wealth size. This means that such decisions are independent of what gains or losses have been realized in the past. This property, along with the assumption of the serial independence of distributions of returns, reduces the informational value of past experience to zero. Portfolio decisions are thus entirely separated from past experience. As for the future, the investor can freely reshuffle his portfolio in every period without incurring any transactions costs. It is therefore pointless for him to be concerned about probabilities beyond the current period. In short, the apparent sequential nature of the decision problem notwithstanding, the above problem is really a static problem. On the other hand, generalization to variable elasticity of marginal utility cases makes manipulations quite hard. A useful extension would be to introduce wages as an additional source of income. Wages or human capital are subject to different types of uncertainty like mortality. The introduction of mortality would call for a modification of the objective functional as well as the addition of life insurance as another asset. A pioneering work in this direction is Yaari (1965). But again, he deals with a special case (the case of perfect insurance) in which the solution is essentially free from the effects of lifetime uncertainty.

There are two fundamental defects in the formulations in the last and the present chapters as a theory of *speculative* demand for money. The first is that they fail to recognize the idea that speculation is always made in anticipation of changes in information (probabilities) in the near future whose nature is such that if the agent acted on the basis of the currently available information, the action may, in the light of the new information, prove to be sub-optimal. The conventional assumption of a once-for-all fixed probabilities rules out such important aspects of speculation. We shall attempt to remedy this defect somewhat in our analysis of precautionary demand for money in Chapter 4.

Another defect, which is related to the first, is that the objective is assumed to be the dollar value of the portfolio and does not go far enough to study the ultimate use of the assets. While the above analysis of the consumer is an attempt to correct this flow, the model has not allowed for wide choices among financial assets. A full analysis should allow the consumer to hold financial assets as well as claims of consumption goods. Whether the consumer wishes to hold consumption goods only so as to minimize risk concerning his future consumption or some mix of commodity claims and financial assets will depend on the measure of risk aversion.

(E) In the last and the present chapters, we have studied the Mean-Variance analysis and the Expected Utility analysis of choice involving risk. The fundamental problem of choice in a risk-taking situation is one of ordering among various distributions of the relevant random variable, e.g., the portfolio return W. The Mean-Variance analysis attains a complete ordering of these distributions by postulating a utility function directly in terms of the mean and the variance. The Expected Utility analysis proposes to weigh distributions by the utility function and to pick the maximum. If, in the latter analysis, one is willing to fully specify the form of the utility function, one should be able to order distributions completely. Even though one is unwilling to give a complete specification of the utility function but willing to specify the utility function to a certain class, one can still derive a criterion on the basis of which to order two distributions. Such an idea has been formalized and studied by a number of people, e.g., Quirk and Saposnik (1962), Hadar and Russel (1969) and Hanoch and Levy (1969). See also Rothschild and Stiglitz (1970, 1971). We call this the Stochastic Dominance Approach.

The term stochastic dominance has a long history and means the following. Let f and g be two *distinct* probability density functions defined on an interval $I = [\underline{x}, \bar{x}]$ of a random variable X. Let the cumulative distributions of f and g be F and G, respectively. Then g is said to dominate f stochastically if, for all $x \in I$, $F(x) \geq G(x)$. This condition means that G lies entirely below F, or, speaking loosely, g lies to the right of f. If X is an economic variable and if a larger value of X is preferred to a smaller one, it is intuitively obvious that the prospect represented by g is preferred to the prospect represented by f. In fact a theorem has been proven to the effect that if $U(x)$ is a utility function with $U'(x) > 0$, then $E_g U(x) > E_f U(x)$, namely, the expected utility of X under g is greater than the expected utility of X under f whenever the above dominance condition holds. But more interesting is the theorem relating to the converse, namely, if $E_g U(x) > E_f U(x)$ for *any* $U(x)$ with $U'(x) > 0$, then $F(x) \geq G(x)$ for all $x \in I$.

The proof of these theorems is not hard. The difference in the expected utility is given by

$$E_g U(x) - E_f U(x) = \int_I (g - f) U(x) \, dx$$
$$= (G(x) - F(x))|_{x=\underline{x}}^{x=\bar{x}}$$
$$- \int_I [G(x) - F(x)] U'(x) \, dx$$
$$= \int_I [F(x) - G(x)] U'(x) \, dx.$$

The last expression is obviously positive if g dominates f, i.e., if $F(x) \geq G(x)$ for all $x \in I$, which proves the first theorem. On the other hand, suppose there is an interval I_1 in which $F(x) < G(x)$. Then the last expression can be written as

$$\int_{I_1} [F(x) - G(x)] U'(x) \, dx + \int_{I-I_1} [F(x) - G(x)] U'(x) \, dx.$$

Even if $F(x) - G(x) > 0$ in $I - I_1$, it is possible to choose an increasing function $U(x)$ to make this sum negative. Hence, to ensure the positivity of this expression for any $U(x)$ with $U'(x) > 0$, we must have $F(x) \geq G(x)$ for all $x \in I$, which is the second theorem.

While it is useful to know these results, we are interested in a more specific class of utility functions, i.e., *concave* functions in decision problems involving risk. To the extent that the utility function is more specified, we should expect a weaker condition on the distributions which enables us to determine the preference ordering between two random variables. Hadar and Russell (1969) have shown that the following condition, called the second-degree stochastic dominance, or SSD for short,

$$\int_{\underline{x}}^x F(y) \, dy \geq \int_{\underline{x}}^x G(y) \, dy, \qquad \text{for all} \quad x \in I,$$

plays the role of the previous dominance condition (which is now called the first-degree stochastic dominance or FSD) for the class of increasing, concave utility functions. In other

words, this condition is both necessary and sufficient for
$E_g U(x) > E_f U(x)$ where $U(x)$ is *any* utility function such
that $U'(x) > 0$, $U''(x) < 0$. The proof is again quite simple.
Writing

$$\int_I [F(x) - G(x)] U'(x)\, dx$$

$$= U'(x) \int_{\underline{x}}^x [F(y) - G(y)]\, dy \Big|_{\underline{x}}^{\bar{x}}$$

$$- \int_I \left[\int_{\underline{x}}^x \{F(y) - G(y)\}\, dy \right] U''(x)\, dx,$$

and applying a similar reasoning, the result follows.[7]

It may be of some interest to see how much more can we
say about stochastic dominance if, in addition to the concavity, we went along with Tsiang (see Chapter 2) to further
restrict the concave utility functions to that class which have
the properties of decreasing absolute risk aversion and increasing relative risk aversion. We learned in Chapter 2 that
the following two functions set bounds on this class of utility
functions:

$$U(x) = B(1 - e^{-bx}), \qquad x > 0, \quad B, b > 0, \tag{3.31}$$

$$U(x) = (1/(1-a))x^{1-a}, \qquad x > 0, \quad a > 0. \tag{3.32}$$

Using (3.31), the SSD condition becomes

$$\int_0^\infty e^{-bx} \int_0^x \{F(y) - G(y)\}\, dy\, dx \geq 0. \tag{3.33}$$

---

[7]More recently, Whitmore (1970) has proposed the notion of the "third-
degree Stochastic dominance" (TSD) under the assumption that $U^{(3)}(x) >
0$. The conditions are that

$$\int_{\underline{x}}^x \int_{\underline{x}}^y \{F(z) - G(z)\}\, dz\, dy \geq 0, \qquad \text{for all} \quad x \in I,$$

and

$$\int_I \{F(y) - G(y)\}\, dy \geq 0.$$

Using (3.32), one gets

$$\int_0^\infty x^{-(1+a)} \int_0^x \{F(y) - G(y)\} \, \mathrm{d}y \, \mathrm{d}x \geq 0. \qquad (3.34)$$

Equations (3.33) and (3.34) show that in either case the condition involves a decreasing weight as x rises from zero to infinity. This means that, in terms of this class of utility functions, the left-hand tail of the distribution really counts. This points to the significance of the skewness of distributions in preferences over prospects involving risk. If one accepts such decreasing weights, a safe asset like money appears to be able to compete well with a wide variety of risky assets.

The formal elegance of the Stochastic Dominance approach apart, the question of our main interest concerns its applicability. In particular, how do its results differ from those obtained from the Mean-Variance analysis? Given the distribution of a set of random yields, how do these two approaches differ in predicting "efficient" portfolios? Porter and Gaumnitz (1972) report on their experimental study on this question. Using the data from the Chicago Price Relative tapes on 925 U.S. stocks for the period 1960–65, they first produced 893 portfolios each consisting of 2 to 10 stocks. Of these, 198 were FSD efficient, 40 SSD efficient and 31 TSD efficient. On the other hand, they found 39 port-folios efficient in the sense of the Mean-Variance analysis, or MV-efficient, for short. In particular, they noted that a total of 24 portfolios were contained in both the SSD-efficient, and the MV-efficient sets. Then they observed that the 15 (= 39 − 24) MV-efficient portfolios eliminated by the SSD test were all low-return, low-variance portfolios, while the 16 (= 40 − 24) SSD-efficient portfolios eliminated by the MV test were found scattered over the middle ranges of return and variance but all of them were very close to the MV-efficient ones. Furthermore, they noted that the TSD test somewhat reduced the conflicts between the SSD and the MV rules.

The fact that the MV-efficient portfolios with low returns

and low variances were systematically eliminated by the
SSD test prompted them to conclude that the highly risk-
averse investor was the one most likely to suffer from the
use of the MV model since it forced on him choices inconsistent with the maximization of expected utility. This
conclusion again seems to deny the relevance of the MV
analysis as a theory of demand for money, a reinforcement
of Tsiang's conclusion. But the reasons are not quite the
same. While Porter and Gaumnitz emphasized the deviation
of the MV-efficient portfolios from the SSD-efficient ones in
the low-return, low-variance range, Tsiang relied on the
implausibility of a point on the MV-efficient frontier in this
range to be chosen as an optimal portfolio. A closer
examination of the matter both in theory and in facts seems
necessary before we can draw a final conclusion.

We wish to conclude this chapter with a remark on the
relevance of the asset theory of demand for money in
general.

First, how good is the hypothesis of maximizing the
expected utility of wealth as an explanation of the actual
behaviour of investors? Although the comparative statics
propositions which can be drawn from a theoretical model of
the expected utility theory are rather meagre, the Stochastic
Dominance approach has opened up a way for empirical
applications of the theory. If one can gain sufficient knowledge of the distribution of various yields, one can test the
predictive accuracy of the theory by comparing actual portfolios of banks and other financial institutions and even
those of households with the SD-efficient portfolios. Second,
assuming that these tests hold sufficient promise, one would
wish to check the efficiency of the asset theory as a theory of
the demand for money relative to an alternative theory
which emphasizes the uncertainty concerning cash requirements. Chapter 4 looks at this alternative theory and its
implications.

References

Arrow, K. J., *Aspects of the theory of risk-bearing* (Helsinki, 1965).

Bellman, R., *Dynamic programming* (Princeton, N.J., 1957).

Bernoulli, D., "Specimen theoriae novae de mensura sortis", (1738); translated as "Exposition of a new theory of the measurement of risk", *Econometrica* (1954).

Cass, D. and J. E. Stiglitz, "The structure of investor preferences and asset returns", and "Separability in portfolio allocation: A contribution to the pure theory of mutual funds", *Journal of Economic Theory* (1970).

Hadar, J. and W. R. Russell, "Rules for ordering uncertain prospects", *American Economic Review* (1969).

Hanoch, G. and H. Levy, "The efficiency analysis of choice involving risk", *Review of Economic Studies* (1969).

Menger, K., "The role of uncertainty in economics" (original in German, 1934); translated in: M. Shubik, ed., *Essays in mathematical economics in honor of Oskar Morgenstern* (Princeton, N.J., 1967) ch. 16.

Merton, R. C., "Lifetime portfolio selection under uncertainty: The continuous case", *Review of Economics and Statistics* (1969).

Mossin, J., "Optimal multi-period portfolio selection", *Journal of Business* (1968).

Von Neumann, J. and O. Morgenstern, *Theory of games and economic behavior* (New York, 1944, 1946, 1953).

Porter, R. B. and J. E. Gaumnitz, "Stochastic dominance vs mean-variance portfolio analysis: An empirical evaluation", *American Economic Review* (1972).

Quirk, J. and R. Saposnik, "Admissibility and measurable utility functions", *Review of Economics and Statistics* (1962).

Rothschild, M. and J. E. Stiglitz, "Increasing risk", *Journal of Economic Theory* (1970, 1971).

Rudin, W., *Principles of mathematical analysis* (New York, 1964).

Samuelson, P. A., "Lifetime portfolio selection by dynamic stochastic programming", *Review of Economic Studies* (1969).

Whitmore, G. A., "Third-degree stochastic dominance", *American Economic Review* (1970).

Yaari, M. E., "Uncertain lifetime, life insurance, and the theory of the consumer", *Review of Economic Studies* (1965).

4

The Transactions Cost Approach

(A) In the preceding chapters, we established the demand for money as a relatively safe asset in a world of uncertainty. In these models, however, holding of money balances is a form of saving competing with consumption spending, while consumption spending apparently requires no use of money. In other words, there is no explicit recognition of the medium of exchange function of money. It is for this reason that many monetary economists hold a negative opinion of these models as a theory of demand for money. In the real world, they contend, there are certain forms of near monies which are as safe as cash, earn interest, and are convertible into cash at very little cost. These near monies will therefore dominate cash as stores of value. What these models tell us is at best the allocation among these near monies or between near monies and other non-monetary assets. The present transactions cost approach is an attempt to provide an alternative theory based on the recognition that purchases of goods must be backed by cash. The recent experience of open inflations in Latin American countries has also called the asset theory into question, for it is hard to justify, in terms of such a theory, people's positive demand for cash in the face of more than 100 percent negative interest on cash per annum. It appears, to be more natural, therefore, to say that the robustness of a money economy comes from money being the dominant medium of exchange. On the other hand, the mere fact that all purchases must be backed by cash is not a sufficient reason for people to *hold* cash balances. In a completely frictionless world, people would still hold no cash. To explain people's transaction balances, therefore, it is necessary to introduce certain elements of frictions or imperfections. Transactions costs we postulate in this chapter capture such frictions.

Baumol (1952) and Tobin (1956) formulated a simple model of transactions demand for cash using a bond interest rate and a broker's fee as the key determinants of the allocation between cash and bonds, and arrived at the familiar "square-root" formula. Consider an individual who receives an income y per period whose length is determined institutionally. Assume that he receives this income in cash at the beginning of the period and that his optimal pattern of expenditure is characterized by a constant stream over the period. Further, assume that he faces an interest rate r per period and the broker's fee is a dollars per transaction. His objective is to maximize the *net* interest income with respect to his portfolio choice, subject to the condition that all spending be backed by cash. If the number of transactions, n, is prescribed, the maximal net income is given by[1]

---

[1]This is a simple dynamic programming problem. Take the income period to be a unit time length, and first consider the case in which $n = 2$. This means that the individual purchases bonds at the beginning and sells them out at some intermediate date, say, t, $0 < t < 1$. For a given t, the net interest income $\Pi_t = (1 - t) \, try - 2a$. Maximizing Π_t with respect to the choice of t, we find $t^* = \frac{1}{2}$ and $\Pi_{t^*} = \frac{1}{4} ry - 2a$. Next consider the case in which $n = 3$. This time, bond sales occur twice. Let t be the time the first sale takes place. For the bond holding up to this t, he earns an interest income $(1 - t) \, try$. For a given t, the maximal interest income in the rest of the period is already known from the solution for the $n = 2$ case as $\frac{1}{4}(1 - t)^2 ry$. The net interest income is therefore $\Pi_t = (1 - t) try + \frac{1}{4}(1 - t)^2 ry - 3a$. Again maximizing this with respect to t, we find $t^* = \frac{1}{3}$, and $\Pi_{t^*} = \frac{2}{6} ry - 3a$. Similarly, for $n = 4$, we get $\Pi_t = (1 - t) try + \frac{2}{6}(1 - t)^2 ry - 4a$, which yields $t^* = \frac{1}{4}$ and $\Pi_{t^*} = \frac{3}{8} ry - 4a$. The formula for general n can be derived easily by induction.

$$\Pi = \max[0, (n - 1/2n)ry - na],$$

where n includes the initial purchase of bonds. Assuming that the net income is positive and that the number of transactions can be treated as a continuous variable, differentiate it with respect to n to get $n^* = (ry/2a)^{1/2}$ for the optimal number of transactions. Since the average balance of wealth held is $y/2$ and since the average balance held of bonds is $(n^* - 1)y/2n^*$, the average cash balance held is $y/2n^*$ or $(ay/2r)^{1/2}$, which shows that the transactions demand for cash is an increasing function of a and y and a decreasing function of r. In particular, if $a = 0$, n^* is infinitely large and the average cash balance is zero. While this square-root formula is allegedly too special to be useful, the inventory-theoretic framework provided by Baumol and Tobin has proven to be extremely important. First, by characterizing money as the medium of exchange they capture the fundamental feature of a money economy – goods do not buy goods; only money can. Second, the introduction of bonds prevents the demand for money from becoming an imposed one, despite such institutional restraints, and makes the demand for money for transactions purposes an interesting problem of choice. We shall look at a few extensions of the Baumol–Tobin model in the rest of this chapter.

(B) One useful extension is to make the model fit for general equilibrium analysis. Feige and Parkin (1971) allowed the consumer to hold commodity inventories in addition to money and bonds, studied his personal equilibrium and, finally, the question of a social monetary optimum.

First, the personal equilibrium is described as follows. Consider a family unit who maximizes the utility function

$$U = U(pq), \tag{4.1}$$

where pq is the dollar volume of commodities consumed during the period, p being a fixed parameter in their model.

The first flow constraint the family faces is

$$0 = y + \Pi - pq - T, \tag{4.2}$$

where y = the labour income for the period in current dollars, T = taxes, and Π = the "net profit from inventory management". The taxes T represent a neutral transfer component and a component to effect interest payments on cash balances. Specifically, they assume

$$T = t + h(r_m), \tag{4.3}$$

where

$$h(r_m) = 0 \quad \text{for} \quad r_m = 0, \qquad h(r_m) = k \quad \text{for} \quad r_m > 0.$$

The net profit from inventory management is given by

$$\begin{aligned}
\Pi = (r_k - \alpha_k)p\bar{K} + (r_b - \alpha_b)\bar{B} + (r_m - \alpha_m)\bar{M} \\
- \alpha_q P\bar{Q} - \beta_b n - \beta_q m,
\end{aligned} \tag{4.4}$$

where $p\bar{K}$ = the average stock of capital, $\bar{B}$ = the average inventory of bonds, $\bar{M}$ = the average inventory of cash balances, $p\bar{Q}$ = the average inventory of commodities, r_k = the rate of return on capital, r_b = the rate of return on bonds, r_m = the rate of return on money, α_k = the cost per dollar of carrying capital inventories, α_b = the cost per dollar of carrying bond inventories, α_m = the cost per dollar of carrying cash balances, α_q = the cost per dollar of carrying commodity inventories, n = the number of bond market transactions during the period, m = the number of commodity market transactions during the period, β_b = the cost per bond market transaction, β_q = the cost per commodity market transaction. Assuming that all transactions are evenly spaced over the period, the average stocks are related to the flow consumption pq by

$$p\bar{Q} = pq/2m, \qquad\qquad m \geq 1, \tag{4.5}$$

$$\bar{M} = pq/2n - pq/2m, \qquad (m \geq n; \quad m = n \text{ means} \\ \text{perfect synchronization}), \tag{4.6}$$

$$\bar{B} = pq/2 - pq/2n, \qquad n \geq 1. \tag{4.7}$$

The stock constraint the family unit faces is

$$\bar{A} = p\bar{K} + \bar{B} + \bar{M} + p\bar{Q}. \tag{4.8}$$

Thus

$$p\bar{K} = \bar{A} - pq/2. \tag{4.9}$$

Substituting (4.5)–(4.7) and (4.9) into (4.4), the following budget constraint is obtained.

$$\begin{aligned} 0 = y &+ (r_k - \alpha_k)(\bar{A} - pq/2) + (r_b - \alpha_b)(pq/2 - pq/2n) \\ &+ (r_m - \alpha_m)(pq/2n - pq/2m) - \alpha_q(pq/2m) \\ &- \beta_b n - \beta_q m - pq - T. \end{aligned} \tag{4.10}$$

The family maximizes (4.1) subject to (4.10) with respect to the choices of pq, n and m. If we hold pq fixed for the moment and carry out maximization with respect to m and n, we obtain the Baumol–Tobin type square-root formulas for $(\bar{M})^*$, $(p\bar{Q})^*$ and $(\bar{B})^*$. Again treating m and n as continuous variables and assuming an interior solution, the optimal numbers of bond and commodity transactions are given by

$$n^* = \{(r_b - \alpha_b - r_m + \alpha_m)pq/2\beta_b\}^{1/2} \tag{4.11}$$

$$m^* = \{(r_m - \alpha_m + \alpha_q)pq/2\beta_q\}^{1/2}. \tag{4.12}$$

Substitution of n^* and m^* into (4.6) yields the optimal average holdings of cash, commodities and bonds:

$$\begin{aligned} (\bar{M})^* = &\{\beta_b pq/2(r_b - \alpha_b - r_m + \alpha_m)\}^{1/2} \\ &- \{\beta_q pq/2(r_m - \alpha_m + \alpha_q)\}^{1/2}, \end{aligned} \tag{4.13}$$

$$(p\bar{Q})^* = \{\beta_b pq/2(r_m - \alpha_m + \alpha_q)\}^{1/2}, \tag{4.14}$$

$$(\bar{B})^* = pq/2 - \{\beta_b pq/2(r_b - \alpha_b - r_m + \alpha_m)\}^{1/2}. \tag{4.15}$$

Note that if $\beta_q = r_m = \alpha_m = \alpha_b = 0$, equation (4.13) reduces to

$$(\bar{M})^* = (\beta_q pq/2r_b)^{1/2},$$

as in Baumol–Tobin. The personal equilibrium will be determined completely when maximization with respect to pq has been carried out.

Feige and Parkin then proceeded to a general equilibrium

by interpreting the household as a representative one accounting for I/N of the economy. This means that the household is now subject to the following two conditions to make individual plans consistent at the aggregate level. First, that taxes T be equal to the expenditures required to service government debts $\bar{B}$ and $\bar{M}$ at the interest rates r_b and r_m, respectively. Second, the inventory demand for goods be equal to the available stock of goods. These conditions may be written as

$$T = r_b\bar{B} + r_m\bar{M} + h(r_m), \tag{4.16}$$

and

$$\bar{W} = p\bar{K} + p\bar{Q} \quad \text{or} \quad p\bar{K} = \bar{W} - pq/2m, \tag{4.17}$$

where $\bar{W}$ is the aggregate available stock of goods.

The fact that the neutral component of the taxes is equal to $r_b\bar{B} + r_m\bar{M}$ should *not* be interpreted to mean that the taxes are imposed in proportion to *individual* inventory holdings. Substituting (4.16) and (4.17) into (4.10), we get

$$\begin{aligned}
0 = y &+ (r_k - \alpha_k)(\bar{W} - pq/2m) - \alpha_m(pq/2n - pq/2m) \\
&- \alpha_q(pq/2m) - \alpha_b(pq/2 - pq/2n) \\
&- \beta_b n - \beta_q m - h(r_m) - pq = 0. \tag{4.18}
\end{aligned}$$

Maximization of the utility function of the representative family unit, $U(pq)$, subject to (4.18) yields the solutions for inventory stocks of the following forms.

$$\begin{aligned}
(\bar{M})^* = &\{\beta_b pq/2(\alpha_m - \alpha_b)\}^{1/2} \\
&- \{\beta_q pq/2(r_k - \alpha_k - \alpha_m + \alpha_q)\}^{1/2}, \tag{4.19}
\end{aligned}$$

$$(p\bar{Q})^* = \{\beta_q pq/2(r_k - \alpha_k - \alpha_m + \alpha_q)\}^{1/2}, \tag{4.20}$$

$$(\bar{B})^* = pq/2 - \{\beta_b pq/2(\alpha_m - \alpha_b)\}^{1/2}. \tag{4.21}$$

These solutions represent solutions in a state of social optimum. By comparing them with the solutions (4.13)–(4.15), Feige and Parkin noticed that the personal optimal solutions would correspond to the social optimal solutions if the following conditions are met:

$$r_m = r_b = r_k - \alpha_k, \tag{4.22}$$

which may be written for money (and similarly for bonds)

$$(r_k - \alpha_k) - (r_m - \alpha_m) = \alpha_m. \tag{4.23}$$

The left-hand side of (4.23) represents the *private* opportunity cost of holding cash. The right-hand side of (4.23) is the real *social* opportunity cost of carrying money. Thus (4.23) states simply that the private and the social opportunity costs be equal to each other in the social optimum, which is characterized by the rate of interest on money being equal to the net real rate of return on capital. If we start from a situation where $r_m = 0$ and $\alpha_m > 0$, and move (in a comparative statics sense) to the social optimum in which $r_m > 0$, cash balances will increase, whereas bond and commodity inventories will decrease. This means that given $\bar{W}$, more real capital will be made available for productive purposes, according to (4.14) and (4.17). This, they argued, would augment the consumption flow and consequently the social welfare.[2]

The models presented above have postulated a set of positive transactions costs. But if these costs are commissions charged by brokers and warehouses, they are themselves market prices and therefore should be determined in a general equilibrium framework. On the other hand, if they are real costs of transactions incurred by transactors themselves, these costs should still be explained. One way to handle this problem is to define these costs as time costs and absorb them in a leisure–work choice framework. Saving (1971) used this idea and formulated a model which produced a system of demand functions for commodities, leisure, bonds and money. An interesting feature of his model is the existence of multiple monies, e.g., cash, demand deposits at commercial banks, commercial papers and credit cards, and possible substitutions among these monies. This is an important suggestion. The need for a

---

[2]We shall return to the question of a monetary optimum in Chapter 13.

proper analysis of the relationship among various types of
monies is clear not only to settle the issue on the definition
of money but also to understand the working of the money
market in various phases of economic fluctuations.

(C) Another obvious extension is to introduce uncertainty
via cash needs. This extension enables us to analyze the
so-called "precautionary" demand for money.

Let us first consider an investor whose initial wealth is
$A > 0$. He can hold this wealth in three ways: cash M which
yields zero return, a short-term bond S which yields a net
interest of r percent, and a long-term bond L which yields a
net interest of R percent. These returns are assumed to be
certain, and we further assume $0 < r < R$. What is uncertain
is the spending needs which must be fully backed by cash.
The investor, however, has a subjective probability of cash
needs N to be represented by a probability density function
$f(N)$ defined on a line segment $[\underline{N}, \bar{N}]$ where $\underline{N}$ is a certain
minimum cash need, and $\bar{N}$ is a certain finite maximum cash
need. So long as N does not exceed M, the investor may pay
out of cash in hand without cost. However, if N should
exceed M, he must sell bonds and make payments which
involves a positive transactions cost. We make a simple
assumption that the sale of S costs c dollars per transaction,
and the sale of L costs C dollars per transaction, with $c < C$.
Finally, we assume that the investor maximizes the expected
value of his wealth at the end of the period. Formally, his
problem is

$$\begin{aligned}
\text{Max.}_{\{M,S,L\}} V = &\int_{\underline{N}}^{M} [M - N + S(1 + r) + L(1 + R)]f(N)\,dN \\
&+ \int_{M}^{M+S} [(S + M - N)(1 + r) + L(1 + R) - c] \\
&\qquad \times f(N)\,dN \\
&+ \int_{M+S}^{\bar{N}} [(L + S + M - N)(1 + R) - c - C] \\
&\qquad \times f(N)\,dN, \qquad\qquad (4.24)
\end{aligned}$$

subject to

$$A - M - S - L = 0, \qquad M \geq 0, \quad S \geq 0, \quad L \geq 0. \qquad (4.25)$$

Equivalently, maximizing $V + \lambda(A - M - S - L)$ with respect to (λ, M, S, L) in the usual manner, the first-order conditions for an interior maximum are

$$A - M - S - L = 0,$$

$$\int_{N}^{M} f(N)\,dN + (1 + r)\int_{M}^{M+S} f(N)\,dN + (1 + R)\int_{M+S}^{\bar{N}} f(N)\,dN$$

$$+ cf(M) + C\,(M + S) - \lambda = 0, \qquad (4.26)$$

$$(1 + r)\int_{N}^{M+S} f(N)\,dN + (1 + R)\int_{M+S}^{\bar{N}} f(N)\,dN$$

$$+ Cf(M + S) - \lambda = 0, \qquad (4.27)$$

$$1 + R - \lambda = 0. \qquad (4.28)$$

The comparative statics results can be readily obtained from

$$\begin{bmatrix} 0 & -1 & -1 & -1 & d\lambda \\ -1 & -rf(M) + cf'(M) + B & B & 0 & dM \\ -1 & B & B & 0 & dS \\ -1 & 0 & 0 & 0 & dL \end{bmatrix}$$

$$= \begin{bmatrix} -dA \\ -\left[\int_{M}^{M+S} f(N)\,dN\right]dr - \left[\int_{M+S}^{\bar{N}} f(N)\,dN\right]dR - f(M)\,dc - f(M+S)\,dC \\ -\left[\int_{N}^{M+S} f(N)\,dN\right]dr - \left[\int_{M+S}^{\bar{N}} f(N)\,dN\right]dR - f(M+S)\,dC \\ -dR \end{bmatrix}$$

$$(4.29)$$

In (4.29), $B \equiv Cf'(M + S) + (r - R)f(M + S)$. The second-order conditions turn out to be that $B < 0$ and $cf'(M) - rf(M) < 0$. The results are summarized in the following table:

Effect on

		M	S	L
Increase in	A	0	0	1
	r	−	+	−
	R	0	−	+
	c	+	−	+
	C	0	+	−

The first row of the table states that an increase in the initial wealth goes entirely to the highest-yielding asset. The second and the fourth rows predict reasonable responses in the portfolio when the parameters of the middle asset changes. The third and the fifth rows state that the changes in the parameters of the asset at the end of list induce adjustments only between that asset and the one immediately before it. Although our three-asset illustration somewhat obscures the general nature of the solution, the basic feature of this type of models is that the adjustments are always confined to those between adjacent assets. So we see that the predictions of this type of precautionary demand models about portfolio choice are considerably different from those of the risk–return models. For a similar analysis with many assets, see Gray and Parkin (1973). More on this point in Section E below.

(D) Generally speaking, comparative statics results of stochastic models are difficult to derive, and often indeterminate. One wonders then what made the comparative statics results of the model in the previous section determinate and so simple. Clearly, it was the assumption of risk neutrality. What can we say if the individual is risk-averse?

In order to see the effect of risk aversion, let us consider a similar simple model of a consumer who faces a prospect of random cash needs. At the beginning of a period, he has an initial wealth of A dollars which he allocates between money M and bonds B. One unit of the bond sells at a price $1/(1 + r)$ dollars and it promises the holder one dollar at the end of the period. The consumer carries out his planned consumption at the end of the period after the bonds have matured. But we assume that during the period, he faces uncertain cash needs. For example, an old friend may pop in, his car may break, or he may fall ill. All these accidents necessitate cash spending, and comprise the sources of uncertainty mentioned above. Of course he can secure a maximal degree of "flexibility" to meet such contingencies by carrying all his wealth in the form of cash. But this would mean foregoing the interest. On the other hand, if all the wealth is to be held in the form of bonds, he must sell part of his bonds whenever such contingencies arise. We assume that if bonds are sold before maturity, he not only fails to earn interest but also incurs an additional cost in the form of a transactions cost. Hence the portfolio choice problem.

His budget constraint for the initial portfolio allocation is obviously

$$A - M - B/(1 + r) = 0. \tag{4.30}$$

We assume that his objective is to maximize the expected utility of *planned* consumption, $EU(c)$. Once the portfolio allocation has been determined, then C is given as follows:

$$
\begin{aligned}
C &= B + M - N, &&\text{if} \quad N \le M, \\
&= B - \frac{1+r}{1-t}(N - M), &&\text{if} \quad N > M.
\end{aligned}
\tag{4.31}
$$

where N denotes the accidental cash needs. We assume that the domain of N is $[0, \bar{N}]$, where $\bar{N}$ is less than A. The parameter t, $1 > t > 0$, represents the (proportional) transactions cost mentioned above. Figure 4.1 may be useful to see how the values of C were derived.

In Figure 4.1, the solid line with slope $(1 + r)$ represent equation (4.30). Let P be the portfolio allocation point. Since

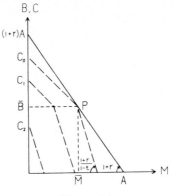

Figure 4.1

cash does not bear interest, the value of the portfolio at the end of the period will be the point designated as C_0, if no accident happens. When accidents happen, the consumer must spend his cash. If the cash need is less than $\bar{M}$, say N_1, then he simply runs down his cash balance, and the amount of money available for his planned consumption reduces to C_1. When the cash need exceeds $\bar{M}$, he is forced to sell his bonds. For example, if $N = N_2 > \bar{M}$, then the amount of money available for his planned consumption becomes C_2. It is obvious that when no accidents are expected to happen, the consumer will put all of his money in bonds.

His problem can now be formally stated as

$$\text{Max.} \int_0^M U(B + M - N)f(N)\,\mathrm{d}N$$
$$+ \int_M^{\bar{N}} U\left(B - \frac{1+r}{1-t}(N - M)\right)f(N)\,\mathrm{d}N, \qquad (4.32)$$

subject to (4.30), $M \geq 0$, $B \geq 0$. In (4.32), U is a twice-differentiable concave utility function, and $f(N)$ denotes the p.d.f. of N.

Suppose an interior maximum exists. Then it is characterized by (4.30),

$$A - M - B/(1 + r) = 0,$$

$$\int_0^M U'(C_{\mathrm{I}})\,dF + \frac{1+r}{1-t}\int_M^{\bar{N}} U'(C_{\mathrm{II}})\,dF - \lambda = 0, \tag{4.33}$$

$$\int_0^M U'(C_{\mathrm{I}})\,dF + \int_M^{\bar{N}} U'(C_{\mathrm{II}})\,dF - \frac{\lambda}{1+r} = 0, \tag{4.34}$$

where

$$C_{\mathrm{I}} = M + B - N,$$

$$C_{\mathrm{II}} = B - \frac{1+r}{1-t}(N - M),$$

$$dF = f(N)\,dN,$$

and λ is the Lagrangian multiplier on the constraint (4.30).

Now what kind of comparative statics results do we expect from this model? If we tabulate the results as in the previous section, we have:

Effect on

		M	B
Increase in	A	?	?
	r	?	?
	t	+	−

Namely, the only definite result is the effect of a change in the transactions cost. All other effects are ambiguous. The nature of ambiguities can be seen from the following equations:

$$\frac{\partial M}{\partial A} = \frac{1}{|J|}\left[-\frac{r}{1+r}\int_0^M U''(C_{\mathrm{I}})\,dF + \frac{t}{1-t}\int_M^{\bar{N}} U''(C_{\mathrm{II}})\,dF \right], \tag{4.35}$$

$$\frac{\partial M}{\partial r} = \frac{B}{(1+r)^2}\left(\frac{\partial M}{\partial A}\right) + \frac{1}{(1+r)|J|}\left[\frac{t}{(1-t)^2}\int_M^{\bar{N}} U''(C_{\mathrm{II}}) \right.$$
$$\left. \times (M - N)\,dF - \frac{1}{(1+r)^2}\int_0^M U'(C_{\mathrm{I}})\,dF \right], \tag{4.36}$$

where $|J| > 0$ denotes the Jacobian determinant of the system (4.30), (4.33) and (4.34). In both equations, the two terms in the square brackets have opposite signs; the first terms are positive and the second negative.

Although no general propositions can be established in this context, we can make a few observations. First, when the consumer is risk-neutral, i.e., $U''(\ ) = 0$, it follows immediately that $\partial M/\partial A = 0$, $\partial M/\partial r < 0$, as in the previous section. Second, when the consumer is risk-averse, the degree of risk aversion and the market parameters are all combined in determining the effects in which we are interested. If we specify the degree of risk aversion, however, we can say something. For example, if the U function has a constant absolute risk aversion, i.e., $-U''(x)/U'(x) = a = $ constant, then $\partial M/\partial A = 0$. To show this, first calculate the values of the two integrals from (4.33) and (4.34) as

$$\int_0^M U'(C_\mathrm{I})\, \mathrm{d}F = \frac{t}{t+r}\, \lambda, \tag{4.37}$$

$$\int_M^{\bar{N}} U'(C_\mathrm{II})\, \mathrm{d}F = \frac{r(1-t)}{(t+r)(1+r)}\, \lambda. \tag{4.38}$$

Next, using $U''(x) = -aU'(x)$ in (4.35), we have

$$\frac{\partial M}{\partial A} = \frac{a}{|J|}\left[\frac{r}{1+r}\int_0^M U'(C_\mathrm{I})\, \mathrm{d}F - \frac{t}{1-t}\int_M^{\bar{N}} U'(C_\mathrm{II})\, \mathrm{d}F\right]. \tag{4.39}$$

Finally, substituting (4.37) and (4.38) into (4.39), we have $\partial M/\partial A = 0$, as was to be shown. Note this paradoxical result. In the terminology of Chapter 3, money has become "the" risky asset. But why not bonds? In this model, money is indeed a risky asset, and so are bonds. The intervention of the random cash needs in effect makes both assets risky so far as planned consumption is concerned. So this is a portfolio choice problem in which all assets are risky. Recall that all the determinate results we derived in Chapters 2 and 3 were for the cases in which there was a riskless asset. In these cases, the riskless asset served as the measuring rod. But once the riskless asset disappears, there is no obvious way to evaluate the price of risk, and I suspect that certain paradoxical results may come out in such cases. The above result is just an example. If money is indeed a risky asset, the kind of inference Arrow and Tsiang drew from the empirical demand for money function about the risk aversion measure does not seem valid. Thirdly and finally, the effect of a change in the interest rate seems to be even more complex. An increase in the interest rate has the effect of pushing out the budget line for a given initial money wealth, which raises the potential for planned consumption. But, on the other hand, the increase in the interest rate increases the opportunity cost of selling the bonds prior to maturity. In terms of Figure 4.1, the semi-broken curves show a stronger "kink" at $B = \bar{B}$. Thus for a given distribution of N and for a given amount of M, planned consumption becomes more variable whenever N exceeds M. To avoid a greater variation in planned consumption, the consumer may well want to hold a greater amount of cash in the face of an increase in the interest rate.[3]

(E) This section is devoted to a brief survey of the literature on the theory of commercial bank behaviour. There is a good reason to study the behaviour of commercial banks, given the key part they play in determining the effects of monetary changes on the rest of the economy. But we do not yet have a definitive theory of commercial banks as firms. Given the diverse activities of commercial banks, a workable theory of production and cost is not easy to establish. Our purpose here is a much more limited one of comparing the relevance of the two approaches, the risk–return approach and the liquidity requirements approach, in describing the behaviour of commercial banks.

[3]For an interesting discussion on a similar subject, see Goldman (1974).

Let us begin with the risk–return approach. In this approach, commercial banks are taken to be just ordinary investors who attempt to allocate exogenously given amounts of funds among a number of assets so as to maximize profits modified by risk considerations. Despite its obvious failure to capture the special nature of banks, as firms, this approach has been a dominant approach in empirical studies of the commercial bank behaviour. Perhaps the best study to date is that by Parkin, Gray and Barrett (1970). In this paper, the authors employ a strongly specified theoretical model of expected utility maximization and apply it to the quarterly portfolio data of the U.K. commercial banks during the 1953–1967 period. Letting Π be the random profit per period, they postulate a utility function $U(\Pi)$ for each bank which is specified as

$$U(\Pi) = a - c\, e^{-b\Pi},$$

where a, b, c are positive constants. Furthermore they assume that Π is normally distributed with mean u_Π and variance σ_Π^2. When these two assumptions are combined, the expected utility of Π becomes

$$EU(\Pi) = a - c\,\exp\left[-\frac{b}{2} u_\Pi + \left(\frac{b}{2}\right)^2 \sigma_\Pi^2 \right],$$

so that maximizing $EU(\Pi)$ is equivalent to maximizing $[u_\Pi - (b/2)\sigma_\Pi^2]$, a special form of the family of utility functions postulated in the MV analysis. Hence the solution has all the properties of that in the MV analysis. As for the vector of assets and liabilities, they assume that only part of the list of assets are banks' choice variables, while all others are exogenous. Specifically, they take call loans, treasury bills, commercial bills and government bonds as banks' choice variables. Of these the amount of call loans is assumed to be subject to randomness. The same is true of all the assets and liabilities which are not in the choice set. Finally, as for the returns on assets and liabilities, they assume that they are all random, except those which are prohibited by law. Taking note of a number of restrictions on the regression coefficients and applying restricted least squares estimation method, they arrive at a reasonably satisfactory result, with many of the coefficients on interest rates significant and possessing right signs, and with R^2 ranging from 0.80 to 0.99. On the basis of this result, they discuss effects of various hypothetical policy measures. But in general, the MV model has not done well at all in explaining the portfolio behaviour of commercial banks. No other similar studies have been able to claim the degree of success achieved in the Parkin–Gray–Barrett paper. This fact suggests that one should perhaps look at the alternative approach seriously.

The alternative approach, which emphasizes the stochastic nature of bank deposits as the major source of banks' funds, dates back to Edgeworth (1888, p. 113) who declared that:

> "Probability is the foundation of banking. The solvency and profits of the banker depend upon the probability that he will not be called upon to meet at once more than a certain amount of his liabilities."

Referring mainly to the currency reserve of the Bank of England whose liabilities doubled between 1844 and 1873, he argued that a less-than-double increase in its reserve during the same period could be justified but that the size of an adequate reserve would depend crucially on the probability distribution of the random currency demand on the part of the public. In particular, he distinguished between the case where individual demands are mutually independent (in which case an increase in the reserve by a factor of $\sqrt{2}$ would do) and the case where individual demands are mutually dependent via a common cause (in which case large and positive covariances would exist between individual demands). While the fundamental nature of the problem was noticed clearly by Edgeworth, he did not pursue the problem much further. Edgeworth's idea was later exploited by Orr and Mellon (1961) in their model of commercial bank behaviour. In their model, which is quite similar to the one presented in Section C above excepting for its explicit recognition of the reserve requirements, they concentrate on the effect of the size of a bank's reserve at the beginning of the planning period (which is treated as a parameter and not part of the bank's choice variables) on the size of the new deposit liabilities the bank is willing to create. Starting with a given amount of (excess) reserves, the bank faces an uncertain prospect of reserve losses during the period. Recognizing such uncertainty the bank decides on how much deposit liabilities to create so as to maximize its expected profits. They show that the possibility of reserve losses cause the bank to create less deposit liabilities than in the certainty case (where the bank would hold zero excess reserves), although the size of such deposit liabilities depend on the interest and transactions cost parameters of the model and also crucially on the availability of liquid short-term assets. There are a few other models of similar nature, e.g., Morrison (1966, ch. II) and Klein (1971). These papers differ in emphasis, but the basic idea is the same.

In his book, Morrison (1966) has applied his model to the explanation of the excess reserves held by the U.S. commercial banks expecially during the 1930's. Again his model is a partial model of commercial banks and he concentrates on their demand function for reserves. His main conclusion on the basis of regression analysis during that period is that the interest sensitivities of reserves were not infinitely large, i.e., banks were *not* in a liquidity trap, but that their liquidity preference curve *shifted* to the right during that period. But we have yet to learn, in terms of complete empirical systems of banks' portfolios, how this liquidity approach compares with the pure portfolio approach.

References

Baumol, W. J., "The transactions demand for cash: An inventory theoretic approach", *Quarterly Journal of Economics* (1952).

Edgeworth, F. Y., "The mathematical theory of banking", *Journal of the Royal Statistical Society* (1888).

Feige, E. L. and J. M. Parkin, "The optimal quantity of money, bonds, and commodity inventories, and capital", *American Economic Review* (1971).

Goldman, S. M., "Flexibility and the demand for money", *Journal of Economic Theory* (1974).

Gray, M. R. and J. M. Parkin, "Portfolio diversification as optimal precautionary behaviour", in: M. Morishima, ed., *Theory of demand* (Oxford, 1973).

Klein, M. A., "A theory of the banking firm", *Journal of Money, Credit & Banking* (1971).

Morrison, G. R., *Liquidity preferences of commercial banks* (Chicago, Ill., 1966).

Orr, D. and W. G. Mellon, "Stochastic reserve losses and expansion of bank credit", *American Economic Review* (1961).

Parkin, J. M., M. R. Gray and R. J. Barrett, "The portfolio behaviour of commercial banks", in: K. Hilton and D. F. Heathfield, eds., *The econometric study of the United Kingdom* (Edinburgh, 1970).

Saving, T. R., "Transactions costs and the demand for money", *American Economic Review* (1971).

Tobin, J., "The interest elasticity of transactions demand for cash", *Review of Economics and Statistics* (1956).

Part II

Markets

Man is an animal that makes bargains; no other animal
does this – no dog exchanges bones with another.

Adam Smith

In Part I above, we saw various ways of formulating the
demand for money as the choice problem of individuals.
There money was thought of as the source of liquidity to
meet unpredictable spending needs, as an asset offering a
surer rate of return, or as an instrument which economizes
the real costs associated with exchange and storage. Each of
these formulations represents an effort to rationalize individuals' demand for money.

If money were just another commodity, the theory of
money would be nearly complete when individuals' demand
has been established. In the case of usual consumer goods,
an individual's taste for them can be defined without
reference to his environment. There are, to be sure, some
commodities, like automobiles, whose exact use value to an
individual can only be determined by specifying the road
condition, availability of maintenance services, etc. But individual preferences for ordinary commodities can be
defined largely independently of the environment. In contrast, the utility or the use value of money to an individual
depends essentially on the environment, for such a value lies
not in its value as a commodity but in its services in
connection with his social act of exchange. It is obvious that
money would be totally useless to Robinson Crusoe. It is

also true that if the environment were such that the markets are complete and perfect in the sense of Arrow–Debreu, there would again be no use for money. To understand money, therefore, it is necessary to study the environment individuals live in. The environment we call markets. The role of money, if any, lies in its capacity to provide individuals with a better environment, better in the sense of facilitating exchange and coordination among individual plans and generating a more efficient allocation of scarce resources.

Historically, Adam Smith (1776) was among the first economists to recognize the importance of exchange activities and the role of money. Smith singled out the power of exchange as the unique capacity of man and made it the precondition for the division of labour and the resulting efficient mode of production (Book I, ch. III). He also argued how money ("some one commodity or other...few people would be likely to refuse in exchange...") could facilitate exchange by allowing people to avoid the difficulties of attaining the double coincidence of wants (Book I, ch. IV). But Smith never explained how "some one commodity or other" had come to gain general acceptability in exchange. He simply dismissed this question as "natural". As is often the case, natural things are hard to explain.

The neoclassical utility theory made one significant contribution to the theory of exchange. The classical labour theory of value had been unable to explain why people desired exchange in the first place, because when two commodities of the same value were exchanged there were apparently no gains to either party. It was the convex preferences of the neoclassical utility theory that gave a definite answer to this basic question. Apart from this contribution, however, the neoclassical theory abstracted entirely from the problem of exchange. True, we speak of neoclassical models of "pure exchange". But these models have absolutely no implication for the problem of exchange. To illustrate, consider the following miniature general equilibrium model due to C. Menger consisting of 3 traders and 3 goods. Suppose that trader 1 has one unit of good A but desires good B; trader 2 has one unit of good B but desires good C; and trader 3 possesses one unit of good C but wants good A in exchange. According to the neoclassical theory, this model has an equilibrium at a price vector $(1, 1, 1)$, at which the goods have changed hands to the right traders. The theory also predicts that the equilibrium will actually be realized. But if we think for a moment how to implement such exchanges, we will see that there is a problem. It is a pity that the economists who did serious studies of exchange – Walras, Jevons, Menger, Edgeworth – were all founders of the neoclassical school but that their efforts in this direction have been largely ignored in the subsequent development of the neoclassical theory. The main purpose of this part is to study some ways of formulating meaningful models of a monetary economy, following, wherever possible, the lead given by these forerunners.

The program of Part II is as follows. In Chapter 5 we study the problem arising from the afore-mentioned peculiar nature of the demand for money in the context of a conventional general equilibrium model. This is followed by a discussion of Starr's attempt to formalize the notion of the double coincidence.

In Chapter 6 we look at the problem raised by Menger concerning the origin and the evolution of money. This is a problem of historical dynamics. Monetary models usually postulate money as something which commands general acceptability and attempt to explain, in a comparative statics sense, how a society with money benefits from it relative to one without. Menger contended that this was not the problem of money calling for an explanation. The enigma of money was how a society consisting of a set of atomistic and egoistic individuals has developed such a universal medium of exchange. A simple model will then be introduced to explain the evolution of money.

Chapter 7 turns to the problem of coordinating individual

plans or the problem of market equilibrium. From the point of view that this problem is fundamentally an informational problem, we first look at the theories of Walras and Edgeworth. The problem is then investigated in a more general form following the lead given by Arrow and Stigler.

Chapter 8 deals with the role of money as a store of purchasing power in intertemporal resource allocation. Arrow asserted that money claims are conducive to an efficient resource allocation over time at less cost than commodity claims in a world of uncertainty. We wish to examine the validity of this theorem. Samuelson, though in a different context, showed the superiority of money over other (capital) goods in the attainment of an efficient intertemporal resource allocation. These studies suggest an important proposition that the superiority of money as a store of value comes from its being the medium of exchange or equivalently from its ability to embody general purchasing power.

Chapter 9 concludes Part II with a discussion of Temporary Equilibrium models and of expectations in an economy with incomplete markets.

5

Money and General Equilibrium Theory

(A) The demand for money does not come from individuals' physiological needs but derives from its services in connection with their exchange activities. An individual's demand for money would therefore be zero if no one else wanted it. This interdependence of individual preferences for money poses a difficult problem for general equilibrium theory.

The internal consistency of competitive general equilibrium systems was established by a number of existence proofs by Arrow–Debreu (1954), Gale (1955) and others. If we denote the vector of accounting prices of n commodities by p and the vector of market excess demands for these commodities by $Z = Z(p)$, an equilibrium is defined by a certain semi-positive p^* such that $Z(p^*) \leq 0$, $p^*Z(p^*) = 0$. To establish the existence of such a p^*, certain assumptions or postulates are required regarding preferences and technology. At the level of $Z(p)$, these postulates may be summarized by the following [see Hahn (1965)]:

(H) $Z(p) = Z(kp)$ for any $k > 0$, $p \geq 0$ (Homogeneity)
(W) $pZ(p) \equiv 0$ for any $p \geq 0$ (Walras' Law)
(C) $Z(p)$ is continuous over $p \geq 0$ (Continuity)
(B) $Z(p)$ is bounded from below (Boundedness)
(S) $Z(0) > 0$ (Scarcity)

Given (H)–(S), the existence of an equilibrium is proven

easily. First, from (S), $p = 0$ is not a candidate for p^*. Hence we can concentrate on semipositive prices, $p \geq 0$. By (H), we can normalize prices so that $p \in S$ where S is an $(n-1)$-dimensional unit simplex, i.e.,

$$S = \left\{ x \colon x_j \geq 0, \sum_{j=1}^{n} x_j = 1 \right\}.$$

Second, define a mapping $q = q(p)$ by

$$q_i = (\max[0, p_i + hZ_i(p)]) \bigg/ \left(\sum_{j=1}^{n} \max[0, p_j + hZ_j(p)] \right),$$

where h is a certain positive number. Notice that by interpreting q as prices to be established on next "day", the above mapping can be viewed as a plausible price adjustment process. By (B), $Z_j(p)$ never goes to minus infinity for any j and for any $p \in S$. Hence by choosing h small enough, the denominator of the above mapping is assured to be positive so that the mapping is meaningful. Furthermore, $q_i \geq 0$ for all i and $\sum_{i=1}^{n} q_i = 1$. Namely, $q \in S$. By (C), $q = q(p)$ is continuous. Thus $q = q(p)$ is a continuous mapping from S into itself. By Brouwer's Fixed Point Theorem, then, there exists a fixed point, i.e., there exists a p^* such that $q(p^*) = p^*$, or writing in full

$$p_i^* = \max[0, p_i^* + hZ_i(p^*)] \bigg/ \sum_{j=1}^{n} \max[0, p_j^* + hZ_j(p^*)].$$

If $p_i^* = 0$ for any i, then from the above equation, $p_i^* + hZ_i(p^*)$ cannot exceed zero, or $Z_i(p^*) \leq 0$ for that i. For a set of positive p_i^*'s, (W) leads to

$$\sum_{+} [Z_i(p^*)]^2 = 0,$$

where $\sum_{+}$ stands for a summation over the indices i for which $p_i^* > 0$. This means that $Z_i(p^*) = 0$ whenever $p_i^* > 0$. It has thus been shown that the fixed point p^* is indeed an equilibrium price vector.

The introduction of (a token) money offers a challenge to

this line of logic. Let $\bar{p} = (p, p_m)$ be the $(n + 1)$ price vector where p_m is the accounting price of money. Then we may write the $(n + 1)$ vector of excess demand functions as

$$Z(\bar{p}, M) = Z(p, p_m M),$$

where $M \geq 0$ is the existing money stock. An equilibrium may be defined as before by a $\bar{p}^* \geq 0$ such that $Z(\bar{p}^*, M) \leq 0$, $\bar{p}^* Z(\bar{p}^*, M) = 0$. But if we follow the above reasoning, there is no assurance that $p_m^* > 0$. But $p_m^* = 0$ means that the economy is no longer a money economy. To ensure that the economy remains a money economy, p_m must remain positive. But the peculiar nature of the demand for money denies appeal to any non-satiation or scarcity assumption to the effect that $Z_m > 0$ when $p_m = 0$. Hahn argues that in order to prove the existence of an equilibrium of a money economy, one ends up postulating (1) $p_m > 0$ and (2) $Z_m > 0$ at $M = 0$ for any $p \geq 0$, $p_m = 0$. The first postulate says that we exclude zero exchange value of money at the outset. The second postulate states that the economy has an inherent desire to use money.[1] But these are precisely the kind of propositions to be deduced logically on the basis of an explicit theory of exchange. For the purpose of monetary analysis, there is therefore not much point in dwelling on these neoclassical models which have no underlying exchange theory. So let us proceed to a more productive exercise.

(B)   In this section we study an illuminating paper by Starr (1972). His major contribution lies in his formalization of the concept of double coincidence of human wants and the conditions for the attainability of an exchange equilibrium in a barter and a monetary economy.

Following Jevons (1875), Starr begins his analysis with a

---

[1]Starr (1974) lately made an appeal to taxes to be paid in money in order to prevent the price of money from becoming zero.

discussion of barter and monetary exchange (p. 291):

> "Barter is not merely the exchange of goods against goods, but rather the exchange of reciprocally desired goods. A barter transaction is one in which, for each trader, excess demand is not increased for any commodity and excess supply is not increased for any commodity.
>
> The concept of double coincidence has two parts. The first is that all trade in a barter economy satisfies some ultimate want. When goats are traded for apples it is because the owner of the goats has an excess supply of goats and an excess demand for apples; the owner of the apples has an excess supply of apples and an excess demand for goats. The second part of the double coincidence condition is the idea that the only compensation a trader receives for supplying a second trader's wants is received from the second trader."

To exemplify the difficulty of barter exchange, Starr uses the three-commodity, three-trader example of Menger described earlier. While the model clearly has an equilibrium, its implementation by means of barter is not possible, for no double coincidence of wants between two traders can take place. This example shows quite clearly that the Walrasian "pure exchange" model is not suited for the analysis of exchange. In fact, the Walrasian model may be interpreted as a barter model without the double coincidence condition, i.e., all commodities are equally acceptable in exchange. From the point of view of monetary theory, however, the double coincidence condition is essential.

> "... When money is introduced to this family of models it is defined to be the commodity to which the standard restrictions on desirability of commodities

traded do not apply. Money is the only commodity that can be accepted in trade though the recipient has no excess demand for it; money is the only commodity that can be given in trade though the donor has no excess supply of it."

Starr proposes to perform a comparative analysis of a pure exchange economy, one without, and the other with, a commodity called "money". Otherwise the two economies are identical. To facilitate comparison, the "classical dichotomy" between value and monetary theory is assumed. Thus the relative prices are determined solely by real forces. If we denote the price vector for the barter economy by p^B, the corresponding price vector for a money economy is $p = (p^B, p_m)$. There are N goods in the barter economy. Money is taken to be the $(N + 1)$st good. Throughout the paper, the existence of an exchange equilibrium is assumed.

First the barter economy: Let a_{ij}^n be the quantity of good n going from trader j to trader i. If we let T be the set of all traders and $|T|$ be the number of traders in T, an *exchange*, $A^B = [a_{ij}^k]$, is a $|T|^2 \times N$ matrix with $a_{ij} = -a_{ji}$. Starr characterizes the barter exchange as satisfying the following three conditions.

Condition 1 (Price Consistency): For each row of A^B, a_{ij}, $p^B \cdot a_{ij} = 0$. This condition states the plain fact that the transaction between any pair of traders involves exchanges of commodities of the equal market value, i.e., transactions between any pair of traders must be cleared between them.

Condition 2 (Monotone Excess Demand Diminution): Let $d_i(p^B)$, $p^B \geq 0$, be the excess demand correspondence. Then for each $i \in T$ there exists $w_i \in d_i(p^B)$ such that

(i)
$$\text{sign } a_{ij}^k = \text{sign } w_i^k \quad \text{or} \quad a_{ij}^k = 0, \qquad \text{for} \quad j \in T, \quad k = 1, \ldots, N,$$

and

(ii) $\left|\sum_{j\in T} a_{ij}^k\right| \le |w_i^k|.$

This condition states (i) that each transaction reduces, if anything, the size of the excess demands, a reflexion of the voluntary nature of exchange, and (ii) that no trader over-fulfills his excess demands. Conditions 1 and 2 jointly capture the notion of double coincidence of wants.

Condition 3 (Excess Demand Fulfillment): For each $j \in T$,

$$\left(\sum_{j\in T} a_{ij}\right) \in d_i(p^B).$$

This condition relates to the implementability of individual desired bundles by exchange.

   An equilibrium price vector is a $p^B \ge 0$ such that for each $i \in T$, $x_i \in d_i(p^B)$ and $\Sigma_{j\in T}\, x_i = 0$. The main result for barter is summarized in Theorem 1 which states that if p^B is an equilibrium price vector there is an exchange satisfying *any two* of the three conditions at p^B. To illustrate this theorem, consider the three-commodity, three-trader example. Recall that trader 1 has one unit of good A but wants good B; trader 2 has one unit of good B but wants good C; and trader 3 has one unit of good C but wants good A. An equilibrium price was $(1, 1, 1)$. Consider, in particular, the following three patterns of exchange.

(1) No exchange at all.
(2) Trader 1 grabs good B from trader 2; trader 2 grabs good C from trader 3; and trader 3 grabs good A from trader 1.
(3) Trader 1 takes good B from trader 2 in exchange for good A (by coercion); trader 2 takes good C from trader 3 in exchange for good A.

These three patterns of exchange, though not very

reasonable, are always possible. Exchange (1) clearly satisfies Conditions 1 and 2, but not Condition 3; Exchange (2) clearly satisfies Conditions 2 and 3, but not Condition 1; and Exchange (3) clearly satisfies Conditions 1 and 3, but not Condition 2. The important implication of this theorem is that the three conditions *cannot* generally all be satisfied by a *single* barter exchange.

Next, the money economy. Money being the $(N + 1)$st good, a monetary exchange is now a $|T|^2 \times (N + 1)$ matrix, $A = [a_{ij}^k]$, with $a_{ij} = -a_{ji}$. In view of the assumed dichotomy between the real and money variables, the prices of money, p_m, is set arbitrarily at unity. So the price vector in the money economy is $p = (p^B, p_m) = (p^B, 1)$. Note also that all traders' excess demands for and excess supplies of the money good are taken to be irrelevant or zero. Taking this special nature of the money good, a monetary exchange A is said to be monotone excess demand diminishing at p if A^B is monotone excess demand diminishing at p^B. Likewise, A is said to be excess demand fulfilling at p if A^B is excess demand fulfilling at p^B. Then, if p is an equilibrium price vector for a monetary economy, there exists a monetary exchange A that is price consistent, monotone excess demand diminishing, and excess demand fulfilling at p (Theorem 2). The proof of the theorem is revealing. First choose $x_i \in d_i(p)$ for all $i \in T$ so that $\Sigma_{i \in T} x_i = 0$. Second, for $k = 1, \ldots, N$, choose a_{ij}^k so that

$$\text{sign } a_{ij}^k = \text{sign } x_i^k = -\text{sign } x_j^k,$$

or

$$a_{ij}^k = 0,$$

and

$$\sum_{j \in T} a_{ij}^k = x_i^k.$$

In other words, for a prescribed equilibrium vectors $\{x_1, \ldots, x_{|T|}\}$, compare x_i^k and x_j^k for all k and for all pairs

(i, j). If x_i^k and x_j^k have opposite signs for any k and (i, j), a_{ij}^k is chosen to have the same sign as x_i^k. Otherwise a_{ij}^k is set at zero. Furthermore, the magnitudes of a_{ij}^k are chosen so that the total amount of good k going to trader i, $\Sigma_{j \in T} a_{ij}^k$, exactly fulfills his excess demand for good k. Third, as for the money good, let

$$a_{ij}^{N+1} = - \sum_{k=1}^{N} p^k a_{ij}^k = \sum_{k=1}^{N} p^k a_{ji}^k,$$

i.e., all traders finance their net purchases solely by cash. Evidently, the above construction of a_{ij}^k $(k = 1, \ldots, N)$ is excess demand diminishing and excess demand fulfilling. Such a choice of a_{ij}^k $(k = 1, \ldots, N)$ is always possible. What remains is the price consistency condition. But this condition is clearly met by the a_{ij}^{N+1} above. The existence of a universally acceptable good makes it always possible to clear the transactions between any pair of traders while maintaining the other two conditions for mutually beneficial trades. In other words, a monetary exchange in effect wipes out the monotone excess demand dimination condition which, in combination with the price consistency condition, poses so much trouble in barter. Thus for every acceptable barter exchange there is a corresponding acceptable monetary exchange. But the converse is obviously untrue. In the three-commodity, three-trader example, there was no acceptable barter exchange. But once we give one dollar of money to any one trader, an acceptable monetary exchange becomes possible. Hence there are more acceptable monetary exchanges than acceptable barter exchanges. This increase in the chance of attaining an acceptable exchange due to the introduction of money is what constitutes the social benefit of money.

Illuminating as it is, Starr's formulation leaves some of the basic questions unanswered. First it does not explain what money is and how money has come into being. Money is simply assumed to be something which commands general acceptability. Second, is the potential benefit at the society's level a sufficient reason for the existence and use of money by individuals? According to the individualistic approach, the answer is negative. Third, is the double coincidence of wants condition a reasonable characterization of a barter economy? If a primitive economy used some physical good, say, rocks, as a medium of exchange among traders, has it realized the full potential benefit of money? We think not. While we cannot claim to have the answers to all these questions, we shall consider the problem of dynamics in the next chapter and also remark on the individual vs. state theorizing of money and on the desirability of a synthesis along the line of the game theory at the end of Chapter 7.

References

Arrow, K. J. and G. Debreu, "Existence of an equilibrium for a competitive economy", *Econometrica* (1954).

Gale, D., "The law of supply and demand", *Mathematica Scandinavica* (1955).

Hahn, F. H., "On some problems of proving the existence of an equilibrium in a monetary economy", in: F. H. Hahn and F. P. R. Brechling, eds., *The theory of interest rates* (London, 1965); also in: R. W. Clower, ed., *Monetary theory* (1969).

Jevons, W. S., *Money and the mechanism of exchange* (London, 1875); also an excerpt in: R. W. Clower, ed., *Monetary theory* (1969).

Smith, A., *The wealth of nations* (London, 1776).

Starr, R. M., "The structure of exchange in barter and monetary economies", *Quarterly Journal of Economics* (1972).

Starr, R. M., "The price of money in a pure exchange monetary economy with taxation", *Econometrica* (1974).

6

The Origin and
the Evolution of Money

(A)   Throughout Part I and also in the previous chapter, we made an assumption that money was useful, that its desirability was fully recognized by all the economic agents in the system. It was the common belief among these agents that made money money. For such a belief to continue, everyone's expectation that the money he offers will be accepted by his partners must be realized consistently. While modern history shows that such expectations have been realized with an extraordinary consistency, a science cannot be built on such a belief. Firstly, there have been cases, though all under unusual situations, where the belief fell to the ground and the economy went close to barter. Secondly, and more importantly, such a historical theory cannot answer the question as to how money came into existence. To the best of my knowledge, this question has never been answered properly. Economists conventionally have been content with enumerating a number of properties – homogeneity, divisibility, cognizability, portability, durability, etc. – that observed dominant media of exchange have possessed. This may be a satisfactory answer to the question: What sort of a commodity does a society tend to choose as money, *given that the society knows the usefulness of having a general medium of exchange*? This, however, is a secondary question and a much easier one than the primary question pertaining to the conditional clause italicized above, and especially the dynamic aspect of it.

As for this primary question, perhaps the best account to date was given by Menger (1892, pp. 239–240):

> "It is obvious even to the most ordinary intelligence that a commodity should be given up by its owner in exchange for another more useful to him. But that every economic unit in a nation should be ready to exchange his goods for little metal disks apparently useless as such, or for documents representing the latter, is a procedure so opposed to the ordinary course of things.... What is the nature of those little disks or documents, which in themselves seem to serve no useful purpose, and which nevertheless, in contradiction to the rest of experience, pass from one hand to another in exchange for the most useful commodities, nay, for which everyone is so eagerly bent on surrendering his wares? Is money an economic member in the world of commodities, or is it an economic anomaly? Are we to refer its commercial currency and its value in trade to the same causes conditioning those of other goods, or are they the distinct product of convention and authority?
>
> . . . .
>
> The problem, which science has here to solve, consists in giving an explanation of a general homogeneous course of action pursued by human beings when engaged in traffic, which, taken concretely, makes unquestionably for the common interest, and yet which seems to conflict with the nearest and immediate interests of contracting individuals.
>
> . . . .
>
> ... it is clear that the choice of the precious metals by law or convention, even if made in consequence of their peculiar adaptability for monetary purposes, presupposes the pragmatic origin of money, and

selection of those metals, and the presupposition is unhistorical. Nor do even the theorists above mentioned honestly face the problem that is to be solved, to wit, the explaining how it has come to pass that certain commodities ... should be promoted amongst the mass of all other commodities, and accepted as the generally acknowledged media of exchange. It is a question concerning not only the origin but also the nature of money and its position in relation to all other commodities."

Thus, according to Menger, the fundamental problem of money is not why certain metals have become money, nor whether the society benefits from having a general medium of exchange, which was the question tackled by Starr, but how a general medium of exchange has evolved in a society through unconcerted actions of egoistic individuals.

Having stated the problem, Menger (1892, pp. 242–243) proposes a theory of saleableness of goods:

"These difficulties [of barter exchange] would have proved absolutely insurmountable obstacles to the progress of traffic, and at the same time to the production of goods not commanding a regular sale, had there not lain a remedy in the very nature of things, to wit, *the different degrees of saleableness (Absatzfälligkeit) of commodities.* The difference existing in this respect between articles of commerce is of the highest degree of significance for the theory of money, and of the market in general. And the failure to turn it adequately to account in explaining the phenomenon of trade, constitutes not only as such a lamentable breach in our science, but also one of the essential causes of the backward state of monetary theory. The theory of money necessarily presupposes a theory of the saleableness of goods."

To evaluate the saleableness, Menger seems to propose two measures. One (p. 243) is the difference between the purchase price of a good (the number of units of the most saleable good to be given up) and its selling price (the number of units of the most saleable good to be obtained on immediate resale). The other (p. 245) is the expected time cost involved in the sale of the good at an "economic" price. Menger's discussion of the saleableness ends with a consideration of its determinants. One point to be noted in this context is his emphasis on the conditions of the market as against the physical characteristics of commodities as the determinants of the saleableness. Of the eighteen items he enumerates on pp. 246–247, only some refer to the latter. The significance of this point should not be overlooked, for one of the basic errors committed by monetary theorists even today is to try to build the theory of money on the basis of the physical properties of the goods chosen as media of exchange, ignoring the social nature of money in the sense that you want it because other people want it.

Having laid down the theory of the saleableness, Menger (1892, pp. 248–249) describes the genesis of media of exchange as follows:

> "... When anyone has brought goods not highly saleable to market, the idea uppermost in his mind is to exchange them, not only for such as he happens to be in need of, but, if this cannot be effected directly, for other goods also, while he did not want them himself, were nevertheless more saleable than his own. By so doing he certainly does not attain at once the final object of his trafficking, to wit, the acquisition of goods useful to *himself*. Yet he draws nearer to that object. By the devious way of mediate exchange, he gains the prospect of accomplishing his purpose more surely and economically than if he had confined himself to direct exchange.
>
> ... Men have been led, with increasing knowledge

of their individual interests, each by his own economic interests, without convention, without legal compulsion, nay, even without any regard to the common interest, to exchange goods destined for exchange their wares for other goods equally destined for exchange but more saleable.

. . . .

... And so it has come to pass, that as man became increasingly conversant with these economic advantages, mainly by an insight and by the habit of economic action, those commodities, which relatively to both space and time are most saleable, have in every market become the wares, which it is not only in the interest of everyone to accept in exchange for his own less saleable goods, but which are also those he actually does readily accept. And this superior saleableness depends only upon the relatively inferior saleableness of every other kind of commodity, by which alone they have been able to become *generally* acceptable media of exchange.

. . . .

But the willing acceptance of the medium of exchange presupposes already a knowledge of these interests on the part of those economic subjects who are expected to accept in exchange for their wares a commodity which in and by itself is perhaps entirely useless to them. It is certain that this knowledge never arises in every part of a nation at the same time. It is only in the first instance a limited number of economic subjects who will recognize the advantage in such procedure, an advantage which, in and by itself, is independent of the general recognition of a commodity as a medium of exchange, inasmuch as such an exchange always and under all circumstances, brings the economic unit a good deal nearer to his

goal,... But it is admitted that there is no better
method of enlightening anyone about his economic
interests than that he perceive the economic success
of those who use the right means to secure their own.
Hence it is also clear that nothing may have been so
favourable to the genesis of a medium of exchange as
the acceptance, on the part of the most discerning and
capable economic subjects, for their own economic
gain, and over a considerable period of time, of
eminently saleable goods in preference to all others."

To summarize, Menger makes three points in his discussion of the genesis of media of exchange which deserve
attention. First, the peculiar interdependence among individual tastes for a medium of exchange mentioned above,
i.e., your willingness to accept it depends on your expectation about the same willingness on the part of your traders.
Second, money is not a product of legal compulsion or of
any social contrivance, but is a product of unconcerted
efforts among individuals, each pursuing his own economic
interests. Third, the evolution of money as a learning process
on the part of generations of individuals. This dynamic
theory is in sharp contrast with the classificatory, comparative static, discussions of barter and monetary exchange
so prevalent in the literature.

(B) In this section we present a simple model which for-
malizes some of the points raised by Menger. Our objectives
are threefold. First, we wish to formulate a model of
exchange where people choose between direct exchange and
indirect exchange purely on selfish, economic grounds and
where an individual's preferences for a medium of exchange
depends crucially on other people's preferences for it.
Second, we wish to formulate a model which explains the
process of monetization where a certain commodity gradually emerges in the role of a universal or dominant medium

of exchange. We do not wish to postulate the existence of a universal medium of exchange, for the historical process of monetization was never a sudden jump from a barter to a money economy but a gradual process of learning. Third, we wish to be able to measure the social gain from having a dominant medium of exchange and its nature. Let me begin with a sketch of the model.

We consider an economy at a certain historical time. The economy is inhabited by many (unspecified) individuals, and there are n goods ($n \geq 3$). We suppose that the number of individuals is substantially larger than the number of goods. Individuals are classified according to (1) the type of good he originally supplies and (2) the type of good he ultimately demands. An individual who originally supplies good i and ultimately demands good j will be referred to as an individual of type (i, j). We take the distribution of these types as the fundamental datum of the model. The supply of good i by an individual of type (i, j) is assumed to be fixed for each period. This period also determines the frequency of his exchange activities. The preferences of an individual of type (i, j) are assumed to depend on three arguments, the amount of consumption of good j, the amount of consumption of good i, and the amount of leisure enjoyed during the period. His utility function therefore has the form $U(x_j, x_i, H - T)$, where H is the total number of hours in the period and T is the number of hours consumed in exchange activities. We assume that U is an increasing, concave function in all its arguments. For simplicity, we write $V \equiv H - T$. The individual maximizes such a utility function subject to

$$x_i = \bar{x}_i, \tag{6.1}$$

and

$$x_j = e_{ij} s_i, \tag{6.2}$$

where $s_i, 0 \leq s_i \leq x_i$, is the number of units of x_i traded and e_{ij} is the exchange rate of good i for good j or the price of good i in terms of good j. Hence his problem is essentially one of time allocation, i.e., the choice of T. Since this T plays a central part in our model, we wish to take time to explain it.

We suppose that the transactions time consists of two elements. One is the time spent by a trader in finding the right type of partner. If, for example, an individual is of type (i, j) and if he opts for a direct barter, he must find an individual going from good j to good i. The other element is the time spent by a trader in setting an exchange rate acceptable to him and his partner, given that he has found a right type of partner. As for the first element, we assume that it depends on the relative frequency with which the individuals of the desired type are distributed in the economy. Let us denote, for each type (i, j), the relative frequency of this type by f_{ij}, and the fraction of individuals of type (i, j) going for an indirect exchange via good k by Π_{ij}^{k}. We interpret Π_{ij}^{i} as the fraction of individuals of type (i, j) who do not participate in exchanges at all, and Π_{ij}^{j} as the fraction of individuals of type (i, j) going for a direct barter. Obviously, $\Pi_{ij}^{k} \geq 0$ and $\Sigma_{k=1}^{n} \Pi_{ij}^{k} = 1$ for all (i, j). In any period, the relative frequency of individuals going from i to j, p_{ij}, consists of three categories:

(1) that portion of type (i, j) going for a direct barter,
(2) that portion of type $(i, k), k \neq i, j$, going from i to medium j,
(3) that portion of type $(k, j), k \neq i, j$, going from medium i to j.

If we assume that the individuals engaged in indirect barter are evenly distributed between the first leg and the second leg of transactions, we may write p_{ij} as

$$p_{ij} = \Pi_{ij}^{j} f_{ij} + \frac{1}{2} \sum_{k \neq i, j} (\Pi_{ik}^{j} f_{ik} + \Pi_{kj}^{i} f_{kj}). \tag{6.3}$$

Remember that the f_{ij}'s are the fixed data of the model, whereas the Π_{ij}^{k}'s are to be determined through individual choices as explained below. We assume that the first element of the time cost, given these p's, is measured by the expected number of searches to meet an individual of the right type.[1]

In general, if there are s objects to choose from a total of S, the probability of picking one of the s objects for the first time on the kth trial is given by

$$\frac{_{S-s}C_{k-1}}{_sC_{k-1}} \cdot \frac{s}{S-k+1}, \qquad 1 \le k \le S-s+1,$$

where C stands for "combinations".

The expected number of searches is therefore given by

$$E(s, S) = \sum_{k=1}^{S-s+1} \frac{_{S-s}C_{k-1}}{_sC_{k-1}} \cdot \frac{sk}{S-k+1}. \tag{6.4}$$

If we write $s = Sp$, we can write $E = E(p, S)$, where p is the relevant probability. Hence, if the individual described above opts for a direct barter, the cost is given by

$$T_{ij}^{j} = tE(p_{ji}, S), \tag{6.5}$$

where t is the amount of time consumed per inspection of traders, and S is the total number of traders.

The second element of time cost is the time spent by a pair of partners of the right types to arrive at mutually acceptable terms of trade. This is the cost of "higgling" emphasized by Edgeworth. This element of cost would certainly be substantial in trade under poorly organized markets under consideration, and a full analysis would require a comprehensive model of sequential decisions. But we shall not pursue this problem of higgling here in order to concentrate on the first type of time costs.

Let us illustrate the choice problem of an individual of type (i, j). First, taking his choice of exchange route as given, consider his choice between exchange and autarchy (no exchange). Maximizing $U(e_{ij}s_i, \bar{x}_i, H - T_{ij})$ with respect to

---

[1]The use of these probabilities as a measure of trading costs was first examined by Robert Jones of Brown University in his Ph.D. dissertation (1976).

$\bar{x}_i \geq s_i \geq 0$, the first-order condition for a maximum becomes[2]

$$e_{ij} U_{x_i} - U_{x_i} \leq 0 \leq s_i.$$

Let s_i^* be the solution. If $s_i^* = 0$, the individuals will definitely choose not to exchange. If $s_i^* > 0$, we compare the two utilities, one with exchange

$$U(e_{ij} s_i^*, \bar{x}_i - s_i^*, H - T_{ij}),$$

and the other without exchange

$$U(0, \bar{x}_i, H).$$

The individual will engage in exchange if and only if the former utility is greater than the latter. This implies that for a given choice of the exchange route and the time cost T_{ij}, there exists a critical exchange rate $\underline{e}_{ij}$ such that he will engage in exchange if $e_{ij} \geq \underline{e}_{ij}$. Clearly, $\underline{e}_{ij}$ depends on his taste and the time cost T_{ij}.

Next, consider his choice of the exchange routes. We must now distinguish among different time costs corresponding to different exchange routes. Denote by T_{ij}^k the time cost to be incurred if he opts for an indirect exchange via good $k, k \neq i$. As a special case these routes include a direct exchange, i.e., $k = j$. Strictly speaking, the exchange rate will also vary from one route to another, and hence, we must specify it by e_{ij}^k. But we shall simply assume that the exchange rates are the same for all exchange routes, i.e., $e_{ij}^k = e_{ij}$ for all $k \neq i$. This assumption reduces the problem of choice of exchange routes to a simple one of comparing various time costs T_{ij}^k. Naturally, the optimal exchange route is the one for which T_{ij}^k is minimal. Let k^* be the medium good corresponding to a minimum T_{ij}^k. Having found k^*, we are back to the first problem. Note that for an indirect exchange, the time cost is the *sum* of the two terms corresponding to the two legs of transaction, i.e.,

$$T_{ij}^k = t[E(p_{ki}, S) + E(p_{jk}, S)]. \tag{6.6}$$

[2]The expression $x \leq 0 \leq y$ means a Kuhn–Tucker inequality, i.e., $x \leq 0, y \geq 0$ and $xy = 0$.

Having made the choice of the exchange routes the centrepiece of the model, we are naturally curious about the plausibility of indirect exchange. The following table tabulates the expected number of searches for selected values of p and S. The figures in the first and the second columns have been calculated from (6.4). The figures in the last column show the limiting values as S goes to infinity and have been obtained from the formula: $\lim_{S \to \infty} E(p, S) = 1/p$. [See, e.g., Feller (1950, p. 47).]

p	$S = 5$	$S = 10$	$S = \infty$
0.1		5.5000	10.0000
0.2	3.0000	3.6666	5.0000
0.3		2.7638	3.3333
0.4	2.0000	2.2000	2.5000
0.5		1.8333	2.0000
0.6	1.50000	1.5714	1.6666
0.7		1.3750	1.4285
0.8	1.2000	1.2222	1.2500
0.9		1.1000	1.1111
1.0	1.0000	1.0000	1.0000

Clearly, E increases with an increase in S and decreases with an increase in p. Two things are to be noted. First, as S increases, the room for advantageous indirect barter increases. For example, a direct barter at $p = 0.2$ is even with an indirect barter at $p = 0.6$ for $S = 5$, but for $S = 10$, it is even with an indirect barter at $p = 0.5$. For $S = \infty$, it is even with an indirect barter at $p = 0.4$. The same observation can be made for other probabilities generally. Second, though not shown in the table, an increase in the number of commodities increases the number of types of individuals. With a greater number of smaller probabilities competing, it is highly likely that the choice among different trade routes becomes more sensitive and the room for advantageous indirect barter will increase. These observations suggest that in a small community with a simple life style, the potential gain from indirect exchanges, if it existed, would be small.

With this remark, we shall concentrate on the limiting form $E(p, S) = 1/p$. Thus $T_{ij}^k = t(1/p_{ki} + 1/p_{jk})$. The relative advantage of an indirect barter over the direct one depends on the sign of $(1/p_{ki} + 1/p_{kj} - 1/p_{ji})$. It remains to explain how individuals obtain the knowledge of these p's. We shall assume that individuals estimate these probabilities on the basis of more or less subjective guesses and consequently with some errors. We may then say that instead of $1/p_{ij}$, individuals take $1/p_{ij} + X_{ij}$ to be the relevant probability. The term X_{ij} is a random term whose dispersion represents the diversity of individual estimates. Hence for given (p_{ji}, p_{ki}, p_{jk}), individuals of type (i, j) will partly abstain from exchange, partly go for a direct barter and the rest will go for indirect exchanges via a variety of media. The situation faced by an individual of type (i, j) can be summarized as follows. Given his estimates of the probabilities, he would choose an indirect route via good k^*, if $T_{ij}^{k^*} < T_{ij}^k$, for all $k \neq i, k^*$, i.e.,

$$X_{k^*i} + X_{jk^*} - X_{ki} - X_{jk} < 1/p_{ki} + 1/p_{jk} - 1/p_{k^*i} - 1/p_{jk^*},$$

and   (6.7)

$$X_{k^*i} + X_{jk^*} - X_{ji} < 1/p_{ji} - 1/p_{k^*i} - 1/p_{jk^*}, \qquad (6.8)$$

and if the route via k^* yields him a higher utility than that enjoyable in his autarchy position, i.e.,

$$U(e_{ij}, s_i^*, \bar{x}_i - s_i^*, H - T_{ij}^{k^*}) > U(0, \bar{x}_i H),$$

or, defining $\hat{T}_{ij}^{k^*}$ as that value of $T_{ij}^{k^*}$ at which the two utilities become equal to each other,

$$X_{k^*i} + X_{jk^*} < \hat{T}_{ij}^{k^*}/t - 1/p_{k^*i} - 1/p_{jk^*}. \qquad (6.9)$$

The conditions that he choose a direct exchange or autarchy can be given in a similar manner. For simplicity, we assume that these X's have a common distribution with a zero mean.

Thus we write $X = X_{ij}$ (for all i, j), $Y = X_{ki} + X_{jk}$ (for all i, j, k), $Z = X_{ki} + X_{jk} - X_{ji}$ (for all i, j, k), and $W = X_{ki} + X_{jk} - X_{k'i} - X_{jk'}$ (for all k, k', i, j). We further assume that the cumulative distributions of these random variables are given by

$$F_X(x), \quad F_Y(y), \quad F_Z(z), \quad F_W(w).$$

Then the fraction of individuals of type (i, j) that will opt for an indirect exchange via good k is given by

$$
\begin{aligned}
\Pi_{ij}^k = {} & F_Y(\hat{T}_{ij}^k/t - 1/p_{ki} - 1/p_{jk}) \\
& \times F_Z(1/p_{ji} - 1/p_{ki} - 1/p_{jk}) \\
& \times \prod_{k' \neq i, j, k} F_W(1/p_{k'i} + 1/p_{jk'} - 1/p_{ki} - 1/p_{jk}).
\end{aligned}
\tag{6.10}
$$

The fraction of individuals of type (i, j) that will opt for a direct exchange is given by

$$
\begin{aligned}
\Pi_{ij}^j = {} & F_X(\hat{T}_{ij}^j/t - 1/p_{ji}) \\
& \times \prod_{k \neq i, j} [1 - F_Z(1/p_{ji} - 1/p_{ki} - 1/p_{jk})].
\end{aligned}
\tag{6.11}
$$

Finally, the fraction of individuals of type (i, j) that will choose to stay in the autarchy position is given by

$$
\begin{aligned}
\Pi_{ij}^i = {} & [1 - F_X(\hat{T}_{ij}^j/t - 1/p_{ji})] \\
& \times \prod_{k \neq i, j} [1 - F_Y(\hat{T}_{ij}^k/t - 1/p_{ki} - 1/p_{jk})].
\end{aligned}
\tag{6.12}
$$

Hereafter we shall denote the whole set of fractions Π_{ij}^k for all i, j, k by Π. Note that the domain of Π is a Cartesian product of $n(n - 1)$ unit simplices, say P, and that equations (6.10)–(6.12) define a mapping from P into itself, in view of (6.3).

Now, how can this model explain the evolution of a universal medium of exchange? For this purpose the model must first be made dynamic. We may therefore imagine an economy extending over time and in which different individuals come and go generation after generation. Individuals estimate the p's on the basis of their observations in the past. To formalize such a learning process, we assume that the individuals' estimates of the p's are formed with a one-period lag. The dynamic process begins at a certain historical time with a given set of Π's. Call it $\Pi(0)$. The $\Pi(0)$ may very well represent a state of pure direct barter with a large number of individuals in their autarchy position. But, as they recognize the potential gains from indirect exchange, they change their trade patterns which in turn changes Π. The dynamic process continues over time, and as a limit, will hit a steady state in which the Π's no longer change. This equilibrium Π, Π^*, may possibly represent a state in which a certain commodity k has been exalted to the position of a universal or a dominant medium of exchange.

Under this dynamic assumption, equations (6.10)–(6.12) can be written as

$$\Pi(t+1) = \phi[\Pi(t)], \qquad t = 0, 1, 2, \ldots . \tag{6.13}$$

Once we specify an initial value $\Pi(0)$, (6.13) will generate a path of Π over time. Unfortunately, despite the great simplifications we already made it is not easy to study the dynamic properties of system (6.13) to the full. We must therefore be content with a few observations.

First, the position of equilibrium, i.e., the nature of Π^* is such that $\Pi^* = \phi(\Pi^*)$. The existence of such a Π^* can be assured if we assume that the F functions are all continuous and if we adopt the convention that $1/p = \infty$ whenever p is zero. Thus when any one p is zero, the expected transactions time containing it is infinite. But since individuals always have an option of not participating in exchange, such a transaction will be automatically excluded from consideration. Hence the mapping ϕ is always meaningful.

Suppose that the Π^* corresponded to a state of complete specialization in a single medium of exchange in some good k^*. Then $p_{ij} = 0$ for all $i, j \neq k^*$. For all such (i, j), from (6.10)–(6.12), we have

$$\Pi_{ij}^k = 0 \quad \text{if} \quad k \neq k^*, i, \tag{6.14}$$

$$\Pi_{ij}^{k^*} = F_Y(\hat{T}_{ij}^{k^*}/t - 1/p_{k^*i} - 1/p_{jk^*}), \tag{6.15}$$

$$\Pi_{ij}^{i} = 1 - F_Y(\hat{T}_{ij}^{k^*}/t - 1/p_{k^*i} - 1/p_{jk^*})$$
$$= 1 - \Pi_{ij}^{k^*}. \tag{6.16}$$

On the other hand, the substitution of these Π's in (6.3) yields $p_{ij} = 0$ for all $i, j \neq k^*$. Similar results can be readily obtained for those individuals whose resource or ultimate demand coincides with k^*. Thus, the state of complete specialization in a unique medium is a candidate for an equilibrium. In such an equilibrium, individuals benefit from lower transactions costs, and for the society as a whole, more goods are offered for exchange. There is, however, no obvious reason why the above dynamic system should necessarily converge to this kind of special equilibrium. If the parameters of the system are such that no indirect exchange has a comparative advantage over direct ones at $\Pi(0)$, the system will stay in the initial state of direct barter. Even some mediate positions can be candidates for equilibrium.

Secondly, there is the problem of stability. For the purpose of explaining the evolution of money as the "general, homogeneous course of action pursued by human beings", a vague promise of existence is not enough. In fact, the observed robustness of a monetary economy should be taken as evidence of the stability of the monetary equilibrium. While the formal stability analysis of the dynamic system (6.13) is not very helpful, it suggests that a fully monetized equilibrium is likely very stable. Indeed once a unique medium has been established, people's estimation errors will diminish and this in turn helps to preserve the given monetary equilibrium.

Thirdly, we have so far assumed that all monies are commodity monies. This assumption was essential at the initial stage of primitive, direct barter. But once some indirect exchange routes have been established, a token money poses no difficulty and our model can handle it in exactly the same way. As equation (6.3) shows, a good need not be wanted ultimately in order to be accepted in exchange.

Fourthly, the account given above of the origin and the evolution of money was a purely individualistic one in contrast to a rather naive form of social compact theory of money popular in the literature. While we make no claim about the superiority of the former, we have at least shown that it is possible to explain money on purely individualistic grounds and that the resulting theory clearly bears out the interdependent nature of the demand for money, the benefit money renders to the society, and the observed robustness of a monetary economy.

(C)   Several models of general equilibrium that take explicit account of exchange activities have appeared in the literature. They include Hahn (1971), Niehans (1971), Karni (1973) and Brunner and Meltzer (1971). Hahn draws a distinction between "anonymous" goods and "named" goods in classifying commodities. Anonymous goods are those goods which can be identified without using the name of the agents, i.e., those goods whose ownership is irrelevant. Named goods, in contrast, are those goods whose ownership does matter. Market activities are thought of as activities which transform named goods into anonymous goods. Hahn assumes that no named goods can be bought in the market but that these transforming activities require resources. Hahn's money is a good which has the following three properties:

(1) For transactions at all time t, no market is required to transform it from the named state to the anonymous state.
(2) A given quantity of the good at t can be transformed into an equivalent quantity of the good at t', $t' > t$, by storage without the use of any resources.
(3) The good does not enter into the utility functions.

These properties imply that agents, at a positive exchange

value of money, are always willing to accept money in exchange for goods. In this sense, "the set of market activities feasible under this regime will in general be larger than the set when there is no such good" [Hahn (1971, p. 436)]. Hahn also presents a proof of the existence of a market equilibrium with such exchange activities in the presence of money.

Niehans formulates a model of exchange with transactions costs where these costs are made to be the given parameters of the model specific to individual goods. Thus, he assumes that to exchange one unit of good i requires a transactions cost of c_i (reckoned in the units of some numeraire good). Given the cost structure, Niehans studies the implications of costly exchanges for the market equilibrium, and makes predictions as to which good emerges in the role of the medium of exchange and under what conditions. Karni's paper is quite similar to Niehans'.

All these formulations have some common features. First, transactions costs are treated as the given data and money is postulated to be the best good in terms of these costs. No explanation is offered concerning these costs or the determinants thereof. Second, these models are all static in the sense used in the previous section. On the other hand, these models incorporate storage activities and are somewhat more operational than ours. Their models and ours may therefore be regarded as complementary. The paper by Brunner and Meltzer is a good reading on various aspects of the problems of monetary theory but calls for a more precise formalization.

References

Brunner, K. and A. Meltzer, "The use of money: Money in the theory of an exchange economy", *American Economic Review* (1971).

Feller, W., *An introduction to probability and its applications*, Vol. I (New York, 1950).

Hahn, F. H., "Equilibrium with transactions costs", *Econometrica* (1971).

Jones, R. A., *A theory of the origin and the evolution of money*, Ph.D. dissertation (Brown University, 1976).

Karni, E., "Transactions costs and the demand for medium of exchange", *Western Economic Journal* (1973).

Menger, C., "On the origin of money", *Economic Journal* (1892).

Niehans, J., "Money and barter in general equilibrium with transactions costs", *American Economic Review* (1971).

On Market Adjustments

(A) In the models discussed so far, we ignored the problem of coordinating individual plans. In the Starr model of Chapter 5, an equilibrium price vector was assumed to be known. In the model of Chapter 6, we recognized the possibility of individuals' failing to conclude acceptable exchanges, but we did not consider the consequence of such failures. In general, the amount of information necessary for the computation of an equilibrium price vector is prohibitively high. Consequently actual trade takes place at more or less "false" prices. Being false prices, these actual prices cannot coordinate individual plans perfectly. Frustrations will arise. Frustrated individuals may react to their failures. The dynamic process of equilibration will therefore be an extremely complicated process. But we cannot dodge this problem of coordination, for it is the central theme of macroeconomics of which monetary theory is an important part. We wish therefore to devote the present chapter to the study of market adjustments. We shall first look at the theories of Walras and Edgeworth. Then we turn to more modern theories which treat the problem as one of information.

(B) Walras' Theory of Tâtonnement:

> "What must we do in order to prove that the theoretical solution is identically the solution worked out by the market? Our task is very simple: We need

only show that the upward and downward movements of prices solve the system of equations of offer and demand by a process of groping ['par tâtonnement']."

Contrary to Walras' expectation, the problem has turned out to be far from "very simple". Firstly, Walras failed to state his theory of tâtonnement in a clear and consistent manner. In his discussion of the theory in the pure exchange situation (lesson 5, pp. 84–86; lesson 14, pp. 182–185), Walras allowed for actual trading at false prices, but when he moved to the situation involving production (lesson 20, p. 242), he explicitly ruled out trading at false prices by introducing fictitious "bons" (tickets) which enable people to recontract freely. If we take the former interpretation, the very proof he set out to do in the above quote becomes vital but generally impossible. If we take the latter interpretation, the logical consistency of Walras' theory is preserved, but the theory loses its realistic flavour. Jaffé (1967) explains the tâtonnement process as the process of "groping" or "blindly feeling its way" for the very reason that no one in the actual world is presumed to know in advance the parameters or the solution of the equations. This interpretation is consistent with Walras' intended proof. But once we allow for trading at false prices, we immediately face the problem of distributional effects. In order to prove the identity between the mathematical solution and the solution worked out by markets in this manner, we would need some strong assumptions on the individuals' preferences to ensure that the market demand for any commodity depends on the aggregate amounts of initial endowments but not on their distributions among individuals. Walras (lesson 14, p. 185) actually wrote down a theorem called the Theorem of Equivalent Distributions which reads:[1]

"Given several commodities in a market in a state of general equilibrium, the current prices of these com-

[1] My emphasis.

modities will remain unchanged no matter in what way the ownership of the respective quantities of these commodities are redistributed among the parties to the exchange, *provided, however, that the value of the sum of the quantities possessed by each of these parties remains the same.*"

In proving this theorem (pp. 182–185), Walras calculated the "value" of individuals' wealth at the mathematical equilibrium prices, which is evidently preposterous and invalid. What Walras did, in terms of an Edgeworth–Bowley box, is to restrict changes in distributions to the line connecting the original distribution point and the corresponding point of intersection of offer curves. This is tantamount to ruling out trading at false prices! Hence Jaffé's verdict that "actually Walras failed in this attempt [at proving the equivalence of the two solutions]". Some economists, notably Patinkin (1965) and Negishi (1962), have adopted the other interpretation of the tâtonnement on the basis of Walras' use of tickets in the theory of production. The reason Walras introduced tickets in the production theory is obviously to exclude irreversible transformations of resources due to production. It is therefore hard to ignore all the preceding discussion of trading at false prices and identify the tâtonnement process with free recontracting.

   Secondly, there is the problem of convergence or stability. Putting the question of the location of equilibrium aside, how does a system of multiple markets get to an equilibrium? Walras wrote down as the law of the establishment of equilibrium prices the familiar excess demand hypothesis (p. 172). According to Walras' description, we start with a randomly cried vector of prices and the corresponding vector of excess demands. Pick one commodity and find a level of price of that commodity that equates the demand and the offer of the same commodity, other prices given. Then move to the second commodity and find the market clearing level of its price, given the above-mentioned equilibrium price of the first commodity and other prices (still held at the initial level). Then move to the third commodity, and so on. When we have gone to the end of the list, we will have obtained a new vector of prices. At this new price vector, the demand and the offer of the first commodity will generally be different, calling for another sequence of price adjustments. But the crucial fact, according to Walras, is that the excess demand for the first commodity evaluated at the new price vector will be smaller than that evaluated at the initial price vector. Thus the system asymptotically converges to the equilibrium. In the light of modern stability analysis, Walras' discussion of convergence is weak.[2]

Newman (1965, ch. 4, pp. 101–103) has emphasized the general equilibrium nature of the tâtonnement process. As he noted, the word "tâtonnement" appears for the first time (lesson 12, p. 170) when Walras begins to discuss the establishment of equilibrium prices in a multi-commodity context, and Walras calls the sequential adjustments in these multiple markets the theory of tâtonnement (p. 470). The implication of this is that the theory of tâtonnement refers to interactions among markets rather than the groping process in a single, isolated, market. Looked at from this angle, Walras' theory of tâtonnement emerges as a profound theory. Agents in each market have only to adjust the price of their commodity in accordance with the excess demand in their own market, without regard to the conditions in other markets. The informational requirements are minimal. And yet, when people do the same in all markets, the system as a whole converges to a position of general equilibrium, by virtue of the convergence theorem. In fact, given the theorem of equivalent distributions, the system converges to *the* equilibrium position. But as we already noted, neither the

---

[2]The above one-at-a-time method of Walras is known as the Gauss–Seidel Iteration in the theory of approximations. The adjustment process following this method, however, may not converge (see, e.g., Hildebrand 1956, p. 439).

uniqueness nor the stability of the equilibrium of the Walrasian system is guaranteed.

There is one reason why Walras was sloppy on these points, and that is his strong belief in the efficiency of the functioning of markets (pp. 83–84):

> "The markets which are best organized from the competitive standpoint are those in which purchases and sales are made by auction, through the instrumentality of stockbrokers, commercial brokers or criers acting as agents who centralize transactions in such a way that the terms of every exchange are openly announced and an opportunity is given to sellers to lower their prices and to buyers to raise their bids. This is the way business is done in the stock exchange, commercial markets, grain markets, fish markets, etc. Besides these markets, there are others, such as the fruit, vegetable and poultry markets, where competition, though not as well organized, nevertheless operates quite adequately ... In fact, the whole world may be looked upon as a vast general market made up of diverse special markets where social wealth is bought and sold. Our task then is to discover the laws to which these purchases and sales tend to conform automatically. To this end, we shall suppose that the market is perfectly competitive, just as in pure mechanics we suppose, to start with, that machines are perfectly frictionless."

And on p. 106 (my emphasis):

> "The rapidity and reliability of the practical solution leave no room for improvement. It is a matter of daily experience that even in big markets where there are neither brokers nor auctioneers, the *current* equilibrium price is determined within a few minutes, and

considerable quantities of merchandise are exchanged
at that price within half or three quarters of an hour."

The sentences that follow this quote on p. 106 indicate that
Walras thought of the mathematical solution as a good
approximation to the practical solution. But if so, why did he
attempt to prove the equivalence of the two solutions?
Furthermore, his "current" equilibrium price is not an element of the general equilibrium price vector which will only
be reached after many rounds of groping. For consistency
Walras would have to believe not only that individual markets establish their current equilibrium prices quickly enough
but also that market interactions bring the whole system into
equilibrium just as quickly. But this kind of belief defies our
experience. Modern stability analysis along the Walrasian
tradition was initiated by Samuelson (1941)[3] and has been
studied intensively since then. For a comprehensive summary, see Newman (1959), Negishi (1962), and Arrow and
Hahn (1971, chs. 11–13). These studies, however, failed to
establish the convergence of the system under general conditions. One of the restrictive assumptions employed in these
studies is that of perfect competition. But in the real world
perfect competition hardly exists. Above all, information is
scarce and no auctioneers are there to centralize transactions. Under these conditions, the position of equilibrium
itself depends on the environment. We shall have more to
say on this point later.

  Before concluding this section, we shall briefly look at the

---

[3]Samuelson wrote the multiple market adjustment equations $dp_i/dt = k_i ED_i(p)$, where p is the price, ED is the excess demand, k is some
positive number representing the speed of adjustment. Note that this
adjustment rule is different from that of Walras. Yet another rule which is
informationally more centralized is to recalculate the whole vector of
prices simultaneously as an equilibrium solution to the linear system using
the observed ED's and the gradients of the excess demand functions
evaluated at the point of observation. This rule is known as Newton's
method of approximation.

tâtonnement theory with money. Walras (lesson 30) expounded his tâtonnement process with money, where money is a paper money and is "neither a commodity nor anything that can serve as the numéraire". Referring back to (1.5), repeated here for convenience,

$$o_u = q_u - \frac{\alpha p_a' + \beta p_b' + \cdots + \varepsilon p_a'}{p_u'},$$

and aggregating it over individuals, the market equilibrium in the money market can be written as

$$Q_u - \frac{d_\alpha p_a' + d_\beta p_b' + \cdots + d_\varepsilon p_a'}{p_u'} = 0. \qquad (7.1)$$

Needless to say, that equation (7.1) is not always satisfied. If not, an adjustment in p_u' would take place. Denoting $d_\alpha p_a' + \cdots + d_\varepsilon p_a'$ by H_α, such an adjustment may be written

$$\mathrm{d}p_u'/\mathrm{d}t = k[H_\alpha/Q_u - p_u'], \qquad k > 0. \qquad (7.2)$$

Walras' exposition of the tâtonnement process with money is suspiciously simple. What causes such simplicity is his assumption of a virtual dichotomy between the real and the money sectors. Walras (pp. 326–327) wrote:

> "On referring back to the various terms that enter into the composition of H_α, we perceive that they are not absolutely independent of p_u', since p_u' figures in the term of $o_u p_u'$ of the equation of exchange which, together with the equations of maximum satisfaction, enables us to deduce the quantities $\alpha, \beta, \ldots, \varepsilon$ for any party to the exchange and, consequently, the aggregate quantities $d_\alpha, d_\beta, \ldots, d_\varepsilon$ for all parties together. We must admit, however, that the dependence of these items on p_u' is very indirect and very weak.
>
> . . . .
>
> The equation of monetary circulation, when money is not a commodity, comes very close, in reality, to

> falling outside the system of equations of [general] economic equilibrium. If we first suppose [general] economic equilibrium to be established, then the equation of monetary circulation would be solved almost without any groping, simply by raising or lowering p'_u according as $Q_u \lessgtr H_\alpha / p'_u$, at a price p'_u which had been cried at random."

We saw in Part I that the microfoundations of the demand for money according to Walras left much to be desired. We must conclude that his treatment of money in the market context is also shaky. Money barely hangs in the system. For the derivation of a precise market adjustment mechanism with money, we had to wait till Patinkin.

Apart from Walras' work proper, it is useful to study the significance of these stability analyses including that of Patinkin. Broadly speaking, there are two possible interpretations of the adjustment processes employed in these analyses. The first is to regard them as algorithms to hunt down the competitive equilibrium prices already built in the system. The second is to regard them as "realistic" adjustment processes actual markets are likely to generate. Walras saw no difference between the two, and this Walrasian belief became a tradition. Thus these analyses postulate a set of excess demand functions which depends only on prices. This means that the agents take these prices always as given, irrespective of whether the prices are equilibrium prices or not. This means also that the agents always have a belief that they can carry out their plans at these prices and that these prices embody all the information about their environment necessary for their planning. In this way, it is ensured the stationary solution of the adjustment processes based on a minimal informational requirement will in fact be a Pareto optimal equilibrium which would require a maximal amount of information or a maximal degree of centralization of the available information. But the above assumptions on the nature of the excess demand functions are self-contradictory in disequilibria where some agents cannot carry out their plans at the given market prices. To carry out their plans successfully in these situations, they will probably make efforts to gather more information primarily regarding the behaviour of others. The resulting response on the part of these agents would be different from the response they would otherwise make. Hence, except for the case of truly atomistic competition, both the adjustment process and the position of equilibrium will depend on the way information is distributed among agents. We shall first study the structure of exchange equilibria along the line of Edgeworth.

(C) Edgeworth's Theory of Exchange: Historically, the study of market equilibria in the intermediate cases of oligopoly originated in Cournot (1838). Under the premise that each individual will act on the assumption that his rivals' outputs are constant, and will strive to maximize his profits with respect to the choice of his output, Cournot was able to produce a determinate solution. In 1883, Bertrand reviewed Cournot's book and objected to Cournot's use of output reaction functions as against price reaction functions. Bertrand thought a more natural hypothesis would be that each assumes his rivals' prices to be fixed while his own price is adjusted. Under this premise he concluded that each oligopolist would undersell others as long as any profit remained, so that the final result would be identical with that of "unlimited" competition. However natural as it may seem, Bertrand's assumption is just as arbitrary and logically just as inconsistent as Cournot's. Further, Bertrand's conclusion that the only consequence is unlimited competition is obviously false. It was Edgeworth that carried the argument further and concluded that the solution would generally be indeterminate. He based his conclusion on the uncertainty of mutual reactions.[4]

---

[4]For an excellent exposition of classical oligopoly theory, read Fellner (1949, ch. 2).

One of the peculiar features of classical oligopoly theory was that it was a partial theory of sellers' behaviour, treating the behaviour of buyers as a given datum to the problem. Typically buyers are there merely to determine a market demand curve, and the important question of locating the market equilibrium on such a market demand curve is left entirely to the whim of the sellers. The partial theory of sellers' behaviour was formulated perhaps on empirical grounds that there were normally many more buyers than sellers. But from the theoretical point of view it was not a useful formulation. Had Cournot and Bertrand formulated the problem in a more general oligopoly–oligopsony framework, the nature of the problem, i.e., the general indeterminacy of the solution, would have been clear from the outset. The distinction between sellers and buyers, though inherent in a money economy, was not a useful distinction, and anyway, an analysis based on such a distinction should logically be preceded by one without such a distinction. Edgeworth's theory of exchange (1881, pp. 35–39) is indeed a general theory of exchange which embraces all possible market structure from bilateral monopoly to perfect competition.

Edgeworth considers a market where two commodities X and Y are traded. Suppose there are a number of owners of X and a number of owners of Y. These owners form the field of competition. Competition is effected through contracting. A perfect field of competition is said to exist if (1) there are indefinitely large numbers of traders on each side and (2) each individual is given unlimited freedom to contract or recontract with any other trader(s). If these conditions are not met, competition will be imperfect. Edgeworth concludes that contract with perfect competition is determinate, but contracts in all other cases are more or less indeterminate. The "evil of indeterminate contract" is twofold. First, the possibility of deadlock – no final settlement is reached whereas some settlement is desired by both parties. Second, the tendency towards "objectionable arts of higgling" in which the buyer, for example, attempts to ascertain the seller's lowest price without disclosing the highest price he is willing to give. Edgeworth's barter process differs from Walras' tâtonnement process in two respects. First, Edgeworth's is an explicit process of recontracting. Second, Edgeworth's traders do much "higgling", while Walras' traders are price-takers. In Walras, market prices are computed dispassionately by an efficient market machine. In Edgeworth they are produced by traders' passion and energy. This difference can hardly be overstated.

Edgeworth begins his analysis of exchange with the simple case where Robinson Crusoe offers Friday wages in exchange for his labour services. Let the wages be X and Friday's labour services be Y, and assume that each possesses a utility function in terms of the quantities of X and Y. Given the initial endowments of these goods, the locus of common MRS's defines a contract curve. I_c^0 and I_f^0 are the indifference curves corresponding to non-trade positions of Crusoe and Friday, respectively. When Crusoe and Friday trade, the feasible portion of the contract curve lies between A_0 and B_0, which defines the set of all Pareto-efficient allocations between Crusoe and Friday. It contains a "competitive equilibrium", say, E, as a special case, but no special significance can yet be given to it. The whole range between A_0 and B_0 represents therefore the possible location of the present two-person-exchange equilibrium. The actual equilibrium position is determined by the arts of bargaining of the traders.

We now proceed to the essence of Edgeworth's theory. How would an increase in the number of traders affect market trading? In particular, if every agent is allowed to freely contract and recontract, how would an increase in the number of traders help reduce the range of indeterminacy? In order to study this problem, Edgeworth introduces a second Crusoe and a second Friday who are identical in nature to the first Crusoe and the first Friday, respectively. Suppose further that the two pairs are initially at the point

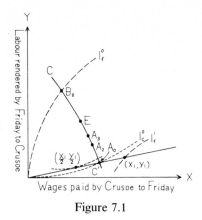

Figure 7.1

A_0, the position most favourable to Friday. In such a situation it is generally possible for one of the Fridays to talk the two Crusoes into a new contract which is more advantageous to all three. The new contract is shown in Figure 7.1 by the two points (x^1, y^1) and $(x^1/2, y^1/2)$, i.e., the Friday locates himself at (x^1, y^1) and the two Crusoes locate themselves at $(x^1/2, y^1/2)$. Namely, the Friday offers y^1 units of labour for x^1 wages which are to be shared equally by the two Crusoes. In order for this to be possible, the point (x^1, y^1) must represent a higher utility for the Friday than I_f^0, and the point $(x^1/2, y^1/2)$ must lie on a higher indifference curve than I_c^0. If the utility functions are strictly quasi-concave, such a mutually advantageous move is generally possible. If so, the original contract A_0 has been *recontracted out* or has been *blocked* by the *coalition* of one Friday and two Crusoes, and hence the contract A_0 is no longer a *viable* contract. So far as the members of the new coalition are concerned they are content with the new positions at which inter-member MRS's are equal. But for the other Friday who has been left out in the cold and has been brought back to the origin, the new situation is totally unacceptable. He will now strike in, with the result that the system will be worked down to a point at least as favourable for the Crusoes as $(x^1/2, y^1/2)$, again blocking the contract reached by the first Friday and the two Crusoes. It is useful to note at this point the following two important properties of equilibrium. First, all the field is collected at one point, for if one couple is at one point and another couple is at another point, then the Friday of one couple and the Crusoe of another couple will generally find it mutually advantageous to form a coalition and strike a new contract, leaving their partners in the lurch. *Second, that common point is on the contract curve*, for, if not, each couple can readily move to the contract curve. Thus when we consider equilibrium we can confine ourselves to the points on the contract curve.

To continue our two-Crusoe two-Friday example, we have seen that if we start from a boundary point on the contract curve which is most favourable to Friday, that initial point is sure to be blocked when a second Crusoe and a second Friday are introduced. By a symmetric argument we can show that the opposite boundary point B_0 will also be blocked. By a continuity argument, any points sufficiently close to these boundary points will also be blocked. This implies that the set of viable equilibrium points (the "core") shrinks with an increase in the number of Crusoes and Fridays. The question is: What do we mean by "sufficiently close", or what amounts to the same thing, what is the set of viable equilibrium points in the two-Crusoe two-Friday case? The answer can be easily deduced from our previous discussion and from the fact that an equilibrium must be on the contract curve. Suppose that all the parties have converged to an equilibrium represented by some point on the contract curve, an interior point of the curve (A_0B_0), say, A_2. Let one Friday attempt to recontract out with two Crusoes. If he is to be successful, he should be able to find a position like (x^1, y^1) such that he is at least as well off as at A_2, and also the two Crusoes are at least as well off at the mid-point of the Friday's new position as they were at A_2, with at least one strict inequality holding. Let us define the "competitive equilibrium" as that point on the contract curve at which the slope of tangency of the two indifference curves passing through that point is the same as the slope of the line connecting that point and the origin. Then it is intuitively clear that as we move from A_0 toward the competitive equilibrium along the contract curve, we will hit a point, some time before we get to the competitive equilibrium, where a mutually advantageous recontract ceases to exist. The first such point is designated in Figure 7.1 as A_2. The point E in the figure represents the competitive equilibrium. By a symmetric argument, if we start from B_0 we will identify a similar point B_2 (not shown) somewhere between B_0 and E. The set of points on the contract curve bounded by A_2 and B_2 will form the core for the present two-Crusoe two-Friday exchange, which is smaller than the corresponding core for the one-Crusoe one-Friday case.

In a similar manner, Edgeworth proceeds to the three-Crusoe three-Friday case. Starting at A_2, he now considers the possibility of blocking by a coalition of two Fridays and three Crusoes. For this case, the analysis is the same except that $(x^1/2, y^1/2)$ is substituted for by $(2x^1/3, 2y^1/3)$. The system works down to a point A_3 which can be shown to lie above A_2. Hence the core shrinks further. Going to the limit when the Crusoes and the Fridays are indefinitely but equally multiplied, the sequences $\{A_2, A_3, \ldots\}$ and $\{B_2, B_3, \ldots\}$ converge to E, the competitive equilibrium. In other words, the indeterminacy disappears asymptotically with the (symmetric) increase in the number of traders, and in the limit, the core shrinks to the competitive equilibrium, establishing the competitive equilibrium as the only viable solution to the exchange problem.[5]

---

[5] A rigorous but extremely readable proof of what has been said above is found in Debreu and Scarf (1963). Arrow and Hahn (1971, ch. 8) is also recommended.

(D) Price Adjustment under Uncertainty: Edgeworth's theory makes clear that the competitive equilibrium is a limiting case. Short of this limiting case of truly atomistic competition, the position of equilibrium is more or less indeterminate. Hence, any model which has the competitive equilbrium as its only stationary solution is a very special model. Furthermore, once we move away from the limiting case, the pricing or higgling becomes an important strategic variable of the market participants. A more realistic formulation must take these aspects into account.

Arrow (1959) questioned the meaning of the adjustment equation

$$dp/dt = h(D - S), \qquad h' > 0, \quad h(0) = 0, \qquad (7.3)$$

as a description of a competitive economy. In his words: "It is not explained whose decision it is to change prices in accordance with (7.3). Each individual participant in the economy is supposed to take prices as given and determine his choices as to purchases and sales accordingly; there is no one left over whose job it is to make a decision on price." Arrow argues that a firm operating in a competitive environment (in the sense of many buyers and many sellers) is a monopolist in the sense of facing a sloping demand curve, and hence that it sets its own price in a manner a monopolist does, except in a (long-run) equilibrium. Consider a competitive market in the above sense but suppose that the aggregate demand and the aggregate supply do not tally at the "market price", e.g., supply exceeds demand. Then starting with the given current price, individual firms will realize that in order to sell more they must reduce the price. If demand exceeds supply, and if the supply is momentarily fixed, individual sellers will perceive the possibility of raising the price in search of greater profits. In either case, the behavioural pattern of competitive firms is the same as that of a pure monopolist, except that they would face greater informational problems concerning the pricing behaviour of competitors. Arrow observes that in such disequilibrium situations, there will not generally be a single market price but multiple prices set by individual firms each acting on the basis of its perceived demand curve. In these circumstances, the adjustment process is apt to be irregular, but there will still be a "broad tendency" for prices to rise when demand exceeds supply, and vice versa. As Arrow points out, the heart of the problem is the lack of information. Even if a firm has a good idea as to what the equilibrium price is like, it need not pay him to lower its price at once to this level, for (1) other sellers may not be aware of this or may be otherwise unwilling to lower their prices, and (2) buyers may not be well-informed so that it can capture some buyers at the above-equilibrium price.

All these ideas can be formalized readily along the line suggested by Stigler (1961). Let us consider a hypothetical single market for a homogeneous commodity. Let there be S sellers and B buyers. We wish to study how the terms of trade, i.e., the prices of the commodity, are determined as a result of the game between sellers and buyers in a world of imperfect information, and its implications for price adjustments. Each seller sets his price and maintains it for the day. In setting his daily price, he is assumed not to know the (current) prices set by other sellers. Thus sellers face an informational barrier. Buyers, on the other hand, are assumed to visit a certain number of sellers each day and buy from the seller with the lowest offer price within their own search set according to their demand schedule. For simplicity, we assume that the number of searches per day is the same for all buyers and is denoted by I. Naturally, $1 \leq I \leq S$. While I itself should really be an important decision variable on the part of the buyer, we shall treat it as a fixed parameter representing the amount of information available to buyers. We also assume that the search set chosen by a buyer is random (although this is typically untrue in the real world where there is more or less a lasting relation between sellers and buyers).

How would a seller set his price? We assume that he has a

certain probability notion of rivals' prices whose p.d.f. (assumed identical for $S - 1$ prices) is given by $g(p)$, with

$$G(p) = \int_0^p g(q)\, dq.$$

Then the probability that he actually sells his wares to a shopper at his price p is $[1 - G(p)]^{I-1}$. Since there are S sellers and B buyers, the expected sale is given by $(B/S)[1 - G(p)]^{I-1}d(p)$, where $d(p)$ is the (common) demand curve of an individual buyer. This quantity may be viewed as his perceived demand curve. One can easily verify that this demand curve is downward sloping, with elasticity

$$E_{xp} = (I - 1)pg(p)/[1 - G(p)] + e_{xp}, \tag{7.4}$$

where e_{xp} is the elasticity of individual demand functions. Clearly, the larger I is (the better informed the buyers are), the higher the elasticity of demand perceived by a seller. Note that it is I, and not S, that matters. If the buyer's information is minimal, i.e., $I = 1$, $E_{xp} = e_{xp}$. This means that each seller faces individual buyers in isolation, which is the case of a pure monopolist. All that the seller must know is the individual demand curve; there is no need to conjecture the rivals' behaviour. A similar, but a more drastic, economy of information obtains when I is infinitely large (which means S is also infinitely large). But in all mediate cases, a correct perception of the demand curve requires a knowledge of both the individual demand curve and the rivals' pricing behaviour.

Having determined the demand curve, we can bring in the supply side in the usual manner and determine the daily supply using the condition $MR = MC$. Suppose this is done. A particular day opens and sales and purchases take place. Because of the assumed lack of information, however, the market will not necessarily clear. Some sellers will find their sales less than they desired, while others will find more demand than they can meet. What would these sellers do by way of planning for tomorrow? A host of factors will be responsible for the determination of the responses on the part of these sellers, the crucial ones being (1) the pattern of conjectures made by sellers about rivals' pricing, (2) the durability of the commodity, and (3) the possibility of new entry and exit. When these factors are at work, there need not be a simple and predictable relation between an excess demand and a consequent price increase, even at the individual level. On the other hand, it is extremely difficult to deduce, on the basis of "reasonable" assumptions on these factors, a price adjustment process counter to the broad excess demand hypothesis.

The above model can be made dynamic by introducing some learning process, for example, about the estimation of rivals' pricing. The stationary solution of this type of model generally ranges from a "competitive" equilibrium to a "monopoly" equilibrium, depending on the informational structure. The stability of such a dynamic process will also be affected by the speculative elements caused by the lack of information.

We wish to conclude this chapter with a discussion of stability analysis and a remark about the implications of the core theory of markets for the theory of money. First, the stability analysis. The basic model employed in conventional stability analysis is a model of pure exchange with free recontracting. The studies show that to ensure stability of this system, certain conditions must be met regarding the form of the excess demand functions. The model was then extended to one with trading at false prices or one with production, and the stability of these extended models has been studied. Arrow and Hahn (1971, ch. 13) made a further extension to include money as the sole medium of exchange. But there are two things in common among all these models: (1) that resources (as well as tastes and technology) are fixed, and (2) that expectations are static. The mathematical results notwithstanding, it is hard to imagine how an economy with fixed resources and static expectations can be very unstable. We may, therefore, take these static models to be categorically stable. Arrow and Hahn in fact find that all the above static models are similar in respect of stability. If we take this position, and if we are to seriously look for the sources of instability in an aggregative economy, they must be found somewhere else, i.e., in the factors ignored in these models. We can identify them with dynamic expectations and changing resources due to the existence of (reproducible) capital goods. The fundamental instability of competitive processes with capital and speculation as demonstrated by optimal and other growth models provides strong evidence for this view.

Second, what implications does the core theory have for the theory of money? To answer this question, we must first realize that the theories which have been proposed to explain the origin and the evolution of money have all gone to one extreme or the other. That is, money has been made either purely a product of social compact or an unintended product of selfish individual actions. Knapp's "State Theory" is an example of the former, while Menger represents the latter type of theory. The former takes all the analytical content out of the theory. The latter, on the other hand, unduly limits the capacity of man who, unlike other animals, is indeed capable of bargaining and cooperating with others. It seems that money can be best described as a product of such cooperative actions of a group of individuals.

In his doctoral dissertation, Wiens (1975) pursued this avenue, the cooperative game approach to the theory of money. Wiens considers an exchange economy in which each individual is endowed with a certain bundle of goods and with a certain degree of efficiency in the exchange activity which is called his "transactions technology". These transactions technologies are individual-specific and generally vary from one individual to another. Now a "barter economy" is defined as an economy in which each individual must carry out exchanges using his own technology. In contrast, a "monetary economy" is one in which the economy as a coalition does all the tradings on behalf of its members, using *its* transactions technology. Wiens identifies the coalition's technology with a subset, possibly the most efficient, of technologies owned by its members. In other words, the coalition is a name for a set of specialized traders. By assumption, exchange activities consume real resources. To cover such real resource costs, the coalition buys goods from its members and sells them back at a higher price. Under certain assumptions concerning the derivation of the coalition's technology from its members, Wiens proves that if the coalition chooses the two sets of prices so as to maximize its "profits" subject to the market clearance condition, and if all the profits are paid out to its members according to the values of their goods sold to the coalition, then the resulting allocation is a core and a competitive allocation which is Pareto-superior to the core allocation attainable in a barter economy.

Some of the interesting implications of this analysis are the following. First, the thesis, while it does not deal with the dynamics of the evolution of money, suggests that the greatest source of benefit of money is in its facilitating the division of labour. Indeed in Wiens' formulation a barter economy is capable of having some media of exchange or triangular trades so long as each trader uses his technology to exchange goods. Second, Wiens proves that a sufficient condition for the economy to remain a monetary economy is that the latter is more efficient than any feasible barter economies (only) at the economy level. But above all, this kind of approach has an advantage over the conventional one in which money is just an additional good and which attempts to establish money on the strength of individuals' demand for it. The notion of the coalition and the core neatly integrates man's self interest with his ability to perceive the benefits from social interaction.

References

Arrow, K. J., "Toward a theory of price adjustment", in: M. Abramovitz, ed., *The allocation of economic resources* (Stanford, Calif., 1959).

Arrow, K. J. and F. H. Hahn, *General competitive analysis* (San Francisco, Calif., 1971).

Cournot, A. A., *Researches into the mathematical principles of the theory of wealth* (Paris, 1838; New York, 1897).

Debreu, G. and H. Scarf, "A limit theorem on the core of an economy", *International Economic Review* (1963).

Edgeworth, F. Y., *Mathematical psychics* (London, 1881).

Fellner, W. J., *Competition among the few* (Clifton, N. J., 1949).

Hildebrand, F. B., *Introduction to numerical analysis* (New York, 1956).

Jaffé, W., "Walras' theory of tâtonnement: A critique of recent interpretation", *Journal of Political Economy* (1967).

Negishi, T., "The stability of a competitive economy: A survey article", *Econometrica* (1962).

Newman, P. K., "Some notes on stability conditions", *Review of Economic Studies* (1959).

Newman, P. K., *The theory of exchange* (Englewood Cliffs, N.J., 1965).

Samuelson, P. A., "The stability of equilibrium: Comparative statics and dynamics", *Econometrica* (1941).

Stigler, G. J., "The economics of information", *Journal of Political Economy* (1961).

Walras, L., *Elements of pure economics* (Paris, 1926; Homewood, Ill., 1954).

Wiens, E., *Money as a transaction technology – A game-theoretic approach*, Ph.D. dissertation (University of British Columbia, 1975).

8

Money and Intertemporal Resource Allocation

(A)   The general equilibrium models presented so far in this part have focused attention on the medium of exchange function of money. The time interval between the two legs of transactions has been considered too short for storage activities to count. But in reality the time horizons of economic agents are long and the money good is durable. Under such circumstances the store of value function of money gains significance. Our interest here is the allocative efficiency of an economy where money, or more generally, money claims are used as a store of value. Why, if at all, does an economy with money claims tend to do better than an economy with only commodity claims in terms of the intertemporal allocation of resources? If so, where does such superiority of money claims come from? How is this superiority related to money being the general medium of exchange? It seems fair to say that definitive answers to these questions have not yet been found. We shall therefore study the suggestive papers by Samuelson, Arrow and others.

(B)   In his famous pure consumption–loan model (1958), Samuelson studied the intertemporal allocation problem in a society inhabited by a succession of mortal individuals. Each individual lives for two periods, his working period and retirement. During the working period he earns one unit of wage income (in kind) which he allocates for consumption over the two periods. If his tastes are such that he must consume positive amounts in both periods, he must save part of his wage income in the first period. The main question concerns the form of such savings. Samuelson makes an assumption that all individuals are alike. Under this assumption, no intra-generation borrowing and lending is possible. Lending the saving to the existing older generation is useless because the older generation will be dead by the time the loan becomes due. The only generation with whom he would wish to trade at interest is the generation immediately after his. But that generation is yet to be born. Thus the only way in which to keep saving is to carry the goods he earned over to the second period. But this would yield at most a zero rate of return (when the good keeps perfectly and is costless to carry). Now we suppose that the population is growing at a positive rate n so that each generation is to be followed by a generation $(1 + n)$ times its size. This means that in any period the total savings being made by the working generation is greater than the dissavings of the retired generation by the factor $(1 + n)$. The excess of the former over the latter represents the net savings of the society which is never consumed. This intertemporal resource allocation is evidently suboptimal. The reason for the suboptimality is this. There is no market or instrument through which individuals can effect inter-generational trades. Such an instrument, Samuelson asserted, could be introduced in the form of the "social contrivancy of money".

Suppose the government (whose very existence is due to a social compact) offers the working generation notes which promise to pay the holder $(1 + n)$ times the original value of his saving a period from now, provided the saving is deposited with the government. In the simple world of Samuelson with only one commodity, such a value may well be reckoned in the units of that good, that is, these notes may be commodity claims. But even here, there is an important difference between money claims and commodity claims. In the case of commodity claims, the government must know what n is, whereas in the case of money claims, the government needs no such knowledge, as we shall show very shortly. But until then we tentatively interpret these notes as commodity claims. If individuals have faith in the government, they would be willing to deposit their savings with the government in exchange for such notes, because if they did not they could earn at best a zero interest on their savings, whereas the notes promise an interest rate n. The government, upon collecting the savings, give them away to the older generation. Consumption by the older generation is thereby enhanced. The balance sheet of the government after these transfers shows zero assets and liabilities equalling $(1 + n)$ times the original deposits which are falling due in a period.[1] After a period, the depositors, who are now in their retirement, claim their principal and interest from the government. But the latter has no difficulty in redeeming its debts, for the principal and interest being claimed are precisely the same as the amount of saving forthcoming from the working generation. All it has to do is to issue similar notes and collect their savings. The process continues in this manner without an end. What has happened is that with the introduction of such notes, a market for inter-generational trades has been opened up, so that all the individuals can enjoy a positive interest rate on their savings equalling the natural growth rate of the economy. The consumption opportunity set for each individual has been expanded and everyone is now better off. So long as the interest rate promised by the government does not exceed n, the "ponzi game" can go on indefinitely.

We have so far taken these notes to be commodity claims. Let us now suppose that the notes are money claims, that is, they embody general purchasing power. In the initial period, the government issues notes denominated in some unit of account (other than the commodity) in proportion to the physical amount of savings collected. Call the price of the commodity so determined p_0. The total amount issued of

---

[1]Cass and Yaari (1966) used this fact to argue that no private enterprise would wish to undertake the role of the government.

these notes is then $p_0L_0(1-c_1)$, where L_0 is the size of the working generation and c_1 is their per capita consumption. Suppose the government promises a nominal interest on money at the rate i so that the stock grows to $p_0L_0(1-c_1)(1+i)$ in a period. This total stock of notes will be used in the next period to purchase the amount of savings forthcoming from the next generation in the next period. The money price of the commodity in this purchase will then be

$$p_1 = p_0L_0(1-c_1)(1+i)/L_1(1-c_1) = p_0(1+i)/(1+n),$$

or the real rate of return on money, $p_0(1+i)/p_1 = 1+n$, irrespective of the amount of these notes issued or the interest promised on them by the government. Hence the theorem: the intertemporal resource allocation where money claims are used as instruments is Pareto-efficient, irrespective of the way the government manages them. The advantage of money claims over commodity claims is that with money claims the government need not know the future endowments in effecting such an efficient allocation. In this sense, money claims dominate commodity claims.

Diamond (1965) raised the following interesting question: Can a decentralized economy attain the same efficient allocation using productive capital goods as stores of value but without the social contrivance of money? Let $F(K, L)$ be the production function with the usual properties of constant returns to scale and diminishing returns to substitution. K is the amount of capital and L is the amount of labour. Individuals are now assumed to save in the form of such productive capital. Assume that the younger generation works in collaboration with capital. Such capital is owned by the older generation and is assumed to have been rented to the younger generation at the marginal productivity rental rate. The distribution of the total output is done according to the marginal productivity theory, namely, the older generation gets $(1+F_K)K$ and the younger generation gets F_LL. The path of capital stock over time can be determined by solving the following maximization problem of the younger generation. Each individual of the younger generation maximizes his two-period utility function $U(c_1, c_2)$ subject to the constraint that $c_2 = (w - c_1)(1 + r)$, where w is the marginal productivity wage and r is the (expected) marginal productivity rental rate on capital one period hence. This yields a solution (c_1^*, c_2^*) as functions of w and r. His saving is then $(w - c_1^*)$. Hence $(w - c_1^*)L$ is the total saving by the younger generation which constitutes the capital stock for the next period. Using the familiar transformation $F(K, L)/L = f(k), k = K/L$, this relation can be written as

$$k_{t+1} = [w(k_t) - c_1^*(w(k_t), r(k_t))]/(1 + n), \tag{8.1}$$

where

$$w(k_t) = f(k_t) - k_t f'(k_t) \quad \text{and} \quad r(k_t) = f'(k_t).$$

Once we specify the forms of the production function and the utility function, we can study both the steady state and the stability of this dynamic system. But consider, in particular, the steady state characterized by the constancy of k, and the implied rate of return on capital $r(k)$. Is there any assurance that this equilibrium r be equal to n? Diamond, using Cobb–Douglas assumptions, has demonstrated that there is no such assurance. The equilibrium r may be greater or smaller than n. What the decentralized capitalist system therefore lacks is an Invisible Hand. A scheme that stores goods is not conducive to an efficient intertemporal resource allocation even if the goods are capable of being productive and even if all the usual barriers to statical Pareto optima are absent.

These studies show clearly that dynamic efficiency in resource allocation is a much more inclusive concept that its statical counterpart. The fundamental source of difficulty here lies in the enormous informational requirements. If physical goods were to be used to effect an efficient allocation, their rates of return must be quoted correctly. But correct price configurations presupposes a precise knowledge of technology, tastes and demography for all the relevant future dates, for these physical rates could not adjust themselves quickly. Money claims, in contrast, have a convenient property that their rates of return adjust automatically to changes in these data. In particular, money claims prevent the system from carrying goods at interest rates lower than the natural growth rate of the economy, and thereby preclude paths that are dynamically inefficient in the Phelps–Koopmans sense.

We are thus led to believe that there is something special about money claims which make them superior to commodity claims in connection with the problem of intertemporal resource allocation. Samuelson's clear-cut results, we must admit, depend on a number of strong assumptions. First, Samuelson mostly confines his analysis to steady states where individual tastes and technology are stationary. This assumption makes the estimation of n rather an easy task. Second, he makes the real rate of return on money to any generation independent of the amount of money issued to the succeeding generation by assuming a peculiar rule according to which the government sells money claims to the public. But if a different rule is adopted, the real rate of return to any generation may become dependent on the amount of money issued to the succeeding generation. In order to ascertain the full implications of money, it seems essential that we reconsider the problem in a more general temporary equilibrium framework in which the future social endowments are uncertain. For this purpose, we shall first look at the famous study by Arrow.

(C)   Arrow (1952, 1964) and Debreu (1959) have proposed a novel way of dealing with the allocation problem under uncertainty. The idea is to extend the notion of commodities to include, besides the usual physical characteristics of the commodities, the time at which the commodity is to be delivered and the state upon which the delivery is contingent. The location of such delivery may also be included in the list of characteristics with respect to which the commodities are to be distinguished from one another. Arrow and Debreu postulate a set of individuals whose preferences are defined over the space of such "contingent commodities" and consider an economy in which these individuals trade these contingent commodities in accordance with their preferences and subject to their budget constraints. The main virtues of this approach are (1) that no special tools are necessary to study the allocation problem under uncertainty: the analysis is formally identical to that which is conventionally applied to the study of allocation under certainty; and (2) that the problem of uncertainty is translated into the incompleteness of markets.

In his paper Arrow considers a pure exchange economy consisting of I individuals $(i = 1, 2, \ldots, I)$, C commodities $(c = 1, 2, \ldots, C)$ and S states $(s = 1, 2, \ldots, S)$. The number of contingent commodities is therefore $S \times C$. Let x_{sc} be the amount of commodity c produced in state s and let Π_{is} be the subjective probability of state s assigned by individual i. Also let x_{isc} be the amount of commodity c claimed by individual i if state s occurs. The market clearing conditions for the SC markets are

$$\sum_{i=1}^{I} x_{isc} = x_{sc}, \quad \text{all } s, c. \tag{8.2}$$

Arrow studies the allocation of risk-bearing from the society's point of view first by means of commodity claims and second by means of money claims or securities.

First, the allocation of risk-bearing by means of commodity claims. Let $V_i(x_{i11}, \ldots, x_{iSC})$ be the utility function of individual i which is assumed to be monotone increasing and quasi-concave for every i. Since the only change from the usual certainty case is the increase in the number of commodities from C to SC, if a social planner wishes to solve the problem of maximizing $\sum_{i=1}^{I} d_i V_i$ subject to (8.2) for any positive vector $(d_1, \ldots, d_I)$, he will be able to obtain an optimal allocation of risk-bearing in the sense of Pareto. The

same allocation of risk-bearing can be attained by competitive markets. Namely, if (x_{isc}^*), all i, s, c, is any optimal
allocation, then there exists a set of money incomes y_i for
individual i, and a set of prices $(\bar{p}_{sc})$ of a unit claim on
commodity c if state s occurs, such that if individual i
chooses the variables x_{isc}, subject to

$$\sum_{s=1}^{S} \sum_{c=1}^{C} \bar{p}_{sc} x_{isc} = y_i, \tag{8.3}$$

taking prices as given, the chosen values of the x_{isc}'s will be
the optimal allocation (x_{isc}^*). Hence:

*Theorem 1:   If $V_i(x_{i11}, \ldots, x_{iSC})$ is quasi-concave for every i,
then any optimal allocation of risk-bearing can be realized by
a system of perfectly competitive markets in claims on
commodities.*

Note the stringent condition imposed on markets. In order
for competitive or decentralized markets to reach an optimal
allocation, individuals must be able to have the SC degrees
of freedom, namely, the economy must provide SC markets
for all the contingent commodities. In other words, the
markets have to be perfect and complete.

   Next, Arrow studies the same allocation problem but this
time by means of money claims or securities. Each security
embodies a vector of money claims payable upon occurrence
of special states. Once any state s occurs, the money transfers determined by the securities take place and then the
allocation of commodities takes place through the "spot"
market (C in number), "in the ordinary way, without further
risk-bearing". The picture Arrow conceives of is very similar
to reality in which "forward" tradings are made using
securities and commodity allocations are effected through
"spot" markets. For simplicity Arrow assumes that there are
precisely S types of securities, where a unit security of type
s promises to pay one monetary unit if state s occurs and
nothing otherwise. Evidently, what is crucial here is the

number of linearly independent vectors of money claims spanned by the collection of securities. Arrow's S types of securities clearly span the whole state space. Under these assumptions Arrow proceeds to show that any optimal allocation of risk-bearing can be achieved by a competitive system using such securities. This is the context of his next theorem:

Theorem 2:   If

$$V_i = \sum_{s=1}^{S} \Pi_{is} U_i(x_{is1}, \ldots, x_{isC})$$

is quasi-concave in all its variables, then any optimal allocation of risk-bearing can be achieved by perfect competition on the securities and commodity markets, where securities are payable in money.

"The social significance of this theorem", says Arrow, "is that it permits economizing on markets; only $S + C$ markets are needed to achieve the optimal allocation, instead of the SC markets implied in Theorem 1."

This is a remarkable theorem showing the superiority of money claims over commodity claims. In terms of the now fashionable information theory, it says that the S prices of securities contain full information about the SC discounted prices of the contingent commodities. But how can this be true?

Arrow's "proof" of Theorem 2 is rather intriguing.[2] For given optimal allocation (x_{isc}^*), let the prices $(\bar{p}_{sc})$ and the incomes (y_i) be determined as before. Let q_s be the price of the security of type s and p_{sc} be the (spot) price of commodity c if state s occurs. Choose these prices so that

$$q_s p_{sc} = \bar{p}_{sc}. \tag{8.4}$$

---

[2]The following discussion is based on my paper "On a theorem of Arrow" (1975).

Given such q_s, p_{sc} for all s, c, an individual will have the same range of alternatives available as in the previous case, and hence, his decision will be the same. The individual i will therefore purchase

$$y_{is}^* = \sum_{c=1}^{C} p_{sc} x_{isc}^* \tag{8.5}$$

units of security of type s. His budget constraint is obviously

$$\sum_{s=1}^{S} q_s y_{is} = y_i, \tag{8.6}$$

and, by assumption, the y_{is}^*'s in (8.5) satisfy (8.6). In order to see how the q_s's get determined, let the total money stock be $y = \sum_{i=1}^{I} y_i$, and notice that no matter which state may turn out, the net volume of claims payable then must equal y, that is,

$$\sum_{i=1}^{I} y_{is} = y, \quad \text{for all } s. \tag{8.7}$$

Substitute (8.5) into (8.7) and multiply both sides by q_s to get

$$\sum_{i=1}^{I} \sum_{c=1}^{C} q_s p_{sc} x_{isc}^* = \sum_{i=1}^{I} \sum_{c=1}^{C} \bar{p}_{sc} x_{isc}^* = q_s y.$$

Dividing through by y, q_s is given as

$$q_s = \left(\sum_{i=1}^{I} \sum_{c=1}^{C} \bar{p}_{sc} x_{isc}^* \right) \Big/ y, \quad \text{for all } s. \tag{8.8}$$

Substitute these q_s's into (8.4) and the spot prices p_{sc} are determined.

Suppose state s occurred. The individual i will then have an income y_{is}^* to allocate among commodities at spot prices p_{sc}. Let $U_i(x_{is1}, \ldots, x_{isC})$ be his utility function which is monotone increasing and concave. His problem is to maximize U_i subject to $\sum_{c=1}^{C} p_{sc} x_{isc} = y_{is}^*$. Let x_{isc}^+ ($c = 1, 2, \ldots, C$) be the solution to this problem. By (8.5), the quantities x_{isc}^* satisfy the same budget constraint. Hence,

$$U_i(x_{is1}^+, \ldots, x_{isC}^+) \geq U_i(x_{is1}^*, \ldots, x_{isC}^*). \tag{8.9}$$

It remains to show that a strict inequality is not possible. Now by the Expected Utility Theorem, the function U_i may be chosen so that

$$V_i = \sum_{s=1}^{S} \Pi_{is} U_i(x_{is1}, \ldots, x_{isC}). \tag{8.10}$$

Suppose the strict inequality holds in (8.9) for at least one s for which $\Pi_{is} > 0$. Then from (8.10),

$$V_i(x_{i11}^+, \ldots, x_{isC}^+) > V_i(x_{i11}^*, \ldots, x_{isC}^*). \tag{8.11}$$

But consider the budget constraint $\sum_{c=1}^{C} p_{sc} x_{isc} = y_{is}^*$ to which the quantities x_{isc}^+ are subject. Multiplying by q_s and summing over s, we get

$$\sum_{s=1}^{S} \sum_{c=1}^{C} \bar{p}_{sc} x_{isc}^+ = y_i,$$

that is, the quantities x_{isc}^+ satisfy (8.3). But by construction the quantities x_{isc}^* maximized V_i subject to (8.3). Hence (8.11) is a contradiction, and in fact the equality holds in (8.9) for all states s for which $\Pi_{is} > 0$. If strict quasi-concavity is assumed on V_i, then $x_{isc}^+ = x_{isc}^*$ for all c, i and s for which $\Pi_{is} > 0$. If $\Pi_{is} = 0$, $x_{isc}^+ = 0$ for all c. So $y_{is}^* = 0$ and $x_{isc}^* = 0$ for all c. In other words, the two-part trading in the second scheme using money claims leads to the same allocation as in the first scheme with commodity claims, and this is how Arrow provided the proof of Theorem 2.

We recall that the S security prices q_s and the SC spot prices p_{sc} were determined, respectively, by (8.8),

$$q_s = \left(\sum_{i=1}^{I} \sum_{c=1}^{C} \bar{p}_{sc} x_{isc}^* \right) \Big/ y,$$

and by (8.4),

$$q_s p_{sc} = \bar{p}_{sc}.$$

This means that *if* $(\bar{p}_{sc})$ are known, then they imply the existence of a set of (q_s, p_{sc}) such that the above-mentioned two-part trading at these prices would lead to the same allocation of risk-bearing as the previous one-shot trading at $(\bar{p}_{sc})$. From this Arrow arrived at the remarkable conclusion stated in Theorem 2. But in the second scheme using securities, there is actually no mechanism that generates the knowledge of $(\bar{p}_{sc})$. When individuals trade in commodity claims as in the first scheme, they naturally reveal more information to the markets than when they trade in money claims. In the former case, they reveal the whole matrix (x_{isc}), whereas in the latter case, they reveal only the vector y_{is}. The two schemes would be identical if all the spot prices were known. But when individuals trade in money claims, the market cannot provide any information on these prices. Individuals will only know how much money they have available if any state s occurs, but they will not know, at the time of purchasing securities, what prices will turn out. The final allocation of risk-bearing depends, however, not on y_{is}'s but on x_{isc}'s, and hence, on p_{sc}'s. Individuals must therefore guess these spot prices which, however, would require knowledge about other individuals' tastes and strategies. Individual's demands for securities and hence for y_{is} would depend on their subjective views on the p_{sc}'s, and there is no assurance that these decisions *will* lead to the same allocation as the one that would be reached under perfect certainty. Thus we must conclude that the two-part scheme will not be so simple as Arrow makes it out to be.

To be specific, the behaviour of an individual under the second scheme facing uncertainty concerning the spot prices can be represented by the solution of the following problem:

$$\underset{(y_{is})}{\text{Max.}} \sum_{s=1}^{S} \Pi_{is} E_{is} U_{is}(x_1(p, y_{is})), \tag{8.12}$$

subject to

$$Y_i = \sum_{s=1}^{S} q_s y_{is}, \tag{8.13}$$

where $U_i(x)$ is an increasing, concave function of x, E_{is} is the expectation taken over the conditional distribution of the spot prices p (a C-vector) given state s, y_{is} is the number of securities of type s purchased by individual i, and $x_i(p, y_{is})$ is the usual demand function. Taking the security prices q_s's as given, the individual solves the above problem for y_{is}'s. Denote them by y_{is}^{**}. For the given social endowments (x_{sc}), these individual decisions would generally lead to the same allocation (x_{isc}^*) if and only if $y_{is}^{**} = y_{is}^*$ for every i and s, where y_{is}^* is defined by (8.5). There is one special case in which the difference between the two schemes disappears. This is the case of Cobb–Douglas utility. The Cobb–Douglas utility function has the property that the proportion of income spent on any good is independent of the prices. In this case, therefore, the individual would attach no value to the information about the spot prices, and y_{is}'s would depend only on the Π_{is}'s. Apart from this exceptional case, the uncertainty concerning spot prices will generally lead to different decisions on y_{is}. In view of (8.7), $\Sigma_{i=1}^{I} y_{is} = y$ irrespective of individual values of y_{is}. Thus what happens when $y_{is}^{**} \neq y_{is}^*$ is that some individuals will have more money and others less relative to the allocation under the first scheme.

The above discussion makes clear that the economy in the number of markets in the second scheme cannot prove the superiority of money claims over commodity claims. On the other hand, as Arrow correctly recognized, money claims dominate commodity claims in the real world. And this calls for an explanation. One way to tackle this problem may be to assume a number of securities, say, S of them as above *and* the same number of contingent commodity claims and study how an individual chooses between money claims and commodity claims. Suppose that there are additional S markets in which one of the C commodities is traded. Let the first commodity be such an instrument. Then the individual's choice problem becomes one of maximizing

$$\sum_{s=1}^{S} \Pi_{is} E_{is} U_i(x_i(p, p_{s1}\bar{x}_{is1} + y_{is})),$$

subject to the constraint

$$y_i - \sum_{s=1}^{S} (\bar{p}_{s1}\bar{x}_{is1} + q_s y_{is}) = 0.$$

The first-order conditions may be written as

$$\Pi_{is}E_{is}[\theta_{is}(p; \bar{x}_{is1}, y_{is})p_{s1}] - \lambda \bar{p}_{s1} \leq 0 \leq \bar{x}_{is1}, \qquad (8.14)$$

$$\Pi_{is}E_{is}[\theta_{is}(p; \bar{x}_{is1}, y_{is})] - \lambda q_s \leq 0 \leq y_{is}, \qquad (8.15)$$

where $\theta_{is}(p; \bar{x}_{is1}, y_{is})$ is the marginal utility of income in state s, and λ is the Lagrangian multiplier on the above budget constraint. Consider a state s for which $\Pi_{is} > 0$, and suppose the optimal y_{is} for this s is positive. For money claims to dominate commodity claims, it must be that

$$p_{s1} \geq q_s E_{is}[\theta_{is}(p; 0, y_{is})p_{s1}]/E_{is}\theta_{is}(p; 0, y_{is}). \qquad (8.16)$$

But if an opposite inequality holds, commodity claims may also be held. The exact functional form of θ_{is} is derived from the utility function U_i. The indirect utility function $U_i(x_i(p, p_{si}\bar{x}_{is1} + y_{is}))$ is a quasi-convex function in the spot prices p, and hence, the effect of variability in p is not transparent. All we can say from (8.16) is that a commodity whose price is highly positively correlated with the marginal utility of income will be a candidate for forward transactions. Generally speaking, nothing prevents the above inequality from being reversed. We must of course recall that we are assuming costless transactions, and in particular, that the commodities purchased forward can be sold at no cost in the spot markets. This is a very strong assumption. If we assume instead that reselling of commodities on spot is costly, money claims become more favourable accordingly. The domination by money claims in the real world must be attributed to some such "imperfections" in the markets as we actually have.

References

Arrow, K. J., "The role of securities in the optimal allocation of risk-bearing", *Review of Economic Studies* (1964); originally in French (1952).

Cass, D. and M. E. Yaari, "A reexamination of the pure consumption loans model", *Journal of Political Economy* (1966).

Debreu, G., *Theory of value* (New York, 1959).

Diamond, P. A., "National debt in a neoclassical growth model", *American Economic Review* (1965).

Nagatani, K., "On a theorem of Arrow", *Review of Economic Studies* (1975).

Samuelson, P. A., "An exact consumption–loan model of interest with or without the social contrivance of money", *Journal of Political Economy* (1958); also in his *Collected scientific papers*, vol. 1 (Cambridge, Mass., 1966).

9

Temporary Equilibrium
and Expectations

(A) In the real world the number of goods is large and the number of possible future states is numerous. But the number of available contingent claims is quite small. The total number of commodity futures markets in the whole world is in the order of 50–60, according to Houthakker (1959) and the future period covered in these markets is far shorter than the time horizons of agents. The situation is much better for money claims (bonds), but the markets are still incomplete. In these circumstances, the agents substitute their subjective future prospects for the prices whenever markets fail to quote them. A temporary equilibrium is an equilibrium of an economy in which agents planned on the basis of such an assumed future and subject to resource constraints resulting from their past actions. A temporary equilibrium is a dynamic concept. It is a snap shot of an economy evolving over time.

The first systematic treatment of the notion of temporary equilibrium is due to Hicks (1939 and 1946, Parts III and IV). In doing this, Hicks paid particular attention to: (1) the distinction between static and temporary equilibrium, (2) the distinction between temporary and intertemporal equilibrium, and (3) alternative specifications of temporary equilibrium models.

First, Hicks compares temporary equilibrium with a static one (pp. 115–116):

"It is true that if one follows the usual course of economists in the past (at least of the vast majority of nineteenth-century economists) and gives one's static theory some slight dynamic flavouring, it can be made to look much more directly applicable to the real world. It can contain most of the staple diet of traditional economics, from the theory of rent and the theory of comparative cost to the theory of monopolistic exploitation; all of which can be established without any consideration of time ever coming into the argument. It can be decked out with illustrations and institutional qualifications, until the skeleton takes on the form of a standard work. But it will still be quite incompetent to deal properly with capital, or interest, or trade fluctuations, or even money – problems where the dating of economic quantities is of the first importance."

He continues (pp. 118–119):

"The stationary state is that special case of a dynamic system where tastes, technique, and resources remain constant through time .... In a stationary state, there can be no tendency for the stock of capital to increase or diminish .... If entrepreneurs do not desire to increase or diminish their stock, their net borrowing must be nil. If the demand and supply for the loans are to be in equilibrium, net saving must therefore also be nil .... It is only in very special conditions that saving and investment will both = 0, for every unit in the economy; and it is only if they do that we can separate out the equations concerning capital and interest, leaving the rest of the price system to be determined as in statics."

Then on pp. 249–250:

"The most obvious difference between any static system of exchange and production, and any dynamic system, consists in the absence of borrowing and lending in the one case and its' presence in the other. In statics, an individual's receipts and expenditures can only differ to the extent of the change in his money balance; in dynamics, the difference can also be made up by a change in his (net) holding of securities.... Securities are something which is bought and sold; therefore they are a kind of commodity; therefore their introduction only changes the formal properties of the system in so far as this special kind of commodity fails to observe the static rules of behavior.... These static rules hold so long as the individual's scale of preferences is independent of the prices fixed on the market. This condition will continue to hold, even in a dynamic system, so long as elasticities of expectations are zero, that is to say, so long as all price expectations and interest expectations are given. If these expectations are given, the demand for securities can be taken as being formally equivalent to a demand for given quantities of physical commodities to be supplied in the future; the price of these commodities (the only part of their price which can vary) being the rate of interest. The fact that the commodities in question are only to be enjoyed at a future date is irrelevant to the determination of prices in the current week; the individual behaves exactly as if he were buying the commodities now. Similarly, when a firm borrows, it behaves exactly as if it were selling commodities to be delivered in the future, selling them at a price also determined by the rate of interest. Thus securities behave exactly like ordinary commodities; the replacement of one of the commodities of static theory by this peculiar sort of commodity does nothing to change the fundamental character of the

system . . . . We may therefore sum up the first step in
our argument. So long as elasticities of expectations
are zero, the temporary equilibrium system works
exactly like a static system and is as stable as that is."

Secondly, as for the comparison between temporary and
intertemporal equilibrium ("equilibrium over time"), Hicks is
not very thorough [this subject was to be developed later in
his Capital and Growth (1965)]. It may therefore be useful to
draw a distinction between the two. A temporary equilibrium
is defined by a vector of prices that clear the markets for all
currently traded goods subject to the historical data and the
state of expectations given at the particular point of time. If
prices adjust fast enough to accommodate any plans currently made by the agents, as Hicks assumes, a temporary
equilibrium always exists. On the next Monday, there will be
another temporary equilibrium, yet another temporary equilibrium on the following Monday, and so on. There is, in
principle, no connection among the sequence of temporary
equilibria. An intertemporal equilibrium requires, however,
that the position of a temporary equilibrium be in line with
those adjacent to it in the sense that the prices established in
that temporary equilibrium were actually expected to prevail
then on previous dates and that the prices expected now are
in fact the correct ones for the future. The deviation of any
temporary equilibrium from its intertemporal counterpart
means that the plans are inconsistent and that the resultant
resource allocation is inefficient over time. Under the
assumption of competition, one can show that every temporary equilibrium meets the statical efficiency conditions in
the usual sense of attaining a point on the *given* production
possibility frontier, if we speak of production efficiency. In
contrast, intertemporal efficiency requires that the succession of points so attained by temporary equilibria be
aligned in such a manner that starting from a certain point on
the production possibility frontier in the first week, the
second week temporary equilibrium will be placed not

merely on one of the many second week production possibility frontiers reachable from the initial position but on an
outer envelope of such a family of frontiers. Thus the
intertemporal equilibrium conditions are much more rigorous
than the temporary equilibrium conditions.

Hicks points out four causes for possible divergence of
temporary equilibrium from its intertemporal counterpart.
They are: (1) inconsistencies among different people's price
expectations; (2) inconsistencies in the plans (in the sense of
inequality between the planned demand and the planned
supply); (3) incorrect estimation of tastes and technology; (4)
systematic bias due to risk aversion (with respect to the
uncertainty of future prices). Of these the first two can be
partially or wholly removed by forward tradings. But the
third represents a type of social risk which cannot be
removed by even perfect futures markets. Hicks believes
that this last fact is mainly responsible for the paucity of
futures markets in the real world. For a similar reason, the
fourth source of divergence cannot be effectively coped with
by forward tradings because the very uncertainty of the
future generates the desire to keep one's hands free to meet
that uncertainty.

Thirdly, there is the important question about the concept
of temporary "equilibrium". As we saw above, the Hicksian
temporary equilibrium is a state of complete market
clearance, based on the assumption of flexible prices. But
what if prices did not adjust that fast? What if the markets
were left uncleared over weeks? Is it still a state of temporary "equilibrium", or is it a temporary disequilibrium?
This is not just a semantic question but a question of
substance related to the notion of the Keynesian temporary
equilibrium. As Hicks himself admitted (1965), the Hicksian
temporary equilibrium, which is characterized by complete
market clearance, is almost a normative concept in a world
in which market non-clearance is the fact of life. And it was
Keynes who stressed the limited capability of the market in
coordinating individual plans. As for the Keynesian unem-

ployment, at least three interpretations have been given in the literature. The first is a dynamic one which stresses slow market adjustments. According to this interpretation, a full-employment equilibrium exists and the behaviour of the system is no different from the neoclassical one, but due to lack of knowledge of the equilibrium prices, groping takes time. Unemployment is thus a disequilibrium phenomenon. The second interpretation stresses the constrained nature of decision making in a state of disequilibrium. In a disequilibrium situation where markets are not clearing at prevailing prices, some individuals are bound to be frustrated, and failures to carry out their plans will affect their subsequent choices. A household which has failed to sell the amount of labour services it desired at the going wage rate will be forced to curtail its spending plan. Likewise, a firm which has failed to sell the amount of commodities it planned at the going prices will be induced to change its production plan. These revised plans now constitute effective demands and supplies to be registered in the market. Unemployment can then be interpreted as a state of equilibrium in terms of these constrained decisions. The third interpretation retains the neoclassical behavioural equations but attributes unemployment to rigidity in some prices in the system. Conventionally, the rigidity in money wages has been singled out as the cause of unemployment. But in a general equilibrium system in which everything depends on everything else, there is no compelling reason why the burden of money wage rigidity must fall on the labour market, just because wages are the price of labour services. Furthermore, money wage rigidity can hardly be the *cause* of unemployment. A more plausible alternative, which is also more in the spirit of Keynes, is to look for the cause of unemployment in the state and nature of expectations. In Keynes' theory, expectations about future prices typically affect the marginal efficiency of capital. Suppose, for example, the marginal efficiency of capital has fallen suddenly for some external reason. Also suppose expectations are unitary elastic so that the marginal efficiency of capital remains unaffected by changes in the current prices. The question is: Can all the markets be cleared by adjustments in the "current" prices alone? If the marginal efficiency of capital is already out of line and is rigid, the current prices may fail to clear all the markets.

We shall postpone further discussions of Keynes' theory until Part III. But it is interesting to note that the existence of a temporary equilibrium, even in the Hicksian framework of flexible prices, depends heavily on the state and nature of expectations, as we shall see below.

(B) Existence of Temporary Equilibrium: The most comprehensive treatment of the Hicksian temporary equilibrium seems to be that by Arrow and Hahn (1971). We wish to give a non-technical account of their analysis.

Arrow and Hahn study the existence of temporary equilibrium in steps. First, they consider the ideal Arrow–Debreu economy with complete futures markets (p. 17). In this economy, all the contracts, spot and forward, are made in the current period. Various forms of uncertainty and risk are assumed to be absent. Thus the time element becomes insignificant, and the model reduces to a static model, except that the number of goods is now increased from, say N, to $N(T+1)$ where T is the length of the future contained in the planning horizons of the agents. The existence of such an equilibrium can be established in the manner discussed in Chapter 5.

Arrow and Hahn then proceed to the case of restricted futures markets (pp. 35–40). Subjective expectations make up for the lack of the market-determined future spot prices. Specifically, they assume that a futures market exists for the $(N+1)$st good. The vector of market-quoted prices p therefore has $N + T$ elements. The decisions made by individual households depend on this p and an NT vector of expected prices, q.[1] Hence we can write the market excess demand functions as $Z(p, q)$, using the notation of Chapter 5. A temporary equilibrium is said to exist if there is a $p^* \geq 0$ such that $Z(p^*, q) \leq 0$. At this stage of their discussion, Arrow and Hahn minimize the role of firms to a point where they make no intertemporal decisions. To show the existence of a temporary equilibrium, they assume:

(W) $pZ = 0$,   for all (p, q) considered,
(H) $Z(p, q) = Z(\lambda p, \lambda q)$,   for all $\lambda > 0$,   for all $p, q \geq 0$,
(C) Z is continuous over S_{N+T} (the domain of the normalized p) for fixed q.

First the case of fixed q: The normalization procedure in (C) means that the future prices have also been normalized. Fixing q means fixing of such a normalized q. For fixed q, write $Z(p, q) = \hat{Z}(p)$ with $p \in S_{N+T}$. With the addition of (B), the boundedness of $Z(p)$ from below, $\hat{Z}(p)$ has all the properties of $Z(p)$ in the static case, except (H). But having normalized p, (H) is not needed for the existence proof. Hence the same proof may be used to establish the existence of a temporary equilibrium in the fixed q case. Secondly, they consider the case where q is a continuous function of $p, p \in S_{N+T}$. Then we can write $Z(p, q) = Z(p, q(p)) = \hat{Z}(p)$, a continuous function of p. The existence of a temporary equilibrium follows at once.

After these preliminary investigations, Arrow and Hahn formulate a more general model of temporary equilibrium (pp. 136–151). The economy is inhabited by two-period maximizers. They include firms as well. Both production and consumption decisions involve two periods. The only goods traded in current markets are the commodities of the current period and bonds. A unit bond is a promise to pay one unit of currency in the next period. We denote the vector of goods traded in by households in the current period by

---

[1]They allow q to vary from one agent to another. To be precise, therefore, q is a collection of q_h's where h identifies agents.

$x = (x^1, x_b)$ and the vector of goods traded in by firms in the current period by $y = (y^1, y_b)$. The corresponding price vector is denoted by $p = (p^1, p_b)$. The superscript 1 refers to the first or the current period, and the subscript b refers to bonds. Bonds are issued by various firms. The uniformity of bond prices reflect the assumption of the absence of risk associated with bond holdings.

The extension of the time dimension for production and consumption activities requires some modifications of the assumptions. First, the dimension of the production possibility set has now expanded from N to $2N$. But firms cannot make decisions on the future variables now, although their future prospects influence current decisions. Since the set of current decision variables is the vector y, it is convenient to absorb the future variables into y. This is done by assuming that firms issue bonds to the extent of their expected net future incomes. Similarly, for households, the future variables which are not executable in the current period are subsumed by defining the "first-period derived utility" which expresses the two-period utility in terms of the current variables alone under the assumption that the value of the second period consumption is determined by the amount of bonds held.

Secondly, the fact that subjective expectations affect current decisions but that no complete futures markets exist to ensure the consistency of these individual plans implies that these expectations could be quite unreasonable. Firms may perceive a possibility of earning infinitely large profits and households may similarly perceive a chance of enjoying an unbounded utility in the second period. It is therefore, necessary to restrict subjective expectations within reason. For the same reason, short sales are ruled out. These assumptions ensure that the current maximization decisions by firms and households have determinate solutions.

Thirdly, an assumption is made to rule out bankruptcies by either households or firms. Thus, their introduction notwithstanding, stocks present no additional difficulty.

Fourthly, the expected future prices are assumed to be either fixed or continuous functions of the current prices. With these modifications, the existence of a temporary equilibrium is shown to be retained.

At present we are witnessing vast research efforts being directed to the reexamination and extension of temporary equilibrium models with a view to constructing a solid general equilibrium model capable of answering important macroeconomic issues such as the coexistence of inflation and unemployment. Taking the Hicksian model as the point of departure, these efforts appear to be moving in two rather opposite directions. One is the move in the Keynesian direction emphasizing the difficulties in market clearance and the importance of quantities as market signals. The other is in a more neoclassical tradition. In contrast to the Hicksian temporary equilibrium model which treats expectations as exogenously given, this latter approach attempts to treat them as endogenous, that is, as part of the solution of the temporary equilibrium model. In this way expectations are assured to be "reasonable". To illustrate the nature of solution of this type of model, let us consider a single commodity, say, X. At the beginning the entire stock of X is in the hands of the suppliers. This stock is to serve the market over two consumption periods. Suppose the suppliers have an option of selling their stocks either in the current period or in the next. This decision depends on two prices, the current price p and the expected future spot price q (given the technical information about storage activities). Let us assume, for simplicity, that the consumers do not speculate and therefore that the market demand curves in the two periods are completely static and identical, depending only on the spot price. If the suppliers know these market demand curves and the aggregate stock of X perfectly, their allocation decisions determine the equilibrium price pair (p^*, q^*) simultaneously and completely. According to this second approach, the economy proceeds *as if* this q^* was the expected price. Needless to say, in more realistic situations, neither the total stock X nor the market demand curves are known with complete accuracy and some "errors" are bound to occur. But the basic idea remains the same. In a word, what this approach aims at is to introduce more "rationality" into expectation formation and thereby achieve a higher degree of determinacy in describing the dynamics of the economic system.

In the rest of this chapter, we discuss the problem of expectation formation and particularly the idea of rational expectations. This is followed by a brief discussion of Radner's temporary equilibrium model which is based on this notion of rational expectation. The discussion of the Keynesian temporary equilibrium models is postponed until Chapter 11.

(C) Expectation Formation: We have seen above that a Hicksian temporary equilibrium is determined by, among other things, the state of expectations. In animating the model, therefore, it is necessary to specify some rules for price expectations. Even if we eliminate exogenous expectations as trivial, there is quite a wide range choice for such rules. How should we go about picking one, or at least, choosing a subset which is in some sense sensible or theoretically justifiable? What are the criteria that any sensible rule must satisfy? We propose the following two criteria: (1) the consistency, and (2) the relevance or the motivation. The consistency criterion states that a sensible expectation formation rule should be self-justifying in some broad sense. Any rule which is systematically and seriously contradicted by experience is not sensible. The relevance criterion states that a sensible expectation formation rule must be feasible under given informational limitations and must arise out of some rational decisions on the part of participants. A rule that employs more information than is available is not sensible. An imposed rule having no motivational basis would not be sensible, even if it were consistent.

All the expectation rules that have been suggested in the
literature fail to meet these two criteria simultaneously.
Expectations of the Cournot type, for example, are inconsistent in a dynamic world, though they could find motivational justification. The Koyck-type distributed lag rule, on
the other hand, seems to be reasonably consistent but lacks a
motivational foundation. It is easy to formulate and solve a
rational decision problem with some relevant expectation
rule for an individual. But when these individual choices are
aggregated, the resulting realized time path of aggregates will
not generally be what was expected by the individuals. The
search for an expectation formation rule that meets both
criteria involves a very complex tâtonnement concerning the
functional form (if one exists) of the expectation function.

There are, in the literature, two opposing views on this
matter, one negative and the other positive. Gordon and
Hynes (1970) expressed a negative view on a search for a
sensible expectation rule, or more generally, on the existence
of any stable *dynamic* relationship between aggregates. Take
a stock market. Suppose there is a firm expectation that
share *A* will appreciate relative to share *B*. Then some
participants will see a chance for a gain and will exploit this
opportunity. The consequence will be that the actions by
these participants have destroyed the initial expectation.
After such speculation or arbitrage, all the shares should
look just as profitable as any other, i.e., the only type of
expectations that can persist is one of complete randomness.
Likewise, any systematic rules of expectation or adjustment
would be discovered sooner or later and exploited and consequently be destroyed. Hence such rules can stay only
temporarily and are therefore dynamically unstable. The
Gordon–Hynes proposition is not convincing in two respects.
First, they are not clear about the time dimension within
which such speculation or arbitrage takes place. The
dynamic adjustments we are concerned with are inherently
short-run in nature and the very lack of information makes
adjustments sluggish. During such a short time dimension,

their conclusion does not apply. On the other hand, if they merely mean that adjustments die out in the long run, their point is trivial. Second, while they are correct in asserting that many adjustment rules are bound to be destroyed by speculation and arbitrage, it does not follow that *all* rules should be destroyed. There may exist some rules, like the "core" of an economy, which survive such activities. Indeed, the question here is very similar to that of the existence of a competitive equilibrium. In the static model, we were concerned with the existence of a price vector that survives arbitrage. In the present dynamic world, we are concerned with the existence of a set of adjustment equations that survives arbitrage, provided such arbitrage operations cannot be completed instantaneously.

Against this agnostic view of Gordon and Hynes, Brock (1972) proposed to search for an expectation formation rule that is perfectly consistent. Let $x(t)$, $0 \leq t < \infty$, denote a certain aggregate quantity, and let $x_t^e(s), t < s$, denote the expectation of x for time s formed at time t. Suppose we write

$$x_t^e(s) = \bar{x} + f_t(s)(x(t) - \bar{x}), \tag{9.1}$$

where $\bar{x}$ is the equilibrium value of x to be explained below, and $f_t(s)$ is an expectation function belonging to the set $F \equiv \{f_t$, for all $t \geq 0$ f_t is continuous, decreasing, $f_t(t) = 1$, $f_t(\infty) = 0\}$. Suppose further that the aggregative behaviour is given by

$$Dx = \phi(x^e), \qquad x(0) = x_0, \tag{9.2}$$

where D is the operator d/dt. x^e is generally the whole profile $x_t^e(s)$, $s > t$, and hence $\phi(x^e)$ is generally a functional. We assume that there is an $\bar{x}$ such that $\phi(\bar{x}) = 0$, and that $x(\infty) = \bar{x}$. Brock's problem is to see if there exists an $f_t(s)$ in F such that if expectations are formed according to this $f_t(s)$ then the actual path of $x(s)$ generated by these expectations coincides with $x_t^e(s)$ for all $s > t$. Suppose we start at time 0 with an arbitrary function $f_0 \in F$, but suppose that the fore-

casts generated by this f_0 were not consistent with observations. Then, at some time point, say, time 1, f_0 is revised to
$f_1 \in F$, according to some rule $f_1 = E(f_0)$. If f_1 were still not
consistent, it would be further revised to $f_2 = E(f_1)$ at time 2.
Precisely what kind of revision rule the map E represents
depends on the nature of the problem. The question Brock
asks is: If such a process continues, will $\{f\}$ eventually
converge to some "equilibrium forecast" $\bar{f}$? If so, will it be
unique? In his view, if an $\bar{f}$ can be found such that it is
independent of the initial condition f_0 and is the unique point
of accumulation of all the sequences in F, then such an $\bar{f}$ will
help to lessen the ad hoc content of macrodynamics. Brock
demonstrates the existence of a unique $\bar{f}$ using a simple
illustrative model. He further establishes a general uniqueness theorem for such equilibrium form of the expectation
function.

   In his illustrative model, x is the continuous measure of
the industry size and he postulates that the rate of entry Dx
is equal to the discounted sum of expected profits. Profits at
any time depends on the price of the product and the price,
in turn, depends on the (expected) size of the industry. Thus,
(9.2) takes the form

$$Dx = \int_t^\infty e^{-\delta(s-t)} \Pi[p(\bar{x} + f_t(s)(x - \bar{x}))] \, ds, \qquad x(0) = x_0.$$

Brock assumes the profit function to be linear, i.e.,

$$\Pi[p(x)] = mx + b, \qquad b > 0, \quad m < 0.$$

Under this assumption, he gets

$$Dx = \int_t^\infty e^{-\delta(s-t)}[m(x + f_t(s)(x - \bar{x})) + b] \, ds,$$

$$\bar{x} = -b/m,$$

$$= m(x - \bar{x}) \int_t^\infty e^{-\delta(s-t)} f_t(s) \, ds. \qquad (9.3)$$

In this linear case, Brock notes that $f_t(s)$ may be written as
$f(s - t)$. Putting $f_s(t) = f(s - t)$ and letting $s - t = y$, (9.3)

becomes

$$Dx = m(x - \bar{x}) \int_0^\infty e^{-\delta y} f(y) \, dy. \qquad (9.4)$$

Upon integration, this can be written

$$x - \bar{x} = (x_0 - \bar{x}) \exp \left\{ mt \int_0^\infty e^{-\delta y} f(y) \, dy \right\},$$

or

$$g(t) \equiv (x(t) - \bar{x})/(x_0 - \bar{x}) = \exp \left\{ mt \int_0^\infty e^{-\delta y} f(y) \, dy \right\}.$$

From this,

$$E(f) = \exp \left\{ mt \int_0^\infty e^{-\delta y} f(y) \, dy \right\} \equiv e^{mtL(f)}. \qquad (9.5)$$

Equation (9.5) defines a mapping E and $\bar{f}$ is a fixed point of this mapping, i.e., $\bar{f} = E(\bar{f})$. To find the form of $\bar{f}$, notice that $\bar{f}$ has the form $e^{\bar{K}t}$, $\bar{K} < 0$. Substituting $\bar{f}(t) = e^{\bar{K}t}$ into $\bar{f} = E(\bar{f})$, we get

$$e^{\bar{K}t} = \exp \left\{ mt \int_0^\infty e^{-\delta y} e^{\bar{K}y} \, dy \right\} = e^{mt/(\delta - \bar{K})}.$$

Thus $\bar{K}$ is identified as the negative root of the quadratic equation $\bar{K}^2 - \delta \bar{K} + m = 0$.

The uniqueness of $\bar{f}$ is established by noting that the $\bar{K}$, which was the fixed point of the map $H(K) = m/(\delta - K)$, is also the fixed point of the iterate $G(K) \equiv H(H(K))$ and that $G(K)$ is a "contraction mapping", i.e., $G(K)$ has a positive slope less than unity in the range $K < 0$. This means that $\bar{f}(t) = e^{\bar{K}t}$ and this $\bar{f}$ generates a self-fulfilling set of forecasts, $\bar{x}_t^e(s) \equiv \bar{x} + \bar{f}(s - t)(x_t - \bar{x}) = \bar{x}^a(s)$ for all s, t, where $\bar{x}^a(s)$ is the path generated by actors forecasting with $f_t(s) = \bar{f}(s - t)$ for all s, t. In other words, if expectations were formed according to $\bar{f}(t) = e^{\bar{K}t}$, expectations would be perfectly self-fulfilling. The particular form of equilibrium forecasts naturally varies from one problem to another. But the very existence of such equilibrium forecasts suggests that a macrodynamic theory could be built on a firmer footing comparable to equilibrium statics. (Equilibrium forecasts are to dynamics as equilibrium prices are to statics.) This means also that such a macro dynamics will logically share the same set of problems as the equilibrium statics, the central one being the informational feasibility of the tâtonnement process. At the abstract level, there are the usual problems of existence, uniqueness and convergence. Brock's discussion is mainly concerned with these problems and he has had a considerable amount of success. In this sense, Brock has extended the conventional equilibrium statics to an equilibrium dynamics. But at the practical level, it is hard to believe that the behaviour of a macroeconomy can be adequately represented by such an "equilibrium" disequilibrium path – much more so than believing that all or most of the transactions are carried out at equilibrium prices in an atemporal model. Notice that the dynamic equation (9.2) is taken as given throughout the above exercise. This means, in a general equilibrium context, that a complete dynamic model describing the path of moving temporary equilibria must be known for any given form of expectation functions. But this would require utilization of information about the future, e.g., the way $\bar{x}$ shifts over time. In other words, while this rule satisfies the first criterion perfectly, it hardly meets the second criterion. We therefore now turn to a rational expectation model which stresses informational limitations.

(D) Radner's model (1972) is the first rigorous temporary general equilibrium model based on the idea of rational expectations. His model, cast in a time–state preference framework, is more general than Arrow and Hahn's in that he deals with a longer time horizon and in that contingent commodity markets partially exist. Extension of the time horizon beyond two periods enables him to differentiate between the near and distant future in terms of varying degrees of fineness in the partitioning of states at different dates.

Radner considers an economy extending through a finite sequence of dates $1, \ldots, T$. The set of all possible states is denoted by S. Each element of S is a particular history of the environment from date 1 through date T. One can imagine an economy starting from a certain "point" in date 1 and facing many alternative paths emanating from it, like branches from a tree, into the future. But the important point is that standing in date 1 and looking ahead, not every individual state can be discerned. What one sees is a very cloudy picture in which only a few branches spread from the root quickly disappearing in a haze. In other words, the set of observable events at date 1 is a very crude partition of S. In date 2 the picture will become little better and the partition a little finer. In general, the perceived partition is expected to become clearer with the passage of time. In Radner's model, the extent of the contingent commodity markets is determined by the extent of the partition of observable events. Namely, a trade contract at date t in event A to deliver a certain amount of commodity h at date u $(u \geq t)$ in event B is *allowable* if event A is observable at date t and if event B in date u is also observable at date t. Radner adds another condition on an allowable contract, namely, that the amount of the commodity involved in such a contract be no greater than a given positive number. While this assumption appears quite innocuous, the magnitude of this positive number proves to be rather crucial in the sense that the existence of temporary equilibrium depends on this number. At any rate, to each type of such allowable contracts there corresponds a price and the set of these prices constitutes the system of commodity prices.

Radner begins his investigation with the case of pure exchange. In this model, each consumer is endowed with a certain fixed initial resource which is assumed to be sufficient to place him in an interior point of his consumption set. Given his initial resource, each consumer engages himself in a set of allowable trades so as to maximize his (expected) utility subject to a sequence of constraints such that for each date–event pair, the amounts of current and forward sales do not exceed the resource in hand net of planned consumption. An equilibrium is defined as a set of prices at the first date, a set of common price expectations for the future, and a consistent set of individual plans for consumers such that, given the current prices and price expectations, each consumer's plan is optimal for him.

Radner then introduces producers and a stock market. Given a commodity price system, each producer engages in production and trading activities. Such a plan generates an amount of revenue at each date–event pair, and these revenues are assumed to be distributed among the share-holding consumers according to the shares held at the immediately preceding date–event pair. There is a stock market where consumers can trade shares at each date except the last. It is assumed that the initial allocation of shares among consumers was determined prior to date 1. An equilibrium of this extended model is defined in a similar manner with the inclusion of stock prices and producers' plans, and Radner studies the existence of an equilibrium of this economy. Because of the existence of uncertainty (due to partial lack of contingent markets), there emerges the possibility of firms' bankruptcies and the resulting problem of discontinuities in the consumers' demand correspondences. The existence proof, on the other hand, depends on the condition that the share prices remain strictly positive at all times. One way of avoiding this difficulty, Radner suggests, is to eliminate such "unprofitable" firms at the outset. This may be justifiable if we are dealing with a full equilibrium. But in the present context of temporary equilibrium with uncertainty, this is not a very satisfactory strategy. Also the dependence of the existence proof on the afore-mentioned positive number calls for an elaboration.

While none of the temporary equilibrium models studied so far has gone very far in terms of positive results, these studies give us an idea as to what sort of difficulties we must face when we move from a full equilibrium to a temporary equilibrium. This information is in itself quite useful.

(E) We conclude this chapter with a brief discussion of a popular expectation formula called "adaptive" expectations and its rationale. Besides its fair success in empirical studies, the attractive features of the hypothesis are its simplicity in form, the fact that it is a pure feed-back mechanism, and the fact that a theoretical justification can be given to it.

Phillip Cagan (1956) appears to be the first to formulate the adaptive expectation hypothesis. This study is concerned with the analysis of price dynamics in a state of "hyperinflation" which is defined as "beginning in the month the rise in prices exceeds 50% and as ending in the month before the monthly rise in prices drops below that amount and stays below for at least a year" (p. 25). The records of seven countries that underwent such hyperinflation in the early part of this century show that during hyperinflation the amount of real cash balances changed drastically in the face of relatively stable levels of real wealth and real income. Since there is little reason to believe that individuals' tastes changed during these periods, the cause should be looked for in the changes in the expected returns from each form in which wealth could be held, including money. Here again, the changes in the relative profitabilities among different forms of wealth did not seem important enough to explain the wide variations in real cash balances. Cagan hypothesized that changes in real cash balances in hyperinflation resulted chiefly from variations in the expected rate of change in prices.

In order to test this hypothesis empirically, the two variables, the desired real cash balances and the expected rate of inflation, must somehow be related to observable magnitudes. The former, i.e., the relationship between desired and actual real balances involves the problem of the

speed of market adjustments, while the latter is concerned
with the theory of expectation formation. These two issues
give rise to a central problem in dynamic aggregative models.
To the best of my knowledge, however, these two types of
adjustments are not observationally distinguishable, i.e., one
cannot derive a reduced form on the basis of which one can
choose one type of adjustment over the other. Recognizing
this difficulty, Cagan adopts a simple assumption that the
desired real cash balances are always equal to the actual,
thus placing the whole burden of adjustment on expectations.

Examining the time series for the seven hyperinflations,
Cagan observed that the actual rate of change in prices at
any moment did not account for the amount of the balances
at the same moment. In many months when the rates of
change in prices were very low, real cash balances were still
much below what they were in previous months when the
rates were higher. This observation leads Cagan (1956, p. 37)
to hypothesize the following: *The expected rate of change in
prices is revised per period of time in proportion to the
difference between the actual rate of change in prices and the
rate of change that was expected.* Formally, if Π^e is the
expected rate of change, the hypothesis can be written as

$$(d\Pi^e/dt)_t = \beta(\Pi_t - \Pi_t^e), \qquad \infty > \beta \geq 0. \qquad (9.6)$$

John Muth (1961) offered a theoretical justification for this
type of adaptive expectations. He asserted that the major
source of defects of dynamic economic models was the lack
of an explanation of the way expectations were formed. The
not-uncommon argument that the assumption of rationality
in economics leads to theories inconsistent with observed
phenomena, he argued, was untrue. Inconsistencies were
precisely due to the fact that dynamic economic models do
not assume enough rationality. Muth then advanced a theory
of expectations that "expectations were essentially the same
as the predictions of the relevant economic theory". This
hypothesis he termed the "rational expectation hypothesis".

In plain words, the rational expectation hypothesis asserts that expected prices are the expected *equilibrium* prices. For example, suppose we have a market where

$$D_t = a - bp_t \qquad \text{(demand)},$$
$$S_t = A + Bp_t^e + u_t \quad \text{(supply)}, \qquad\qquad (9.7)$$
$$D_t = S_t \qquad\qquad \text{(market equilibrium)},$$

where p_t^e is the expected price and u_t is an error term with mean zero. Eliminating quantities from these equations, we get

$$p_t = (a - A - Bp_t^e - u_t)/b. \qquad\qquad (9.8)$$

Taking the expectation,

$$E(p_t) = (a - A - Bp_t^e)/b.$$

Equating p_t^e to $E(p_t)$, we get

$$p_t^e = (a - A)/(b + B). \qquad\qquad (9.9)$$

Muth has shown that the adaptive expectation formula can be derived as a special case of the rational expectation hypothesis when exogenous shocks are cumulative. Turnovsky (1969) has also derived an adaptive expectation formula for an individual firm using the Bayesian approach. These results suggest that for a wide range of realistic problems an adaptive expectation formula is a good representation of the rational expectation hypothesis.

References

Arrow, K. J. and F. H. Hahn, *General competitive analysis* (San Francisco, Calif., 1971).

Brock, W. A., "On models of expectations arising from maximizing behavior of economic agents over time", *Journal of Economic Theory* (1972).

Cagan, P., "The monetary dynamics of hyperinflation", in: M. Friedman, ed., *Studies in the quantity theory of money* (Chicago, Ill., 1956).

Gordon, D. F. and A. Hynes, "On the theory of price dynamics", in: E. S.

Phelps et al., eds., *Microeconomic foundations of employment and inflation theory* (New York, 1970).

Hicks, J. R., *Value and capital* (Oxford, 1939, 1946).

Hicks, J. R., *Capital and growth* (Oxford, 1965).

Houthakker, H. S., "The scope and limits of futures trading", in: M. Abramovitz, ed., *The allocation of economic resources* (Stanford, Calif., 1959).

Muth, J. F., "Rational expectations and the theory of price movements", *Econometrica* (1961).

Radner, R., "Existence of equilibrium of plans, prices, and price expectations in a sequence of markets", *Econometrica* (1972).

Turnovsky, S., "A Bayesian approach to the theory of expectations", *Journal of Economic Theory* (1969).

Part III

Macroeconomy

The importance of money essentially flows from its being
a link between the present and the future.

J. M. Keynes

Macroeconomic theory deals with a number of key aggregates such as national income, employment, capital stock,
total money stock and the general price level. It attempts to
analyze the relationships among these variables. To accomplish this a macro model is formulated. Since a macro model
is a model of an entire economy, it is necessarily a general
equilibrium model. Indeed, macroeconomic theory is nothing
but an *operational* general equilibrium theory specially
designed to suit the analysis of the above aggregates. There
is no presuming that any one of such relationships is powerful enough to render others superfluous.

The construction of a macro model contains a number of
difficulties. To begin with, there is the problem of aggregation. Aggregates for outputs and inputs are not, strictly
speaking, proper aggregates of the underlying individual
quantities, and the behaviour of these aggregates tends to
contain biases and various "noises" due to aggregation. Apart
from this problem, there are primarily two sources of
difficulties in the formulation of a macro model compared
with the type of general equilibrium models employed in
micro theory. One is that a macro theory is concerned with a
temporary equilibrium, and not with a full or statical equilibrium. A temporary equilibrium is a snap shot of a dynamic

path. Variables are changing over time, which leave one with additional degrees of freedom to close the model. To obtain meaningful comparative statics results with a temporary equilibrium model, one must know the comparative dynamics properties of individual or micro solutions completely. For example, to analyze the effect of an interest rate change on aggregate investment, one must know how a given change in the interest rate is interpreted by investors and how their optimal accumulation paths "shift" in response to the new interest rate profile. There is no dodging the need for considering expectation formations. The other difficulty concerns the manner in which markets adjust to accommodate changes in individual plans. The conventional neoclassical general equilibrium analysis postulates perfect market adjustments to preclude possible inconsistencies among individual plans. But from a point of view which stresses this market problem, such a theory is no more than the study of *intentions* and not of their consequences.

Since our subject is monetary theory, our interest lies specifically in the role of money in an aggregative economy. Although this appears to be a rather narrow problem in macro theory, we cannot isolate ourselves from the above difficulties. On the contrary. The issue between Monetarists and Keynesians in a sense stems from a difference in views on the nature of the temporary equilibrium – its time horizon, the extent to which wealth variables are allowed to influence flow magnitudes, the particular phase of cycles in which the economy is situated, the extent to which expectations exert their influences, etc. Monetarists' favourite arena has been the long-run, a time horizon long enough for the stock of money to come to bear simple relationships to income and prices. Keynesians, on the other hand, have tended to favour the short-run, a time horizon short enough for the stock adjustments to be insignificant. As we shall see, however, neither approach can claim to have satisfactorily captured the dynamic nature of macroeconomic behaviour.

The purpose of this part is to study the working and the

policy implications of money in an aggregate economy by contrasting the Monetarist and the Keynesian views on these matters. In Chapter 10 we first study what the quantity theory of money is by following the writings of Friedman and Keynes. This is followed by a discussion on the significance of some of the empirical studies which have been proposed to determine the relative superiority of the two approaches.

Chapter 11 reviews Keynes' theory. We first examine the nature of his temporary equilibrium in comparison with the neoclassical one. We then proceed to his dynamic theory which centres around the notion of the marginal efficiency of capital. In view of the prevalence of the statical, pure flow-type "Keynesian" models and the on-going controversy over the presence or absence of capital theory in Keynes, we emphasize the importance of fusing the flow model and the asset choice model into one.

Chapter 12 is devoted to a study of dynamic aggregative models. We begin with a simple monetary growth model to highlight the role of expectations and of capital accumulation and the interactions between the money and the real sectors. This is followed by an analysis of more short-run models in order to study unemployment, wages and prices more closely.

Finally, Chapter 13 looks at some of the controversial issues in monetary policy, and in particular, the validity of some of the simple and bold rules proposed by Monetarists. We shall first study in some detail the main arguments – their logic and evidence – of Monetarists and Keynesians concerning the relative effectiveness of monetary and fiscal policies in stabilizing the economy. We then move on to the long-run problem of monetary management which became popular after Friedman's optimum quantity thesis. After a critical review of these issues, we take a look at Friedman's automatic rule which appears to have been adopted by the Federal Reserve System in recent years and a number of problems associated with the actual operation of such rules.

10

The Quantity Theory of Money

(A)   What is the role of money in an aggregative economy? How does a change in the stock of money influence other important variables in the system? How can such a knowledge be utilized to prescribe desirably policies? The ultimate goal of monetary theory is to provide satisfactory answers to these questions. Monetary theorists have long been interested in establishing, in particular, the relationship between the stock of money and the general price level. This body of theories has come to be called the quantity theory of money. It has a long history. Smith, Cantillon, Locke, Marshall, Pigou, Newcomb and Fisher, and even Keynes himself, each had his own version of the theory.

   Symbolically, the theory can be put in the form:

$$M/P = k(\ ) \cdot y,$$

where $k(\ )$, the inverse of the velocity of circulation, presumably depends on a host of factors which we do not attempt to specify at the moment. But no matter what these factors are, the list of such factors must be short enough, and the k function must be stable enough in that short list of factors if the quantity theory is to be of any use both in theory and in practice. The question is then: Does a k function exist such that it is so simple and stable as to dominate other relationships and to qualify as the centre-piece in monetary theory? Opinions of economists are still split. So we have Monetarists and Keynesians. In this chapter we attempt to trace out the subsequent development of the quantity theory mainly through the writings of Friedman and his associates on the one hand, and of Keynes and his followers on the other. We do this not so much out of historical interest as for the current significance of the subject. Whether or not one wishes to call the recent resurgence of Monetarism a "counter-revolution", there is no question that the Monetarists have done a remarkable job promoting their set of ideas. U.S. monetary policy for the last several years has been greatly influenced by them and their influence is becoming increasingly more apparent in macro textbooks of recent vintages. In view of these facts, it is necessary that we reflect upon what the Quantity Theory is about and critically examine the alleged proof of superiority of the Monetarist approach.

(B) Our exposition of the quantity theory begins with Keynes. There are two reasons for taking this rather unconventional approach. First, Keynes himself was once a quantity theorist. By studying the development of Keynes' own ideas, we can see clearly where he parted with the theory. Second, the modern version of the quantity theory held by Monetarists has been developed with Keynes' theory in mind and as a counter-attack on the latter. To understand the spirit of the new quantity theory, therefore, it is essential to know Keynes. Even then it is not easy to identify the quantity theory as "restated" by Friedman with the quantity theory as we know it.

As we mentioned above, Keynes was a quantity theorist. He basically viewed, like all others, the determination of the price level as a resultant of the two independent forces. One was the behaviour of the banking system determining the nominal stock of money balances, and the other was the behaviour of the public choosing an optimal stock of real balances. The price level was then to be determined as the ratio of these two quantities. In his *Tract on Monetary Reform* (1924), he wrote a quantity equation of the following form:

$$M/P = m_1 + hm_2 \quad \text{or} \quad P = M/(m_1 + hm_2),$$

where h is the proportion of the bank's cash reserves to their deposits, and P is the price of a "consumption unit", namely, "a collection of specified quantities of the public's standard articles of consumption". Further, m_1 is the number of consumption units which the public required in cash, and m_2 is the number of consumption units which the public required in bank-deposits. He thought that m_1 and m_2 would depend on the community's wealth and its habits. But he was aware of the limitations of such a formula. Its ignoring of expenditues for non-consumption purposes and its failure to allow for the variety of reasons for which bank-deposits were held were apparent. In the process of his deeper investigations into the determinants of the real balances, he was gradually led away from the conventional quantity theory. In his own words:[1]

> "Formerly I was attracted by this line of approach. But it now seems to me that the merging together of all the different sorts of transactions – income, business and financial – which may be taking place only causes confusion, and that we cannot get any real insight into the price-making process without bringing in the rate of interest and the distinctions between incomes and profits and between savings and investment."

[1] In the meantime, a group of monetary economists have developed the so-called "flow of funds analysis". This analysis is concerned with the study of money flows arising from industrial and financial transactions among various sectors of the economy. This kind of study will enable us to gain detailed knowledge of the financial processes and ultimately of the manner in which the money and the real sectors interact. For recent surveys of the flow of funds analysis, see Bain (1973) and Cohen (1972). While this is a promising line of empirical investation as a follow-up of Keynes' original idea, these economists ironically have complained about the lack of theory to guide them.

A Treatise on Money (1930) was Keynes' answer along this line of inquiry.

In this book, Keynes first defines *the community's money income* as the earnings of the factors of production or the cost of production, which consists of wages and salaries, the normal remuneration of entrepreneurs, interest on capital and regular monopoly gains and rents. The difference between the actual remuneration and the normal remuneration of entrepreneurs is called *profits*. Thus profits are not a part of the community's money income. The "normal" remuneration of entrepreneurs at any time is defined as "that rate of remuneration which, if entrepreneurs were open to make new bargains with all the factors of production at the currently prevailing rates of earnings, would leave them under no motive either to increase or to decrease their scale of operations" (p. 125).

Secondly, by *savings* he means the difference between the community's money income and its money expenditure on current consumption. By *investment*, on the other hand, is meant the net increment of the capital of the community. The *value of investment* is therefore equal to the sum of savings and profits.

Now let E = the money income, I' = the cost of production of new investment, S = savings, R = the volume of consumption goods purchased by consumers, C = the volume of new investment, O = the total output (by appropriate choice of units, $O = R + C$), and P = the price of consumption goods. Then we have

$$PR = E - S = \frac{E}{O}R + I' - S,$$

or

$$P = \frac{E}{O} + \frac{I' - S}{R}. \tag{10.1}$$

Further, letting P' = the price of new investment goods, Π = the price level of output as a whole, I = the value of new investment, we get for the general price level:

$$\Pi = \frac{PR + P'C}{O} = \frac{E - S + I}{O} = \frac{E}{O} + \frac{I - S}{O}. \tag{10.2}$$

The first term of these two equations, E/O, is the average unit factor cost or the "rate of earnings per unit of output" and Keynes denotes it as W_1. The second term, on the other hand, represents profits. In (10.1) $I' - S$ is the profits on the production and sale of consumption goods, and the term $(I - S)$ in (10.2) represents total profits. This can be seen easily as follows: The profits made in the consumption-good industry are

$$Q_1 = PR - \frac{E}{O}R = E - S - (E - I') = I' - S.$$

The profits made in the investment-good industry are obviously

$$Q_2 = I - I',$$

and so the total profits $Q \equiv Q_1 + Q_2 = I - S$, which is the second term of (10.2). Hence equations (10.1) and (10.2) can be rewritten respectively

$$P = W_1 + \frac{Q_1}{R}, \tag{10.3}$$

$$\Pi = W_1 + \frac{Q}{O}. \tag{10.4}$$

Equations (10.1) and (10.2) or equations (10.3) and (10.4) are called the *Fundamental Equations* for the value of money [Keynes (1930, pp. 133–138)].

Though these Fundamental Equations are definitional and have no behavioural implications, the basic difference between them and the quantity theory is already evident. The first term W_1 represents the level of factor prices, and this term directly determines the price levels P or Π in equilibrium. But this term is largely independent of the behaviour of the banking system. Thus if money matters, it is primarily by affecting the second term, namely, profits. And money makes its effect felt in the system chiefly through the bank-rate. Keynes thought that a rise in the bank-rate would cause investment to decline *relative to savings*, a theory which he credited to Wicksell. According to this theory, the primary effects of a rise in the bank-rate is a fall in the price of fixed capital goods, and therefore in P', the price of new investment goods and an increase in savings. Its secondary effects will be a fall in the output of new investment goods, and a fall in P, the price of consumption goods, due to the fall in the expenditure for consumption. Indeed P will fall further due to the fall in the incomes of the producers of investment goods, which he called the tertiary effect (pp. 204–205). At this stage, therefore we have a fall in both P and P', and consequent losses to all classes of entrepreneurs, which result in a decline in the volume of employment which they offer to the factors of production at the existing rates of earnings. If the rates of earnings or the factor prices adjust downward smoothly on such an occasion, a new equilibrium will be established at lower prices and lower rates of remuneration. But if not, a state of unemployment will result and continue until the rise in the bank-rate is reversed or by chance something happens to alter the natural rate of interest so as to bring it back to equality with the new market rate (p. 206). As one might expect, Keynes was doubtful of the smooth adjustments in factor prices (p. 270).

Now looking at the problem from the point of view of the demand for money, Keynes divided the total requirements of the monetary circulation between the *industrial circulation* and the *financial circulation*. The former refers to that portion of the requirements which relates to the business of maintaining the normal process of current output, distribution, and exchange and paying the factors of production, while the latter refers to that portion of the monetary requirements which relates to the business of holdings and exchanging existing titles to wealth including stock exchange and money market transactions, speculation and the process of conveying current savings and profits into the hands of entrepreneurs. To be a bit more specific, the industrial circulation consists of: (1) cash and deposits workers carry to meet their personal expenditures (= *income deposits*) and (2) cash and that portion of *business deposits* which is directly related to the process of production and distribution. The financial circulation, on the other hand, consists of: (1) savings deposits and (2) that portion of business deposits held for the purposes of speculative transactions in capital goods and commodities and of financial transactions (pp. 47–48). Of these two types of circulation, the industrial circulation is expected to bear a fairly stable relation to the community's money income, whereas the financial circulation is largely independent of the money income but depends on the bank-rate and the state of expectations about the future. Since the state of expectations plays a crucial role in determining the financial circulation, even if the bank-rate influences profits and profits influence the state of expectations, the connection between the bank-rate and the volume of the financial circulation appears to be somewhat indirect. Thus Keynes drew a conclusion that, contrary to the quantity theory, the total quantity of money would not be associated in any stable or invariant manner either with the level of bank-rate or with the level of prices (p. 219). Keynes viewed the monetary authority as primarily setting the level of bank-rate rather than the total quantity of money. But even with full capability to manipulate the level of bank-rate, the authority would have only a partial influence on the level of prices, for it has no means of acting directly on the first term of the Fundamental Equations. To raise the first term, the monetary authority would have to stimulate entrepreneurs with abundant credit and abnormal profits; to lower it, the authority would have to depress entrepreneurs with restricted credit and abnormal losses. But these moves, especially the latter, would likely be very costly.

As is well known, Keynes considered in the *Treatise* the

snap shot of an economy at a given level of output and studied the forces that would cause changes in profits and consequently changes in output. The working out of the full effect on output of initial disturbances was postponed till the *General Theory*. So far as his views on the nature of the effects of monetary policy are concerned, however, Keynes' position did not change much between 1930 and 1936. The *Treatise* was written in the late 1920's, a period remembered for its speculative booms. It is worth noting that Keynes' departure from the quantity theory was motivated by his observation of the strong speculative demand for money and not by the Great Depression.

(C) As for the quantity theory in a contemporary sense, the first formal statement of the theory is due to Friedman (1956). In this essay he first emphasized that the theory was "a term evocative of a general approach rather than a label for a well-defined theory", and "a theoretical approach that insisted that money does matter". The essay consists of two rather disjoint (theoretical and empirical) parts. At the theoretical level, Friedman defines the quantity theory as a theory of the *demand* for money (as against a theory of output, or of money income, or of the price level which would require specification of the supply side), and he presents a perfectly general theory of asset choices on the part of the ultimate wealth owning units, with money being one of the many assets. Friedman does not consider the distinction between transactions balances and speculative balances or the distinction between households and firms significant. Nor does he think the existence of banks makes an essential change to his analysis. After a general discussion of the nature and the scope of asset choices by the ultimate wealth-owning units, Friedman writes the demand for money function in the following alternative forms:

$$M/P = f(r_b \cdot r_e, DP/P; w; Y/P; u),\qquad (10.5)$$

$$M/Y = f(r_b, r_e, DP/P; w; P/Y; u), \tag{10.6}$$

$$Y = v(r_b, r_e, DP/p; w; Y/P; u)M, \tag{10.7}$$

where $v(\ )$ is the reciprocal of $f(\ )$ and can be identified as
the velocity of circulation of money. In these equations,
r_b = the nominal return on bonds, r_e = the nominal return on
equities, DP/P = the rate of change in the price level or the
nominal return on non-human goods, w = the ratio of non-
human to human wealth, and u = the taste parameters.

Now what use does Friedman make of these general
demand functions to substantiate the Monetarists' position?
Very little. For equation (10.7) to be a complete model of
income determination, it is necessary, as he admits, that the
demand for money is highly inelastic with respect to the
variables in v or that all these variables are taken as fixed.
But both these conditions serve to deny the relevance of
such general demand functions to the type of propositions
advocated by the Monetarists. In fact, criticisms of Friedman's "Restatement" came from inside the Chicago School.
Among them, the most explicit has been Harry Johnson
(1965, p. 396) who wrote:

"...to admit interest rates into the demand function
for money is to accept the Keynesian Revolution and
Keynes' attack on the quantity theory."

Patinkin (1965, pp. 81–82, fn. 8) also recorded his disagreement as follows:

"Its title not withstanding, this is actually much closer
to the Keynesian theory than to the quantity theory –
or to the traditional Chicago theory – which Friedman
claims to be restating. For whereas Keynesian theory
emphasizes the optimal relationship among *stocks* of
assets (which is Friedman's main concern), neoclassical (and traditional Chicago) theory emphasized the
optimal relationship between the *stock* of money and

the *flow* of planned expenditures.... Correspondingly, the latter paid little, if anything, attention to the possible impact on the rate of interest or shifts in tastes relating to the form in which assets are held."

Friedman (1966) has addressed himself explicitly to the question of the interest elasticity of the demand for money. He argues that simply introducing interest rates in the demand function for money is no Keynesian revolution but the Fisherine tradition which he seems to be perfectly willing to accept. Theoretically, this makes velocity subject to variations due to real forces and possibly may invalidate Friedman's proposed automatic rule of monetary policy, as pointed out by Johnson. Friedman dismisses this question by saying that the conditions required for such a possibility are different from those he assumed in making that proposal and are "highly special".

In any case it is clear that Friedman is not taking issue with Keynesians at the theoretical level. His basic premises are that interest rates are essentially real phenomena and that the interest elasticity of the demand for money is quite small in the region of -0.15. Hence, the effects of any plausible systematic changes originating in the real sector can be absorbed into velocity with little harm.

Next, in moving to the empirical part of the "Restatement", one finds there a number of familiar propositions that the quantity theorist "accepts", "holds", or "considers of great importance". They are:

(1) that the demand for money is highly stable – more stable than, e.g., the consumption function;
(2) that the demand for money function plays a vital role in determining such important variables as the level of money income or of prices;
(3) that there are important factors affecting the supply of money that do not affect the demand for money. This fact, along with the stability of the demand function for

money, enables one to trace out the effect of changes in
the money supply; and collecting all these;

(4) that the income velocity of money possesses an extraordinary empirical stability which makes it the centre-
piece of macroeconomic analysis.

It seems fair to conclude that the quantity theory is, above
all, a statement of the observed stability of the velocity in
the long-run, without an explanation of what causes such a
stability. According to Friedman (1959), the long-run velocity
of money for the U.S. economy over the period 1869–1957
has followed a secular downward trend in the face of a
secular increase in real per-capita permanent income with
the elasticity with respect to the latter equal to −0.810. As
such, the quantity theory is comparable to the similar long-
run constancies of the average propensity to consume or of
the capital–output ratio. This kind of knowledge is certainly
useful, but one cannot help being hesitant to call it a theory.
At best, the quantity theory is a "low-brow" theory, if we
use Solow's terminology in growth theory. Given a set of
"stylized facts" about the behaviour of a number of "grand
ratios", simple growth theory does a good job explaining
them. But this theory can spell out no more details of the
growth process. For example, we know that we do not
produce a homogeneous output with homogeneous two inputs. Thus any growth program must lay out the pattern of
changes in the industrial structure. Also this type of theory is
totally incapable of explaining the short-run behaviour which
depends, among others, on the interactions between the real
and the money sectors. The same must be true of the
quantity theory. What can the quantity theory predict about
the short-run behaviour of our economy? How can it explain
the details of the working of money within the system? As
for the first point, Friedman discusses, in the same 1959
article and in many other places, the cyclical pattern of
velocity accompanying short-run fluctuations in output but
this does not constitute a theory for the short-run since

short-run fluctuations of velocity are simply residuals which
the long-run theory has failed to explain – that is, they are
described as variations due to deviations of the actual income from its "permanent" level. As for the second point,
Friedman and other Monetarists have generally been reluc-
tant to explore it in any depth. Perhaps further accumulation
of detailed facts will some day induce them to undertake this
task.

(D) In this section and the next we discuss some empirical
evidence and the light it sheds on the Monetarist–Keynesian
debate. Friedman's empirical work is simply too extensive to
be summarized in a few pages. We therefore take up only
two pieces of his work here. The first one is the well-known
Friedman–Meiselman study (1963) comparing the relative
stability of monetary velocity and the autonomous expenditure multiplier for the U.S. The other is his monetary
interpretation of the Great Depression which occupies a
substantial portion of the monumental book by Friedman
and Schwartz (1963). In this chapter, we are concerned with
the first.

Friedman and Meiselman start out by specifying two
alternative theories, the quantity theory and the income-
expenditure theory, in their simplest forms:

$$Y = a + V'M, \tag{10.8}$$

$$Y = \alpha + K'A, \tag{10.9}$$

where Y = national income, M = the money stock (currency
plus commercial bank deposits), and A = total autonomous
expenditures (net private investment expenditures plus the
government deficit). The purpose of their analysis is to
determine empirically which of the variables, M or A,
explains Y better. In their actual estimation, they use consumption expenditures C as the dependent variable instead
of Y,

$$C = a + VM, \qquad (10.10)$$

$$C = \alpha + KA. \,^2 \qquad (10.11)$$

Friedman and Meiselman divide the observation period 1897–1958 into twelve overlapping subperiods so that each subperiod corresponds to a full cycle (either from peak to peak or from trough to trough). Fitting the above equations for all these subperiods, they have found that M was more closely related to C than was A almost uniformly. The only exceptional subperiod was the period 1929–1939, i.e., the deep depression period. From these results, Friedman and Meiselman (1964, p. 166) conclude:

> "The results are strikingly one-sided. Except for the early years of the Great Depression, money is more closely related to consumption than are autonomous expenditures.... The widespread belief that the investment multiplier is stabler than the monetary velocity is an invalid generalization from the experience of three or four years.... One implication of the results is that the critical variable for monetary policy is the stock of money, not interest rates or investment expenditures."

As for the simplistic nature of the models, Friedman and Meiselman are careful to note that "on a more sophisticated level, when additional variables are introduced, the relative advantage of the two might be reversed". But in their view, "the relationship which explains the most in its simplest version is the relationship that will be most fruitful to explore further and to convert into a more sophisticated model" (p. 174).

[2]Besides these two simplest equations, Friedman and Meiselman also estimated a synthesized equation $C = a + KA + VM$ and an equation which has prices as a third variable. They also ran regressions using quarterly data for the post-W.W.II period.

But is their conclusion about the relative superiority of the quantity theory really robust? Given their statistical results, is theirs a valid conclusion? Hester (1964) contended that the Friedman–Meiselman results were highly sensitive to the choice of A, the autonomous expenditures term. In particular, Hester was concerned about the fact that taxes are a function of income, and hence, that using taxes as a component of autonomous expenditures gave rise to a spurious correlation. He proposed an alternatives measure of autonomous expenditures which is equal to $A + T$ where T denote taxes. When regressions were run using this measure as the explanatory variable. Hester found that the correlation between autonomous expenditures and consumption visibly improved to a point where the relative superiority of the quantity theory was no longer obvious. This result was reconfirmed when a few other related measures were used. On the other hand, Savin (1975), rerunning the simple Friedman–Meiselman equations with second-order autoregressive disturbances and using the maximum likelihood and the Hildreth–Lu estimation methods, found that while the coefficient V in the money model remained relatively unchanged, the coefficient K in the income–expenditure model was highly sensitive to the model specification and the estimation method used.

Shifting to the second question raised above, what does the correlation between contemporaneous M and C or A and C mean? The multiplier effect will take time to work itself out. If the effect spreads out over years, what Y or C in any given year captures is a compound effect of fiscal activities over a number of years preceding it. The coefficient estimated this way obviously does not accurately represent the true coefficient of response. The same is also true of the money model, since Friedman is known for his assertion that the effect of monetary policy has a very long lag. We must conclude that these results cannot provide clearcut evidence one way or the other.

(E) What caused the Great Depression? Despite the numerous writings on the various aspects of this question,[3] no definitive answer exists and one wonders if it ever will. Our purpose here is of course not to tackle this formidable problem but rather review one specific diagnosis given by Friedman and Schwartz (1963, ch. 7). The Great Depression was admittedly an exceptional period. Nonetheless, we can gain some insight into the working of monetary policy by studying why monetary policy failed in that period.

Unlike all others, Friedman and Schwartz attribute the Great Depression (at least its extraordinary duration and severity) to a single cause, the failure on the part of the Federal Reserve System to prevent the money stock from falling at the crucial time. According to Friedman and Schwartz, the vital period was the one year following the crash in the stock market in October 1929. This period in retrospect was a fairly quiet one in which financial markets recovered from the shock and even showed some signs of revival. But in November 1930 the first wave of bank failures started. These failures created a panic in the minds of the public and also of banks. The public withdrew their deposits and the banks sought cash to meet the customers demand and also to protect their own portfolios. Friedman and Schwartz believe that the character of the depression underwent a basic change after these events. Anything done by the monetary authority after the end of 1930 was ineffective. To be specific, Friedman and Schwartz argue that if the Federal Reserve System had engaged itself in a vigorous buying operation during the first year after the crash to the order of one billion dollars (whereas in reality the increase in the System's holding of government securities rose by only 150 million dollars between December 1929 and October 1930), high-powered money would have increased

[3]Kindleberger (1973) cites in his references some 160 books and more than 30 articles.

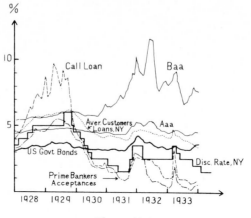

Figure 10.1

by 460 million dollars in the same period instead of actually
declining by 160 million dollars. And this difference in the
volume of high-powered money would have changed the
subsequent path of the economy significantly.

Friedman and Schwartz describe the situation leading to
the first bank failures as follows. They first note that some of
the corporate bond rates, which had been falling in line with
the rates on government bonds and with all the short-term
rates until September 1930, started to move in the opposite
(i.e., upward) direction parallel with the banking crisis (see
Figure 10.1). They then state (p. 312):

> "The reason is clear. In their search for liquidity,
> banks and others were inclined first to dispose of their
> lower-grade bonds; the very desire for liquidity made
> government bonds even more desirable as secondary
> reserves; hence the yield on lower-grade bonds rose,
> while the yields on government bonds fell. The de-
> cline in bond prices itself contributed ... to the sub-
> sequent banking crisis."

Let us now see whether these facts were borne out in the

banks' portfolios (Table 10.1 below), and in particular, in the changes between September and December of 1930. First, as for deposits, the decline was in the order of 600–700 million dollars which is by no standards abnormal in relation to quarterly changes in adjacent periods. Second, looking at the member banks' portfolios and their changes during the above three-month period, total loans and investments declined by some 600 million dollars. This decline was met entirely by liquidation of short-term assets, i.e., open market loans. In the meantime, loans of other categories remained unchanged, but investments increased by some 250 million dollars and this increase came almost exclusively from increased holdings of "Other Securities". These statements remain true well into the mid 1931, and more specifically, until September when Britain left the gold standard. It is true that while the member banks started increasing their holdings of government securities noticeably *after* the events in the last quarter of 1930, it does not seem true that these banks actively contributed to the banking crisis by "first" dumping private securities into the market. One may of course argue that the member banks are not a representative subset of all commercial banks. But this argument does not hold water. The number of member bank suspensions was relatively small (during November 1930, 33 member banks were suspended operations as against total suspensions of 254; during December 1930, these numbers were 56 against 344). But in terms of the amount of deposits involved, the member banks accounted for 53% in November and 57% in December. Given that the member banks' share of total commercial bank deposits was roughly 60% in those days, size was not a major factor in determining deposit safety.

Now if the banks did not take the initiative in liquidating bonds, the public did. Was it because they needed money to finance their ordinary business activities, or was it because the economic conditions in general convinced them to part with bonds? If the former was the reason, the Friedman–Schwartz diagnosis is still valid in that more money would

Macroeconomy

Table 10.1
Classification of loans and investments for all member banks*

	Oct. 4 '29	Dec. 31 '29	March 27 '30
Total of loans & investments	35,914	35,934	35,056
Loans to banks	640	714	527
Loans to others: Total	23,249	23,193	21,494
Secured by stocks & bonds	8,109	8,488	7,730
Secured by real estates	3,152	3,191	3,170
Other loans	11,988	11,515	10,595
Open market loans: Total	2,276	2,243	3,097
Acceptances	163	292	254
Commercial papers	228	291	499
Loans to brokers in N.Y.	1,885	1,660	2,34
Investments: Total	9,749	9,784	9,937
U.S. Gov't securities	4,022	3,863	4,085
Other securities	5,727	5,921	5,852
Deposits: Total (unadj.)	33,004	33,865	32,082
Deposits: Total (adj.)**	33,136	32,486	33,280

*Source: *Federal Reserve Bulletin*, various issues.
**Seasonally adjusted using 1927–8 quarterly weights (0.241, 0.250,

have helped. According to Friedman and Schwartz (their table 15), high-powered money fell from 6,980 million dollars to 6,817 million dollars in the first ten months of 1930, although the decline was not monotonic. In the same period, M_1 (currency plus demand deposits) fell from 25,677 million dollars to 24,986 million dollars, and M_2 (M_1 plus time deposits) fell from 45,295 million dollars to 45,054 million dollars (their table 12). Such a decline in the money stock is the crucial evidence on which Friedman and Schwartz base their verdict. But the fact of the matter was that while the financial markets returned to normal rather quickly after the crash in 1929, the real side of the economy was constantly sliding downwards. The index of industrial production (1923–1925 = 100), which had peaked at 125 in June 1929 and stood (in million dollars).

June 30 '30	Sept. 24 '30	Dec. 31 '30	March 25 '31	June 30 '31	Sept. 29 '31
35,656	35,472	34,860	34,729	33,923	33,073
535	466	631	446	457	599
21,565	21,010	21,007	19,940	19,257	18,713
8,061	7,864	7,942	7,423	7,117	6,842
3,155	3,163	3,234	3,220	3,216	3,149
10,349	9,982	9,831	9,298	8,922	8,722
3,113	3,262	2,233	2,454	2,103	1,563
241	317	370	462	502	338
507	523	366	361	384	296
2,365	2,472	1,498	1,630	1,217	928
10,442	10,734	10,989	11,889	12,106	12,199
4,061	4,095	4,125	5,002	5,343	5,564
6,380	6,639	6,864	6,886	6,763	6,635
33,690	31,839	32,560	31,153	31,566	29,467
33,690	31,966	31,308	32,316	31,566	31,684

0.249, 0.260).

at 121 in August 1929, was 106 in January 1930 and further dropped to 88 in October 1930. The index of factory employment, which stood at 107 in August 1929, was down to 86 in October 1930. In view of this substantial contraction in the scale of economic activities, it is hard to believe how the moderate decline in the money stock mentioned above could have been the major cause for the events which took place in the last two months of 1930. Although Friedman and Schwartz never mentioned, there is no doubt that *real* balances were on the increase throughout this period. As Figure 10.1 shows, rediscount rates had been lowered rapidly and drastically since October 1929, and all the short rates likewise. This trend continued well into the latter half of 1931. But these declines in the short-term interest rates and also in both rates on customer loans and the yield on government bonds could not prevent yields on risky private bonds from shooting up. One might describe this phenomenon as limitation of monetary policy. Lately, Temin (1976) made a comparative analysis of the Keynesian and the Monetarist accounts of the 1930's. While both theories were found more or less incomplete, he gave an edge to the Keynesian theory.

References

Bain, A. D., "Flow of funds analysis: A survey", *Economic Journal* (1973).

Cohen, J., "Copeland's moneyflows after twenty-five years: A survey", *Journal of Economic Literature* (1972).

Friedman, M., "The quantity theory of money: A restatement", in: M. Friedman, ed., *Studies in the quantity theory of money* (Chicago, Ill., 1956); also in his *The optimum quantity of money and other essays* (Chicago, Ill., 1969).

Friedman, M., "The demand for money: Some theoretical and empirical results", *Journal of Political Economy* (1959); also in his *Optimum Quantity of Money.*

Friedman, M., "Interest rates and the demand for money", *Journal of Law & Economics* (1966); also in his *Optimum quantity of money.*

Friedman, M. and D. Meiselman, "The relative stability of monetary velocity and the investment multiplier in the United States, 1897–1958", in their *Stabilization policies* (Englewood Cliffs, N.J., 1963).

Friedman, M. and A. J. Schwartz, *A monetary history of the United States 1867–1960* (Princeton, N.J., 1963).

Hester, D. D., "Keynes and the quantity theory: A comment on the Friedman–Meiselman CMC paper", *Review of Economics and Statistics* (1964).

Johnson, H. G., "A quantity theorist's monetary history of the United States", *Economic Journal* (1965).

Keynes, J. M., *Tract on monetary reform* (London, 1924).

Keynes, J. M., *A treatise on money*, Vol. I (London, 1930).

Kindleberger, C. P., *World in depression 1929–1939* (Berkeley, Calif., 1973).

Patinkin, D., *Money, interest and prices* (New York, 1965).

Savin, N. E., "Friedman–Meiselman revisited: A study in autocorrelation", Unpublished manuscript (1975).

Temin, P., *Did monetary factors cause the great depression?* (New York, 1976).

11

Keynes' Theory

(A) Forty years have lapsed since the publication of the *General Theory* (1936). Yet we cannot say that we have thoroughly digested and formalized Keynes' theory. His theory is broad in scope and contains many important ingredients – a leading role assigned to an independent investment function, wage rigidity and unemployment, theory of the consumption function, money and liquidity preference, durable assets and variable expectations, to name a few. It is not easy to put all these ingredients into one model. This complexity of this theory has long prevented us from seeing this theory as a unified whole, namely from recognizing that all these ingredients were not mutually independent but rather different manifestations of the common cause.

Much of the earlier efforts went into examinations of various parts of his theory, using the classical (or rather neoclassical) theory as the frame of reference. The basic attitude of these earlier writers can be seen most clearly in Klein's question (1947): What are the *minimum* assumptions that are necessary to produce the Keynesian phenomenon of unemployment equilibrium? In answering this question, a "classical" system and a "Keynesian" system were written in the form of symbolic models of static equilibrium and compared. The comparison of the two systems indicated that the Keynesian system differed from the classical one in: (1) the labour supply function, (2) the investment–savings relation, and (3) the demand for money function. The literature produced three explanations for unemployment equilibrium corresponding to these three differences, namely, the rigid wage theory, the I-S inconsistency theory, and the liquidity trap theory, of unemployment.

This way of assessing Keynes' theory is deficient in two respects. First, it is totally static. But as we can easily convince ourselves by reading the *Treatise* and the *General Theory*, he was aiming at a dynamic theory. Take the problem of unemployment. His main concern was not how to prove the existence of an unemployment equilibrium in a statical framework, but was rather what caused unemployment and what dynamic forces were at work in a state of unemployment (*General Theory*, p. vii):

> "This book...has evolved into what is primarily a study of the forces which determine changes in the scale of output and employment as a whole."

One can also recall his dynamic argument against using wage-cuts (even if this were possible) as a cure of unemployment (*ibid.*, p. 269). Secondly, the above method of assessing Keynes' theory fails to see the theory in its entirety by examining various parts of Keynes' theory one at a time. This method would be justifiable if these parts were a collection of independent assumptions. The fact of the matter is, however, that they are not. They all reflect difficulties created by the lack of information. Thanks to the contributions by Clower (1965), Leijonhufvud (1968) and others, we have just begun to understand the basic structure of Keynes' theory as a theory of aggregative behaviour under informational barriers. Looked at from this angle, various parts of his theory begin to fit together. And these informational barriers are not unrelated to money. For money not only separates the act of purchase from the act of sale, but also links the future to the present through its capacity as the major instrument of forward tradings. The informational difficulties arise exactly in connection with these features of a monetary economy (p. vii):

"A monetary economy is essentially one in which changing views about the future are capable of influencing the quantity of employment and not merely its direction."

In describing and evaluating Keynes' contributions, however, one must be careful about distinguishing between what Keynes actually said and what one can make out of Keynes' writings, if one regards historical accuracy as important. For example, is Clower's "Dual Decision Hypothesis" really his? Or is it Keynes'? The question we mentioned earlier, namely, was Keynes' theory static or dynamic, is another example. These questions are quite difficult to answer because the *General Theory* is full of interesting and important observations, assertions, beliefs and conjectures which are merely stated without supporting theory or analysis. Depending on how seriously one takes them, one obtains a variety of interpretations of Keynes' theory. For our purpose, let us agree to use the term Keynes' theory in a rather broad sense to include various contributions made by his followers.

Keynes' theory so defined clearly suggests the need for a reformulation of general equilibrium models in a number of respects. In this chapter we take up two important lines of extensions. First, at the micro level, we need to study the behaviour of individuals confronted with difficulties in market tradings. This would require us to specify the manner in which these difficulties are perceived and interpreted by individuals in making decisions. If we ignore stock variables and long-run expectations, we can use such a model to describe a short-run general equilibrium of the Keynesian type. This part of reformulation is described in the following three sections. But this is not all. As is evident from the above quotations, we must also study the manner in which the future prospects influence current decisions. For this purpose we need to look at the asset markets as part of our general equilibrium system. According to Keynes, the causation of economic changes starts primarily with a change in the state of long-run expectations (his marginal efficiency of capital). This change in the state of expectations causes changes in asset prices (or interest rates). These changes in asset prices, in turn, affect the volume of current investment (and also the volume of current consumption spending). The consequent change in the volume of aggregate demand will then determine the new levels of output and employment through the type of individual choices described above. The existing studies of asset markets in a general equilibrium framework are mainly due to Tobin and his students. These studies of asset markets are needed not so much for completeness sake as for their relevance to monetary policy issues. The precise mechanisms through which a monetary change exerts its influence into the economy can be understood only on the basis of detailed studies of the asset markets, and in particular, the financial asset markets. The monetarist's strategy of by-passing these markets and tying money directly to income is not a very satisfactory one. In Sections E and F, we shall describe this dynamic aspect of Keynes' theory following the writings of Keynes and Tobin.

(B)   Let us begin with Clower's work which seems to be the most significant contribution in this context. Clower (1965) found the purely formal difference between Keynes and the "Classics" in Keynes' denial of the relevance of Walras' Law in the disequilibrium situation of the kind Keynes was concerned with and proposed a "Dual Decision Hypothesis" to rationalize Keynes' theory. As we stressed in Part II, the conventional neoclassical theory abstracts entirely from problems of market transactions. Trading activities are assumed costless and information is assumed perfect. In such a world, if an agent owns a vector of endowments $\bar{x}$, he can be sure to obtain any bundle x provided only that the value of x does not exceed the value of $\bar{x}$, both evaluated at the given market prices. Knowing this, he computes his optimal bundle x^* which will naturally satisfy (in the absence of satiation) $px^* = p\bar{x}$. Walras' Law follows immediately when these individual budget equations are summed over all the agents. The Neoclassics not only used the allocation x^* as the market solution when p was in fact an equilibrium price, but also maintained that if some relevant dynamics of market adjustments were to lead the system to an equilibrium, at that equilibrium all the individual plans written according to the above manner would be realized.

In contrast, Keynes explicitly considered an economy where problems of market transactions were present. From the viewpoint that trading activities do matter, the above budget equations have the implication that all the goods are highly saleable or have the same degree of liquidity. The agent first sells his $\bar{x}$ and then purchases x^* with the proceeds from the sale of $\bar{x}$. This is what is meant by the budget equation $px^* = p\bar{x}$. This equation and its aggregative expression, Walras' Law, therefore have the implication that the first leg of transactions, i.e., the sale of $\bar{x}$, never fails. Such would indeed be a consistent theory as a description of equilibrium. In a disequilibrium situation, however, a closer examination of the trading processes is unavoidable. In examining the sales side of the trading processes, there are two factors to consider. One is the varying degrees of saleableness of various goods. Some goods are easy, while others are difficult, to cash. The other is the varying conditions of different markets. When the demand is strong relative to supply, it will be easier to sell the good, and vice versa. The good in question is labour services. The heterogeneity, immobility and indivisibility of labour services make them difficult to sell compared to other goods. The fact that the demand for labour services is a derived demand also makes it vulnerable to a host of shocks and disturbances created in the economy. Besides, human capital is undoubtedly the least marketable capital asset for various reasons. For the owner of human capital or the supplier of labour services, therefore, how to successfully sell his services is a matter of great concern.

Consider a household which has a potential supply of labour services. Taking the going wage rate as given, he may perform an individual experiment to determine how much labour services to sell and how much of various consumer goods to buy with the wage income. But suppose it has failed to sell its labour services in the way it wished to sell at the going wage rate. The actual sale may be zero but need not be. Under a reasonable assumption on its utility function, the household can be shown to prefer any positive amount of sale (up to the desired amount) to none. If it actually sold a positive amount of labour services $\bar{L}$ which is below his desired amount L^*, its demand for various consumer goods, as it is able to register in the market, would be directly affected by the consequence of the first leg of transactions. Such an effect would naturally be the strongest if the household had no other assets to eat upon and the household could not borrow against its future wage earnings. Generally, if its actual sale falls short of its desired amount, its *effective* demand for goods will be more or less curtailed. And it is such an effective demand that is registered in the market. Also, since $\bar{L}$ is not the household's choice but imposed on it, and since the wage rate is assumed given, its labour *income* is now a datum to the household. Thus, the household's effective demand for consumer goods becomes a function of such labour income, which lends itself to Keynes' notion of the consumption function. Decreased demands for consumer goods by households will be reflected in reduced sales on the part of the sellers of these goods which induces them to adjust their production and inventory levels downward. Such decline in the activity levels of retailers, wholesalers and producers will further result in the curtailment of their demand for labour services. This adjustment process is nothing but Keynes' (dynamic) multiplier process, which bears no resemblance to any of the neoclassical adjustment processes tending toward full employment equilibrium.

In the situation described above, *effective* demands govern the market, but the *notional* demands of the neoclassical type find no place in the system. The usual Walras' Law, which states that the value of the aggregate notional excess demands be identically zero, is irrelevant. What we might have instead is that the value of the aggregate effective excess demands for all the consumer goods (including bonds labour market. It is important to notice that the above difficulties stem from the fact that the economy is a monetary economy. In a barter economy, transactions have only one leg. Sales and purchases are just the opposite sides of the same transactions. Hence these difficulties would not arise in such an economy. Extensive specializations also create problems of coordination. But these specializations themselves were made possible by the existence of money.

(C) Barro and Grossman (1971) have extended Clower's idea to the goods market, following the lead given by Patin-kin (1965, ch. XIII). They argued that the firms would locate actual employment on the notional factor demand curves only if they expected they could sell all the products forth-coming from the given employment at the given prices. If they did not expect so, they would not operate on the notional factor demand curves. In the latter situation, just as the households accepted $\bar{L}$ and adjusted their demands for consumer goods to it, so would firms accept what the goods market can take (which is the aggregate effective demand) and adjust factor employment to it. Just as the households facing an insufficient demand for labour services suffered from utility losses, so would the firms facing an insufficient demand for products suffer from profit losses. And these utility losses and profit losses go hand in hand with each other. For a given set of wages and commodity prices, there may exist a certain level of employment at which the aggregate effective demand for products and the aggregate supply of the same goods tally. Since only effective magnitudes send out signals to the market and since the product market is being cleared, with the labour market being completely subordinate to it, there will be no force in the system pushing the economy toward a higher level of economic activities. The remedy is obviously to somehow increase the aggregate effective demand for products, but this must be sought outside the market. This essentially is the Clower-initiated Dual Decision interpretation of Keynes' theory which makes Keynes' theory quite a new type of general equilibrium theory capable of dealing with many macroeconomic problems its predecessor failed to handle.[1]

(D)   There is, however, one thing the above description of the Keynesian unemployment equilibrium has left unexplained. That is, what makes wages and prices stay where they are? The importance of this question can be appreciated by rewriting the question as follows. Does the Dual Decision theory need an independent postulate about rigid or at least sticky wages and prices? Or, can the Dual Decision theory *explain* sticky wages and prices as part of its implications? This way of posing the question may at first sound offensive, for the majority view holds that if there is to be a single most

[1]This Dual Decision interpretation of Keynes' theory was credited to Keynes himself by Leijonhufvud (1968). But more recently Grossman (1972) expressed an opposite view. Grossman argued that the very insistence by Keynes on firms operating on the notional demand for labour curve showed Keynes' unawareness of such a profound and unifying feature of his own theory. But the above certainly is an interpretation consistent with Keynes' writings.

crucial postulate in Keynes' theory, it is that of sticky wages and prices. But on second thought, one realizes that the term has been used intuitively without any analytical content attached to it. It is also relevant to recall in this context that Keynes never denied the market mechanism in which prices adjust to the market excess demands, and in particular, that he never admitted the significance of artificial price administration either by firms or unions. We thus face a choice between postulating the stickiness and explaining it. In this section, we wish to follow the latter avenue.[2]

Consider the situation described above by the extended Dual Decision theory, i.e., the situation in which both the households and the firms have fallen off their notional schedules, with the current level of employment and production below optimum given the prevailing wages and prices. The households think it impossible to sell more labour services at the going wage rate. This can be interpreted to mean that they have a *perceived* demand curve for labour services such that the marginal wage revenue drops to zero past the current level of employment. Similarly, the firms think it impossible to sell more products at the going prices, meaning that they have a perceived demand curve whose marginal revenue product falls to zero past the current level of sale. Needless to say, these marginal revenues need not fall to zero; they are only required to undergo a sudden decline at the current level of sale to reflect the difficulty of increasing the sale beyond the current level. To put it differently, the Dual Decision theory introduces into the behaviour of agents an element of imperfect competition, and the significance of this fact can hardly be overstated.

In order to study the implication of the above discussion for the flexibility of wages and prices, let us consider the behaviour of the households and the firms in the above situation. Suppose a household attempts to maximize its

[2]The following discussion draws heavily on the idea proposed by Negishi (1974).

utility function $U(x, H - L)$ subject to a budget constraint $wL = px$ and a perceived demand for labour function $w = w(L)$. The first order conditions are given by

$$WL - px = 0, \tag{11.1}$$

$$\frac{W}{p}\left(1 - \frac{1}{\xi}\right) = \frac{U_x}{U_v}, \tag{11.2}$$

where $v \equiv H - L$, and ξ is the perceived elasticity of demand for labour services. When this elasticity is infinite, i.e., when the household believes that it can sell any amount of labour services at the going wage rate W, the above two equations can be solved for x and L, the latter yielding a neoclassical labour supply curve. But in the situation under considera- tion, the elasticity will be small at least beyond the given current level of employment. On the other hand, for levels of L less than the current sale, the household will probably have the freedom to adjust its supply within reason. If we assume that the household has a perfect freedom of this kind, this means that the perceived demand curve is horizontal up to the level of the current sale, possessing a "kink" at the current L. Given this kind of perceived demand function for labour services, the implied labour supply curve will have a jump (upward) at the current level of employment.

Next consider a typical firm whose perceived demand curve has a similar kink at the point of current sale. If the firm, which is otherwise competitive, maximizes profits, its behaviour is characterized by the following conditions:

$$x - F(L) = 0, \tag{11.3}$$

$$\frac{W}{p} = F'(L)\left(1 - \frac{1}{\eta}\right), \tag{11.4}$$

where η is the perceived elasticity of demand for products. Again, adopting a simplifying assumption that its perceived demand curve is horizontal up to the point of current sale, the implied demand curve for labour services undergoes a jump (downward) at the current level of employment. The situation can be visualized as in Figure 11.1. In this figure, real wage W/P is measured along the vertical axis. But since P is a given parameter, one can interpret the axis as measuring the nominal wage rate. While we have chosen here the labour market for illustration, the reader can produce a similar figure for the product market. We let $\bar{L}$ stand for the current level of employment and $\overline{W/P}$ for the current level of real wages. The economy is assumed to be at E.

The question is what, if any, adjustments should we expect of W? Clearly there is no market force at work that compels a change in W. Furthermore, even if the aggregate effective demand has increased as a result of some government action and even if the effective portion of the notional curves has extended beyond $\bar{L}$ as a consequence of such action, there is no reason why W should change, at least within certain limits.

It is useful to note the subtle but important difference between the above interpretation and the conventional one concerning the nature of the position like E. According to the above interpretation, the households would be happy to sell more labour services *if* someone offered them additional jobs at the going wage rate $\bar{W}$. In this sense they are constrained to accept a lower level of employment. But they

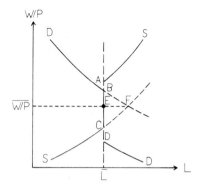

Figure 11.1

are *not* involuntarily unemployed at *E*. In the situation
described in Figure 11.1 the households' optimality condition
(11.2) actually takes the form

$$\frac{W}{p} > \frac{U_x}{U_v}\bigg|_{L=\bar{L}} > \frac{W}{p}\left(1 - \frac{1}{\xi}\right), \tag{11.5}$$

where ξ is the less-than-infinite elasticity of the perceived
demand curve for labour services, evaluated at $L = \bar{L}_+$. So
long as (11.5) holds, the households are at their equilibrium
and have no incentive to sell more labour services. If they
are unemployed, they are voluntarily unemployed. Likewise,
the firms would be willing to hire more labour and produce
more products at the going wages and prices *if* the market
offered them a greater volume of demand. But otherwise
they are quite content with the current level of operation and
they will continue to be so, as long as real wages stay within
certain limits. In a word, the present interpretation yields an
equilibrium account of the Keynesian underemployment,
contrary to the common *dis*equilibrium interpretation.

To summarize: The Dual Decision theory explains the
Keynesian underemployment due to deficient demand as an
equilibrium in which no one has any incentive to increase
employment. At such equilibrium, the burden of deficient
demand falls on both the firms and the households, and wages
and prices have lost their corrective function. Within certain
bounds, a fall in W/P has no stimulating effect on output and
employment. This also means that an increase in the level of
the aggregate demand is not likely to induce an immediate
change in W or P. If we define the flexibility of a price as the
ratio of a percentage change in the price to the rate of excess
demand as measured by the percentage of the current supply à
la Lange, it follows from the above that the flexibility of W or P
is likely very small. We have thus shown that the Dual Decision
theory implies sticky wages and prices.

Before closing this section, a brief comment on the traditional interpretation of the matter seems in order. The traditional interpretation holds that sticky wages and prices imply

something like the Dual Decision process. This begs the whole question of how to explain such stickiness. To cope with this difficulty, economists have tended to depend on such non-market forces as price administration by labour unions and monopolistic firms. But this interpretation not only is unfaithful to Keynes' own view but also unduly limits the scope of his theory. The upshot of the interpretation presented in this section is that it endogenizes and explains the stickiness as an implication of the theory. Furthermore, the traditional interpretation contains a self-contradiction. According to the traditional interpretation, wages and prices are sticky, but employment is always on the firms' notional demand curve. Besides, output adjusts automatically to effective demand. In other words, firms adjust their output level readily to effective demand while maintaining the profit-maximization condition. For this to be always true, wages and prices must be behaving very well indeed![3]

(E) So far, so good. The theory described above explains quite well why unemployment, once it appeared, tends to be self-sustaining. It is also capable of justifying some other features of Keynes' theory, e.g., the consumption function and the multiplier. But this theory does *not* offer us even a clue as to how unemployment came into existence in the first place. Why is it difficult to maintain effective demand at the full employment level? And why is it difficult to push it back to the full employment level, once effective demand has fallen off? To understand the inherent instability of the aggregate demand and the difficulty of controlling it, we must

[3]There is yet another interpretation – a dynamic interpretation – of the Keynesian unemployment equilibrium which was suggested by Patinkin and Leijonhufvud. According to this interpretation, prices are adjusting in the manner the markets tell them to do, but only very slowly due to lack of information. Nagatani (1969) showed that an economy in such a situation might be kept away from equilibrium and caught in a state of *quasi-*equilibrium with unemployment.

now look at the dynamic part of Keynes' theory, namely, his theory of investment and portfolio selection.

The fundamental independent variable in Keynes' system is investment. Savings adjust to investment through an appropriate change in income which, in turn, determines employment. This leading role assigned to investment distinguishes Keynes' theory from the neoclassical theory in which investment and savings are the same thing. And this distinction is important not only at the temporary equilibrium level (*General Theory* vs. *Value and Capital*), but also in the long-run theory of growth (Harrod vs. Tobin–Solow). We recall that in the Hicksian model of temporary equilibrium, the only durable asset by means of which the agents carry out their intertemporal reallocations of their wealths is bonds. The agents, knowing the current spot prices of goods and the bond price but not knowing the future spot prices, make decisions on current demand for goods and for bonds. The uncertainty concerning the future spot prices builds into the agents' demand for bonds an element of *speculation*.[4] But these speculations never disturb the goods market directly.

In contrast, Keynes held a view that expectations would determine the *marginal efficiency* of capital and through it exert a direct influence on investment. Two things are to be noted. First, the difference between speculation and investment. The former in the Hicksian model is a purely financial transaction, and Keynes also has this in his system. Second, the time dimension of expectations relevant to speculation is likely much shorter than that relevant to investment. The long-run nature of the expectations relevant to investment decisions explains why it is rather difficult to control investment by means of the manipulation of the bank rate. Symbolically, Keynes' investment function may be written as

[4]It is true that Hicks (1946, ch. 23) discusses capital accumulation. But the capital he discusses there is synonymous with supply capacity and consequently fails to capture the essential nature of capital in economic dynamics.

$$I = I(r, R),$$

where r is the bond rate and R is the marginal efficiency of capital.

General Theory (pp. 145–146):

> "The schedule of the marginal efficiency of capital is of fundamental importance because it is mainly through this factor (much more than through the rate of interest) that the expectation of the future influences the present. The mistake of regarding the marginal efficiency of capital primarily in terms of the *current* yield of capital equipment, which would be correct only in the static state where there is no changing future to influence the present, has had the result of breaking the theoretical link between today and tomorrow. Even the rate of interest is, virtually, a *current* phenomenon... It is by reason of the existence of durable equipment that the economic future is linked to the present."

The dependence of I on R, along with the high variability of R itself, implies that I as a function of r is a very *unstable* function. This same R is also a determinant of the asset market equilibrium. The causation of change goes in the following order:

$$R \rightarrow r \rightarrow I \rightarrow Y \rightarrow L.$$

With this much of preparation, we can now begin to "animate" the Keynesian temporary equilibrium model to arrive at a Keynesian dynamic model. Since R takes the initiative, the essence of the Keynes' dynamic theory is the analysis of R. Keynes devoted Chapter 22 of the *General Theory* to the analysis of R. To quote (p. 313):

> "Since we claimed to have shown in the preceding chapters what determines the volume of employment

at any time, it follows, if we are right, that our theory must be capable of explaining the phenomena of the Trade Cycle. If we examine the details of any actual instance of the Trade Cycle, we shall find that it is highly complex and that every element in our analysis will be required for its complete explanation. In particular, we shall find that fluctuations in the propensity to consume, in the state of liquidity preference, and in the marginal efficiency of capital have all played a part. But I suggest that the essential character of the Trade Cycle and, especially, the regularity of time sequence and of duration which justifies us in calling it a *cycle*, is mainly due to the way in which the marginal efficiency of capital fluctuates. The Trade Cycle is best regarded, I think, as being occasioned by a cyclical change in the marginal efficiency of capital . . ."

The crucial part of Keynes' account of the cyclical behaviour of R is that related to the later stages of the boom and the onset of "crisis" (pp. 315–317):

"The later stages of the boom are characterized by optimistic expectations as to the future yield of capital goods sufficiently strong to offset their growing abundance and their rising costs of production and, probably, a rise in the rate of interest also. It is of the nature of organised investment markets, under the influence of purchasers largely ignorant of what they are buying and of speculators who are more concerned with forecasting the next shift of market sentiment than with a reasonable estimate of the future yield of capital assets, that, when disillusion falls upon an over-optimistic and over-bought market, it should fall with sudden and even catastrophic force."

. . .

"The explanation of the *time-element* in the trade cycle, of the fact that an interval of time of a parti- cular order of magnitude must usually lapse before recovery begins, is to be sought in the influences which govern the recovery of the marginal efficiency of capital. There are reasons, given firstly by the length of life of durable assets in relation to the normal rate of growth in a given epoch, and secondly by the carrying-costs of surplus stocks, why the dura- tion of the downward movement should have an order of magnitude which is not fortuitous, which does not fluctuate between, say, one year this time and ten years next time, but which shows some regularity of habit between, let us say, three to five years."

Thus, according to Keynes, the marginal efficiency of capital takes the following pattern of movement:[5]

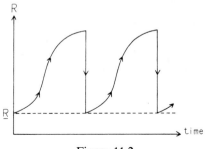

Figure 11.2

Here $\underline{R}$ is the floor value of R corresponding to the state of "collapse". Various Keynesian models of business cycles were attempts to formalize this type of investment cycles, the most imaginative and elegant one having been the non- linear accelerator model by Goodwin (1951, 1965).

[5]The idea that business cycles were mainly due to investment factors as against monetary factors was already clear in the *Treatise* (chs. 18–20), although the emphasis was on prices rather than on output and employ- ment.

We wish to conclude this section with two remarks. First, the apparently still unsettled issue on the role of sticky wages in explaining unemployment. We have argued that the factor responsible for unemployment is the marginal efficiency of capital periodically collapsing and staying at a very low level for a substantial length of time, and that sticky wages and prices are just the consequences of deficient demand caused by the decline in the investment activities. But R is basically the ratio of the future to the current prices. As Leijonhufvud pointed out, it is the stickiness of such price ratios at an abnormal level rather than the stickiness of money wages that prevents the economy from attaining full employment.[6] Such stickiness of R is due to the long-run nature of it, namely, its dependence on the expected profiles of prices over the entire lifetime of the capital equipments under consideration. As Arrow (1968) suggested, the behaviour of the Keynesian investors may be interpreted as reflecting a capital market imperfection in the sense that

[6]Lately, Bliss (1974) expressed a negative view on such an interpretation of the Keynesian unemployment. But his argument, which places the burden entirely on sticky wages, is not convincing. Bliss's argument was that for any given set of expected prices, the current markets can and will achieve an equilibrium as long as the current prices are flexible, and in particular, that the labour market with flexible money wages will attain a full-employment equilibrium. If there is unemployment, it must therefore be due exclusively to rigid money wages. If Bliss were wrong, this would not be because his argument had a logical flow but because his framework was different. The crucial point seems to be whether employment should be treated as a flow (as Bliss did) or as a stock (as Keynes would have thought). Once employment is treated as a stock, employment decisions will become subject to the same set of influences as that which governs investment decisions. I am inclined to think that the stock treatment of employment is the correct approach. Not only is this more realistic but also more in the spirit of Keynes whose main concern was with an economy with *mistakes* and in the process of correcting them. In this sense, the Dual Decision formulation is an odd half-way house which allows for the possibility of mistakes and yet refuses to recognize any realization of mistakes in the form of too high levels of commodity inventories and the stocks of inputs.

the investors ignore the possibility of resale of the capital equipments they have installed. In this regard, an important distinction should be drawn between investors and speculators, the latter being largely free from such time constraints.

Second, what role is money playing during all these times of troubles? A collapse in the marginal efficiency of capital tends to be associated with a rise in the rate of interest reflecting a sharp increase in liquidity preference. But even if the monetary authority took a policy of preventing the rate of interest from rising with a view to offsetting the decline in the marginal efficiency of capital, Keynes did not believe in the effectiveness of such a policy. In Keynes' view, money was neither the cause nor the remedy of the Great Depression. (The monetarist's account of the Depression was the mistake on the part of the monetary authority of curtailing the money supply rather than expanding it.) But Keynes never really elaborated on his view. The *General Theory* contains little formal analysis of money. As he admitted (p. vii):

> "Whilst it is found that money enters into the economic scheme in an essential and peculiar manner, technical monetary detail falls into the background."

This does not mean, of course, that the *General Theory* has little to do with money. On the contrary, Keynes meant it to be a theory of the aggregative behaviour of a monetary economy. But the absence of a detailed analysis of the money and related markets in it prevents us from going much further. So we turn now to Tobin's work.

(F) We confine ourselves here to describing a general equilibrium model of asset markets formulated by Tobin (1969). Empirical studies and policy implications based on this model will be discussed in Chapter 13. The reader should notice the close resemblance between Tobin's model and

Keynes' own writings, especially, his own commentary (1937) on the *General Theory*.

Tobin confines his attention to the capital accounts of economic units, regarding income account variables as *tentatively exogenous data* for balance-sheet behaviour. His objective is to find equilibrium in the market for stocks of assets *conditional upon* assumed values of outputs, incomes and other flows. Underlying his strategy is the behavioural assumption that spending decisions and portfolio decisions are independent. In other words, decisions about the accumulation of wealth are separable from decisions about the allocation of a given wealth.

Let there be n types of assets, financial and real. And let the private sector be composed of m sectors. The government will be the $(m + 1)$st sector. At any point of time, a temporary asset market equilibrium is characterized by an $(m + 1) \times n$ matrix of holdings of assets by various sectors such that for given values of the flow variables, the aggregate quantities of assets held (desired) are equal to the corresponding exogenous supplies. Let r_j be the rate of return on the jth asset $(j = 1, 2, \ldots, n)$, and let f_{ij} be the net demand for the asset j by sector i $(i = 1, 2, \ldots, m + 1)$. For each $i = 1, 2, \ldots, m$, the f_{ij}'s may be thought of as the solution derived à la Mossin. Thus each f_{ij} is generally a function of the vector of n interest rates and the initial wealth w_i which is a given datum at any point of time. By the very nature of the constrained maximization, the f_{ij} functions satisfy

$$\sum_{j=1}^{n} \partial f_{ij} / \partial r_k = 0, \quad \text{for all} \quad k = 1, 2, \ldots, n, \tag{11.6}$$

$$\sum_{j=1}^{n} \partial f_{ij} / \partial w_i = 1. \tag{11.7}$$

These equations imply that the same relations hold for the aggregates

$$f_j = \sum_{i=1}^{m} f_{ij}.$$

The market equilibrium is characterized by a set of n equations of the form $f_j = s_j$ where s_j is the exogenously given supply of assets including government's. Of these n equations, only $(n-1)$ equations are independent and therefore $(n-1)r$'s will be determined.

Tobin illustrates the use of this model in terms of a model which has three assets, money M, government securities S, and real capital K. M and S are measured in the common monetary unit of one dollar. The total private wealth is given by

$$W = qK + \frac{M+S}{p}, \tag{11.8}$$

where p = the price of currently produced goods and capital goods, and pq = the market price of existing capital goods. In other words, q is the ratio of the price of existing capital goods to that of newly produced ones. Thus W is the total private wealth measured in the units of currently produced goods. At a given point of time, the amount of real capital K and the nominal stocks of money and government securities M and S are given. The asset market equilibrium require therefore that the aggregate private demand for each asset be equal to the given supply of it. Tobin lets the *fraction* of W desired to be held in K, M and S be f_1, f_2 and f_3, respectively. He specifies these fractions as functions of the real rates of return r_K, r_M and r_S and the income–wealth ratio Y/W. Thus,

$$f_1(r_K, r_M, r_S, Y/W)W = qK, \tag{11.9}$$

$$f_2(r_K, r_M, r_S, Y/W)W = M/p, \tag{11.10}$$

$$f_3(r_K, r_M, r_S, Y/W)W = S/p. \tag{11.11}$$

Assuming permanently lasting real capital, r_K and q are related through the marginal efficiency of investment R by

$$r_K q = R. \tag{11.12}$$

The real rates on money and securities, r_M and r_S are related to their nominal rates r'_M and r'_S by

$$r_M = r'_M - e,\qquad\qquad(11.13)$$

$$r_S = r'_S - e,\qquad\qquad(11.14)$$

where e is the expected rate of price inflation. An assumption is made here that the securities are short-term so that their market value is independent of r'_S. Equations (11.8)–(11.14) provide six independent equations in the fourteen unknowns, Y, M, S, K, R, r'_M, e, p, q, W, r_K, r_M, r_S and r'_S.

In the "short-run" interpretation of the model, the first eight unknowns are treated as exogenous parameters, and the system is solved for the latter six unknowns, i.e., q, W, r_K, r_M, r_S and r'_S. Appropriate substitutions reduce the model to (11.8), and

$$f_2(R/q, r_M, r_S, Y/W)W = M/p,\qquad\qquad(11.15)$$

$$f_3(R/q, r_M, r_S, Y/W)W = S/p.\qquad\qquad(11.16)$$

In this reduced system, the unknowns are q, r_S and W. Under the additional assumptions: (1) that the own derivatives of f_j are positive, while the cross-derivatives are non-positive (i.e., $\partial f_a/\partial r_b > 0$ if $b = a$, $\partial f_a/\partial r_b \leq 0$ if $b \neq a$), and (2) that government securities absorb changes in requirements for money (i.e., $\partial f_3/\partial (Y/W) = -\partial f_2/\partial (Y/W) < 0$ and $\partial f_1/\partial (Y/W) = 0$), Tobin (1969, p. 25) arrives at the following comparative static results:

Effects on endogenous variables of increase in specified exogenous variables, with all others held constant.

Endogenous variables	M	S	M (at expense of S)	r'_M	Y	R	p	e
q	+	?	+	−	−	+	−	+
r_S	−	+	−	+	+	?	?	−
r_K	−	?	−	+	+	+	+	−
W	+	?	+	−	−	+	−	+

It may be useful to compare this model with the usual Keynesian model. Keynes emphasized the distinction between short assets and long assets, i.e. between assets whose market values are not affected by changes in interest rates due to shortness of life and those whose market values are directly affected by changes in interest rates. Keynes' "bonds" belong to the latter category and in fact Keynes bundled real capital and bonds into one long asset, assuming a fixed relation between r_K and r_S. Under such an assumption, these two rates can be combined into one rate, *the* interest rate. Denote it by r_B. Also denote the total real value of the long assets by B. Then (11.10) may be rewritten as

$$f_2(r_B, r_M, Y/(RB/r_B + M/p))(RB/r_B + M/p) = M/p. \quad (11.17)$$

With M/p, B, r_M and R given, this equation yields a relationship between r_B and Y, which is an *LM* relation. The slope of the *LM* curve in the (Y, r_B) space is given by

$$\frac{dr_B}{dY} = \left(\frac{-\partial f_2}{\partial(Y/W)}\right) \Big/ \left(f_{2r_B} + \frac{RBf_2}{r_B^2}\left[\frac{Y}{Wf_2} \cdot \frac{\partial f_2}{\partial(Y/W)} - 1\right]\right). \quad (11.18)$$

Tobin argues that the bracketted term in the denominator is negative and greater than minus one. The reason is that not all cash balances are held for transactions purposes so that the balances will not increase in proportion to Y. This assumption is sufficient for the *LM* curve to slope upward.

Now the *IS* relation. According to Keynes, the rate of investment will essentially depend on the comparison between the value of capital and its replacement cost. The ratio of the two is Tobin's q. Investment will be related positively to q.

Since $q = R/r_B$, investment demand is negatively related to r_B, given R. If we assume that investment or some other components of aggregative demand for output depends on income in the usual manner, an *IS* curve will be obtained as a negatively sloped curve in the same space. The interaction of the two curves determines a temporary equilibrium pair

(Y, r_B). The value of q in such a short-run equilibrium can be greater than, equal to, or less than unity.[7]

After sketching a general model with more assets, Tobin (1969, p. 29) summarizes the implications of this type of general equilibrium approach as follows:

> "According to this approach, the principal way in which financial policies and events affect aggregate demand is by changing the valuations of physical assets relative to their replacement costs. Monetary policies can accomplish such changes, but other exogenous events can too. In addition to the exogenous variables explicitly listed in the illustrative models, changes can occur, and undoubtedly do, in the portfolio preferences – asset demand functions – of the public, the banks, and other sectors. These preferences are based on expectations, estimates of risk, attitudes towards risk, and a host of other factors. In this complex situation, it is not to be expected that the essential impact of monetary policies and other financial events will be easy to measure in the absence of direct observation of the relevant variables (q in the models). There is no reason to think that the impact will be captured in any single exogenous or intermediate variables, whether it is a money stock or a market interest rate."

This summary well represents the Keynesian's stand.

It should be pointed out, however, that Tobin's dichotomy

---

[7]The "long-run" interpretation of the model runs as follows. One of the conditions for a long-run equilibrium is that the price of existing capital goods be equal to its replacement costs, namely, $q = 1$. Given R, the *IS* relation fixes Y and r_B. Besides, the amount of long assets must bear a certain stable relation to Y in a steady state. Thus B is determined. Given M/P, the *LM* relation determines r_M, the real rate of return on cash balances. The long-run model will be discussed in more detail in Chapter 12.

between the asset markets and the markets for flows is a "tentative" strategy and calls for a more satisfactory synthesis. Following up the line of discussion given in footnote 6, we must eventually face the problem of stocks of various commodities as part of wealth, for it is these stocks that measure the mistakes committed in the past. To try to understand the Great Depression, and macrodynamics in general, without recognizing these stocks is an impossible task. An attempt to reformulate the Keynesian temporary equilibrium in this direction is clearly an urgent task for macroeconomic theorists.

References

Arrow, K. J., "Optimal capital policy with irreversible investment", in: J. N. Wolfe, ed., *Value, capital and growth: Essays in honour of Sir John Hicks* (Edinburgh, 1968).

Barro, R. J. and H. I. Grossman, "A general disequilibrium model of income and employment", *American Economic Review* (1971).

Bliss, C. J., "The reappraisal of Keynes' economics: An appraisal", Discussion Paper No. 55 (University of Essex, 1974).

Clower, R. W., "The Keynesian counter-revolution: A theoretical appraisal", in: F. H. Hahn and F. P. R. Brechling, eds., *The theory of interest rates* (London, 1965).

Goodwin, R. M., "The nonlinear accelerator and the persistence of business cycles", *Econometrica* (1951).

Goodwin, R. M., "A model of cyclical growth", in: R. A. Gordon and L. R. Klein, eds., *Readings in business cycles* (Homewood, Ill., 1965).

Grossman, H. I., "Was Keynes a Keynesian?", *Journal of Economic Literature* (1972).

Hicks, J. R., *Value and capital* (Oxford, 1939, 1946).

Keynes, J. M., *A treatise on money* (London, 1930).

Keynes, J. M., *The general theory of employment, interest and money* (London, 1936).

Keynes, J. M., "The general theory of employment", *Quarterly Journal of Economics* (1937); also in: S. E. Harris, ed., *The new economics* (London, 1947).

Klein, R. L., *The Keynesian revolution* (New York, 1947).

Leijonhufvud, A., *On Keynesian economics and the economics of Keynes* (Oxford, 1968).

Nagatani, K., "A monetary growth model with variable employment", *Journal of Money, Credit & Banking* (1969).

Negishi, T., "Involuntary unemployment and market imperfection", *Economic Studies Quarterly* (1974).

Patinkin, D., *Money, interest and prices* (New York, 1965).

Tobin, J., "A general equilibrium approach to monetary theory", *Journal of Money, Credit & Banking* (1969).

12

Money and Growth: An Introduction to the Theory of Dynamic Aggregative Behaviour

(A) More than a decade ago, Harry Johnson (1962) concluded his survey on monetary theory and policy with a remark that "almost nothing has been done to break monetary theory loose from the mould of short-run equilibrium analysis, conducted in abstraction from the process of growth and accumulation, and to integrate it with the rapidly developing theoretical literature on economic growth". But what do we expect to accomplish by that?

This remark by Johnson needs some clarification. Is it correct to say that monetary theory has been concerned with short-run as against long-run? This is simply not true. On the contrary. Monetary theory has been concerned with long-run. The only sensible interpretation, if not its intention, of the traditional quantity theory is that it is a proposition concerning long-run equilibrium. The same is true of Patinkin's work in the sense that Patinkin's main concern was to explain the transition from one long-run equilibrium to another. Friedman's theory also is a long-run theory. These theories are easily mistaken for short-run theories only because they all deal with a very special kind of long-run equilibrium called a stationary state. In a stationary state no resources are changing, not because we allow too little time for them to change but because we have allowed long enough time for all the resource adjustments to work themselves out. But the "short-run" must be interpreted in the sense of Temporary Equilibrium in which resources and expectations are prescribed more or less arbitrarily. Thus in the true sense of the term, there has never been any short-run theory of money with the exception of Keynes' (but his theory is not thoroughly worked out). From this point of view, we can interpret Johnson as suggesting studies of the long-run effects of money on the real variables in an economy capable of capital accumulation. Specifically, will the stock of capital, real output, real wages and rents, and the amount of real balances in a long-run equilibrium be independent of the manner in which money is supplied? In other words, will the Invariance Principle remain valid in this more general setting? As we shall see shortly, this indeed has been one of the central questions in monetary growth theory.

At a more practical level, the aim of modern growth theory was to provide a simple explanation for the so-called "stylized facts" which appear to characterize the secular trends of a number of important real variables in developed economies: (1) The capital–output ratio remains constant. (2) The capital–labour ratio and output–labour ratio are rising. (3) The rate of interest remains constant. (4) The real wage is rising. (5) The relative shares of capital and labour remain constant. To this list of stylized facts, one may add Friedman's finding: (6) Real balances per capita are rising relative to real permanent income per capita with elasticity 1.810. With this monetary fact added, how should we explain all these facts in terms of a simple model? No matter how we go about formulating our model, one thing is obvious – we cannot avoid specifying the link between the real and the money sectors. Indeed the main value of monetary growth theory lies in its furnishing us with a dynamic framework in which the interactions between the two sectors are explicitly recognized. Such a dynamic framework is equally useful for short-run analysis as we shall illustrate in a later section. We begin with the long-run.

(B) A Neoclassical Growth Model with Money: Can money, as an alternative asset to productive capital, influence the steady state position of the economy? Tobin (1965) was the first to answer this question. His idea was to combine the Wicksellian notion of the cumulative process and the Fisherine notion of the real rate of interest with the neoclassical resource dynamics.

Consider a neoclassical economy in its steady state growing at a given natural growth rate. Given the neoclassical technology, there prevails the marginal productivity rate of return on physical capital which is a function of the capital–labour ratio. If money is useful in such an economy, the real rate on money must be equal to the difference between the natural growth rate of the economy and the rate of monetary expansion. Thus a higher rate of monetary expansion means a lower real rate of return on money. Speaking in a comparative static sense, this would mean that money is now less attractive as a store of value, which would cause a shift in people's portfolios away from money into physical capital. Under certain assumptions on the consumption–saving decisions of the community this would lead to a higher capital–labour ratio in the long-run. In other words, money would be non-neutral.

In order to establish this non-neutrality proposition, Tobin wrote down a formal model. His setting is a two-asset economy, with the usual neoclassical features of technology, factor pricing and population growth. Money is assumed to be purely "outside" money, and any change in its nominal quantity is assumed to be effected by lump-sum taxes or transfer payments. In the model presented below, however, we have made a minor change to accommodate Friedman's equation explicitly,

$$Y = F(K, L), \tag{12.1}$$

$$Y^{\mathrm{d}} \equiv Y + D(M/P), \qquad D \equiv \mathrm{d}/\mathrm{d}t, \tag{12.2}$$

$$C = (1 - s)Y^{\mathrm{d}}, \tag{12.3}$$

$$M^d/PL \equiv m = a(k, e)y^b, \qquad a_k > 0, \quad a_e < 0, \quad k \equiv K/L,$$
$$y \equiv Y/L, \quad b = 1.8, \qquad (12.4)$$

$$DM^s = \mu M^s, \tag{12.5}$$

$$M^d = M^s, \tag{12.6}$$

$$DK = Y - C, \tag{12.7}$$

$$KL = nL, \qquad n > 0, \tag{12.8}$$

$$e \equiv DP/P. \tag{12.9}$$

Equation (12.1) is the usual neoclassical production function with the properties of constant returns to scale and diminishing returns to substitution. Equation (12.2) is the definition of disposable income which consists of real output and the increment in real balances per unit time. Equation (12.3) is the consumption function, and (12.4) is the Friedmanian demand for money function. To accommodate his theoretical tastes, we represented the constant in his empirical equation by the function $a(k, e)$, where the variable k stands for the rate of return on physical capital. The variable e is the expected rate of inflation or deflation so that $-e$ stands for the real rate of return on money. Equation (12.5) specifies the behaviour of the money supply over time. The rate of monetary expansion μ is treated as a policy parameter. Equation (12.6) is the money market equilibrium condition, and (12.7) and (12.8) specify the dynamics of two real resources. Finally, equation (12.9) states that the expected rate of inflation or deflation is equal to the actual rate of inflation or deflation at all times. Note that this is an extremely myopic expectation rule and the dynamic property of the model depends crucially on this special assumption.

The operation of the model is not very difficult. First, rewrite (12.7) in per capita terms using other relevant equations to get

$$Dk = sf(k) - nk - (1 - s)(\mu - e)a(k, e)[f(k)]^b. \tag{12.10}$$

Second, differentiate (12.4) logarithmically with respect to time again making use of other relevant equations to get

$$Dm/m = \mu - n - e. \tag{12.11}$$

In these equations, e is regarded as a function of k and m as we get from equation (12.4),

$$e = e(k, m), \qquad e_k > 0, \quad e_m < 0. \tag{12.12}$$

Thus, (12.10) and (12.11) are a pair of differential equations in k and m. Once we specify the initial values for them, these two equations will determine the time paths of k and m.

Let us first study the long-run equilibrium in which the dynamic variables (k, m) are stationary. Denote the equilibrium values by asterisks. From (12.11), we see that

$$e^* = \mu - n \quad \text{or} \quad (DP/P)^* = \mu - n. \tag{12.13}$$

Substituting this e^* in (12.10), k^* is defined implicitly by

$$0 = sf(k^*) - nk^* - (1 - s)na(k^*, \mu - n)[f(k^*)]^b. \tag{12.14}$$

Using this equation, we can now reexamine the Invariance Principle which asserts that k^* and m^* are independent of μ. From (12.14) we get

$$\frac{\partial k^*}{\partial \mu} = \frac{(1 - s)na_e^*[f(k^*)]^b}{sf'(k^*) - n - (1 - s)n\{a_k^*[f(k^*)]^b + ba^*[f(k^*)]^{b-1}f'(k^*)\}}. \tag{12.15}$$

The numerator is negative by assumption. The denominator can also be taken to be negative since the terms in the curled brackets are definitely negative and the term $sf'(k^*) - n$ is in all likelihood negative. Hence we conclude that $\partial k^*/\partial \mu > 0$. In words, an increase in the rate of monetary expansion stimulates investment in physical capital and leads to a higher equilibrium capital intensity. The average productivity of labour $f(k^*)$ and the marginal productivity of labour $f(k^*) - k^*f'(k^*)$ rise, while the rate of return on capital $f'(k^*)$ falls. Using (12.4), we get the effect of an increase in μ on

m^* as

$$\frac{\partial m^*}{\partial \mu} = a_e^*[f(k^*)]^b$$

$$+ \{a_k^*[f(k^*)]^r + ba^*[f(k^*)]^{b-1}f'(k^*)\}\frac{\partial k^*}{\partial \mu}. \qquad (12.16)$$

The first term represents the direct effect via the fall in the real rate of return on money on the desired real balances which is naturally negative. The second term represents the indirect effect via the change in k^* which is positive. However, when the two terms are combined, we have

$$\frac{\partial m^*}{\partial \mu} = \frac{a_e^*(sf'(k^*) - n)}{D},$$

where D is the denominator in (12.15). Hence we can safely regard the sign of this term as negative. In any case, the Invariance Principle does not hold in this model in which monetary changes are continuous and are translated into changes in the real rate of return on money.[1]

Leaving the evaluation of the so-called "non-neutrality" proposition to the next section, let us now turn to the examination of the dynamic property of this model. As Tobin described, the dynamics of this two-asset economy are generated by the competition between the real rates of return on the two assets. The system is stable if the competition always leads to a narrowing of the return differential whenever it gets too large.

For this purpose we investigate the local stability of the system (12.10), (12.11). Expanding these equations around the equilibrium (k^*, m^*) and taking a linear approximation, we obtain the following system of differential equations:

---

[1]Tobin's model differs from ours in the form of the demand for money function. Tobin wrote it as $M^d/PK = m(k, e)$, $m_k > 0$, $m_e > 0$. But the qualitative results are the same as ours. For details of Tobin's model, see Nagatani (1970).

$$\begin{bmatrix} Dk \\ Dm \end{bmatrix} = \begin{bmatrix} \dfrac{sf' - n(1-s)\{e_k f^b(a+a_c n) + n(a_k f^b + abf^{b-1}f')\}, \ -(1-s)e_m f^b(a+na_c)}{me_k \qquad\qquad\qquad\qquad\qquad\qquad me_m} \end{bmatrix}$$

$$\times \begin{bmatrix} k - k^* \\ m - m^* \end{bmatrix}, \qquad\qquad\qquad (12.17)$$

where all the terms in the coefficient matrix are evaluated at (k^*, m^*). By our previous assumptions, the matrix has the sign pattern,

$$\begin{bmatrix} -(?) & - \\ - & + \end{bmatrix}.$$

Although there remains a slight ambiguity about the sign of the term

$$\partial(Dk)/\partial k\big|_{\substack{k=k^* \\ m=m^*}},$$

it can be shown that the determinantal value of this matrix is negative. This means that the two eigenvalues are real and of opposite sign, and hence that the equilibrium is a saddle point. The dynamic motion near the equilibrium is depicted in Figure 12.1.

Except for the paths indicated by the arrows, the system fails to converge to the long-run equilibrium position. In other words, the equilibrium is unstable in the usual sense of

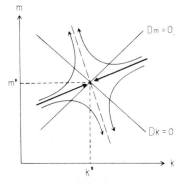

Figure 12.1

economists. What is happening along one of the upward diverging paths, for example, is that while the real rate of return on physical capital keeps rising, the real rate of return on money rises even faster and consequently money wins out in the competition with physical capital.

(C) An Evaluation of Neoclassical Monetary Growth Models: The above model of monetary growth à la Tobin has produced for us more problems than answers. First, the non-neutrality proposition came to the neoclassical minds as a great surprise. Why should the real variables in the long run be affected by money? If the above model predicted non-neutrality, it must have been due to some misspecification of the model. Formally speaking, the last term on the right-hand side of equation (12.14), i.e., the term containing m^*, can be interpreted as a real balance effect. Since it is exactly the non-vanishing of this term in the long run that yields non-neutrality, the alleged non-neutrality is synonymous with the persistence of the real balance effect. The question is then why the real balance effect on the commodity market should persist in the long-run equilibrium.

A number of neoclassical economists voiced a neutrality proposition either in the form of a belief or a proof. Hahn (1969) argued that if a "barter economy" of the Solow–Swan type were capable of attaining a (socially) optimum growth, a monetary economy should certainly be able to do the same, and hence that money was neutral in this fundamental sense. Samuelson (1958) and Cass and Yaari (1967), while they emphasized the vital role of money in attaining an efficient intertemporal resource allocation, also sided with the neutrality proposition. Their neutrality, however, depended on the assumption that the distribution of money was made proportional to individuals' savings which obviously made the return on cash immune to changes in μ. Sidrauski (1967) also came up with a neutrality result on the basis of a formal analysis of the optimizing behaviour of households. The crucial assumption he made was that each household was a permanent entity that grew at the common natural rate. Along with the assumption of a common fixed rate of time preference, this meant that the real rate of return on physical capital was determined directly by the rate of time preference and hence was independent of μ. What all this means is that the neutrality can be established in some special cases.

On the other hand, what positive evidence do we have to support the kind of non-neutrality as predicted by the above model? Levhari and Patinkin (1968) studied models which recognized the utility services of money for the households and the productive services of money for the firms. Their results showed that while the non-neutrality seemed to be rather robust, the direction of the effect on k^* was not independent of the way the use of money was specified in the model. It seems safe, therefore, to conclude that while money is likely to have some permanent effect on the real part of the economy, we cannot be sure of the nature of such effects.

An empirical determination of such an effect is also very difficult. First, the rate of monetary expansion has been extremely variable and there is no obvious way to split the 70–80 year observation period into subperiods with high and low rates of monetary expansion. Secondly, the time series of capital and labour are "input" data and hence subject to cyclical fluctuations. Because of the greater variability of labour input, the capital–labour ratio derived from these data shows counter-cyclical movements, meaning that over cycles, low capital–labour ratios and high rates of monetary expansion come together and vice versa. We are of course not interested in cycles. But given the high variability of μ and the counter-cyclical movements of the capital–labour ratio, a smoothing operation seems too fraught with difficulties to be reliable.

Next, the instability of the growth equilibrium. Many of us find it incredible that our monetary economy should be so unstable. But if our economy is more stable, what is wrong with the above model? Where should we look for stabilizing forces? The literature suggests two explanations.

The first concerns the form of the expectation function. Equation (12.9) is an extremely myopic rule of expectation formation in the sense that people react instantaneously to the rate of actual price change in forming their ideas of the future. But in reality, expectations adapt only with substantial lags. In order to incorporate such a lag, let us replace (12.9) with

$$De = \theta(DP/P - e), \qquad \infty > \theta > 0. \tag{12.18}$$

The coefficient θ represents the speed of adjustment in people's expectations. The smaller this coefficient is, the more lagged the expectations behind the actual price changes. It is obvious that (12.9) is the special case in which $\theta = +\infty$. In order to see the effect of θ on the stability of the system, we find it convenient to use e as the second dynamic variable instead of m. For this purpose, differentiate equation (12.4) logarithmically with respect to time to get

$$\mu - (DP/P) - n = \left(\frac{a_k}{d} + b\frac{f'}{f}\right)Dk + \frac{a_e}{a}De.$$

Substituting for (DP/P) from (12.18) and rearranging terms, we have

$$\left(\frac{a_e}{a} + \frac{1}{\theta}\right)De = \mu - n - e + \left(\frac{a_k}{a} + b\frac{f'}{f}\right)Dk. \tag{12.19}$$

Note the effect θ has on the coefficient in front of De. Here (a_e/a) is some negative number. Given the size of this term, the coefficient can be made positive for sufficiently small values of θ. It can be shown that it was the negativity of this coefficient, due to the absence of the term $(1/\theta)$, that caused instability in our model. Suppose an excess supply was generated in the money market. To restore equilibrium P had to rise. But a rise in P was directly translated into a rise in e which caused a decrease in the demand for real balances. This, in turn, caused a further increase in P and hence a further rise in *e*. With myopic expectations, this process meant a cumulative deviation away from equilibrium. But with expectations sufficiently sluggish, expectations cannot feed on themselves any longer. And this is what happens when

$$\left(\frac{a_e}{a} + \frac{1}{\theta}\right) > 0.$$

The second explanation concerns the manner in which the money supply behaviour was specified in the model. Why should the authority maintain a fixed rate of monetary expansion, especially if the stability of the system is at stake? Suppose instead that the monetary authority adopted the following simple feed-back control rule. Namely, suppose the government pays an interest *i* on its debt, i.e., money, but controls it according to

$$i = i^* + \lambda(DP/P), \qquad \lambda > 0, \tag{12.20}$$

where i^* is some prescribed long-run target interest rate. Revenues required for interest payments are assumed to be collected in the form of another lump sum tax. With the introduction of interest, the real rate of return on money becomes $i - e$, or using (12.20), $i^* + \lambda(DP/P) - e$, which further becomes $i^* + (\lambda - 1)e$ when we assume myopic expectations. When this policy is introduced, it is appropriate to rewrite the $a(k, e)$ function:

$$\hat{a}(k, (1 - \lambda)e - i^*). \tag{12.21}$$

Differentiation of the new *a* function with respect to *e* yields

$$\hat{a}_e = (1 - \lambda)a_e, \tag{12.22}$$

where a_e is the corresponding derivative in the old *a* function. From this it is evident that the sign of $\hat{a}_e$ can be reversed from that of a_e when $\lambda > 1$. Recalling our previous discussion, we recognize that the instability can be removed if $\lambda > 1$, namely, if the government engages itself in a sufficiently vigorous price stabilization policy by means of altering the interest rate. What about a similar policy in terms of the rate of monetary expansion, e.g.,

$$\mu = \mu^* - \lambda(DP/P), \qquad \lambda > 0? \tag{12.23}$$

Interestingly enough, this μ policy has absolutely no effect on the stability property of the model. In reference to equations (12.10) and (12.11), all this does is to replace $\mu - e$ by $\mu^* - (1 + \lambda)e$. The real rate of return on money is not affected directly by the μ policy. The same conclusion has been derived in a similar but more conventional three-asset model dealing with the choice between μ and the bond rate.[2] We must of course be careful in interpreting these results which depend crucially on the way the model is specified. In reality, people's expectations may well depend on the type of μ policy actually chosen; and controlling the (long) rate may not be that simple. But the results suggest at least that the choice of policy instruments for stabilization purposes is important. Even if two instruments have the same effect in the comparative statics sense, they may have different dynamic implications.

We wish to conclude this section with a remark on the dynamic results discussed above. The role of expectations on stability has long been recognized in the literature [see, e.g., Hicks (1939, 1946)]. The result that expectations which are highly sensitive to current changes are detrimental to stability also agrees with our intuition. Essentially the same results have been obtained repeatedly from studies of multiple asset models in general. Monetary growth theory has done a service to provide us with a simple framework in which this basic dynamic property is captured in the choice between money and other assets and in which the important problems concerning stabilization policies are easily handled.

But it would be too hasty to conclude from this that the instability of our economy basically originates in the money sector. By ignoring all the Keynesian problems, namely,

[2]See Stein and Nagatani (1969).

those of an unstable investment function and sticky wages and prices, the neoclassical theory tends to give us a biased view of a dynamic economy. It is therefore necessary to turn our attention to these Keynesian problems.

(D) The Keynes–Wicksell models: The main advantage of introducing money in growth models is to combine the dynamics of resource changes with those of market adjustments. The conventional neoclassical approach has been to dichotomize between the two types of dynamics. When the neoclassicist studies resource dynamics, he takes the market dynamics to always have worked themselves out, while when he studies the market dynamics, he takes resources to remain constant. The neoclassical monetary growth theory discussed so far has followed this convention. Strictly speaking, this dichotomy rests on the assumption that there is a period long enough for markets to clear but short enough for resources not to change. But this is a totally unwarranted assumption. It makes this class of monetary growth models particularly inappropriate as models of short-run dynamics. On the other hand, the conventional short-run models have failed to appreciate the fact that long-run considerations govern the behaviour of the system even in the very short-run. There is a need for a synthesis.

The removal of this dichotomy suggests an approach more in the spirit of Keynes. The main proponent of this alternative approach was Stein (1966, 1970, 1971) who called this class of models the Keynes–Wicksell models. The main features of the Keynes–Wicksell models are: (1) that the investment and savings decisions are made independently with investment taking the lead, (2) that the markets adjust slowly, and (3) that the price changes are explained by the commodity market disequilibria. The following model, adopted from Stein, illustrates the working of the Keynes–Wicksell model. The model deals with an economy where com-

modities, money and bonds exist, along with the two factors
of production, capital and labour.

   The first important building block is the saving–investment
relations. In formulating the investment function, Stein follows the Keynes–Tobin tradition of comparing the value of
existing capital assets (defined as the discounted sum of
expected marginal products over their lifetime) and the supply price (namely, the price of a newly produced unit of
output). Let $R(t)$ be the expected marginal physical product
of existing assets at time t, and $P^e(t)$ be the expected price
of output at time t. Denoting the expected (nominal) interest
rate by $r(t)$, the price of existing assets can be written as

$$\int_0^T R(t)P^e(t) \exp\left\{-\int_0^t r(x)\,dx\right\} dt.$$

If we suppose that investors act on the basis of "averages",
we may rewrite this more simply as

$$P(0)R \int_0^T \exp\{-(r-e)\}\,dt,$$

which, if T is sufficiently large, can be approximated by

$$P(0)R/(r-e),$$

where R and r are appropriate averages of the corresponding
variables defined above, and e is of course a similar average
for expected price changes. Since $P(0)$ is nothing but the
supply price, the ratio of this to $P(0)$, $R/(r-e)$, is equal to
Tobin's q. Investment demand depends positively on the
value of q. Stein writes his investment function as

$$i \equiv I/K = R - r + e - n, \tag{12.24}$$

anticipating the long-run equilibrium conditions that $k \equiv
K/L =$ constant and that $q = 1$. But we shall generally use a
simpler expression,

$$i = i(q), \qquad i_q > 0. \tag{12.24a}$$

It is extremely important to recognize that all these variables

R, e and r (and n for that matter) are expected averages over a very long time period, and hence that equating them with their current values is an invalid procedure, despite the popular practice to do so. This is especially true of R and e for which no markets exist to quote them in the current period. For this reason we denote the long-run average values of these two variables by $\bar{R}$ and $\bar{e}$ and distinguish them from their unbarred current values. As for $\bar{r}$, we represent it by an appropriate current long-term interest rate r.

Next, the savings function, which is also defined as real savings per unit of capital, is assumed to depend on two factors: real output per unit of capital $z(k)$ and net real claims against government per unit of capital θv, where the v are real balances per unit of capital and θ is the total value of the net claims (outside money plus government bonds) per unit of total money stock,

$$s \equiv S/K = s(z(k), \theta v), \qquad s_1 > 0, \qquad s_2 < 0. \qquad (12.25)$$

Possible effects of interest rates on savings are not essential for our analysis and hence are ignored.

The second important feature of the model concerns the way prices change. It is assumed that the proportionate rate of change in commodity prices e is caused primarily by the excess demand for commodities which persist in the short-run. But e may also be influenced directly by $\bar{e}$. Equation (12.26) below assumes that both these forces are at work:

$$e = \bar{e} + \lambda_p(i - s). \qquad (12.26)$$

The coefficient λ_p denotes the speed of adjustment in prices in response to market excess demand. Alternatively, it represents what Lange (1944) called the price flexibility.

The third building block is the behaviour of the financial markets. What Keynes had in mind was clearly a picture of general equilibrium in the multiple markets for financial assets, as we saw in Tobin's exposition. But here we sacrifice such details for operationality and simply represent the financial sector by a standard form of the money market equilibrium. We assume the following demand for money function:

$$m^d \equiv M^d/PK = m(z, R + e, r, \theta v),$$

$$m_1 > 0, \quad m_2 < 0, \quad m_3 < 0,$$

$$0 < \theta m_4 < 1. \quad (12.27)$$

The first element $z(k)$ represents transactions demand for money. The second and the third elements represent the opportunity costs of holding money. Here we used the current values R and e rather than their long-run averages for the reason that speculative activities are short-run in nature. The fourth element θv captures the wealth effect.[3] And finally we assume that the money market clears at all times so that

$$v - m^d = 0. \quad (12.28)$$

The model can be analyzed in steps as follows. First, substitute (12.24a) and (12.25) into (12.26) to get

$$e - \bar{e} - \lambda_p[i(q) - s(z, \theta v)] = 0. \quad (12.29)$$

By combining (12.27) and (12.28), we get

$$v - m(z, R + e, r, \theta v) = 0. \quad (12.30)$$

Equations (12.29) and (12.30) can be solved for (e, r) for given values of $\bar{R}, \bar{e}, k, \theta$ and v. For given levels of these five variables, (1.29) becomes a negatively sloped curve in the (e, r) space. We shall call this an *IS* curve. A similar curve obtained from equation (12.30) is called an *LM* curve. An *LM* curve is also negatively sloped in the same space. But the *LM* curve must have an algebraically greater slope than the *IS* curve as a stability condition.[4] This condition, when written out

---

[3]Real capital is of course part of private wealth. But since we used it as a deflator, it does not appear in this wealth term.

[4]Equation (12.29) and the following dynamic equation associated with (12.30), $Dr = m^d - v$, can be thought of as a pair of differential equations in the variables P and r. Inequality (12.31) is identified as the stability condition for this dynamic system.

in full, becomes

$$1 + \lambda_p i_q q_r(m_2/m_3) > 0. \tag{12.31}$$

Note that this condition imposes a restriction on the size of λ_p for given forms of the behavioural equations. Assuming (12.31), effects on e and r of changes in the five "parameters" are summarized in the table below.

Change in

Effect on	$\bar{e}$	$\bar{R}$	v	θ	k	v subject to $\theta v = $ const.
e	+	+	+	?	?	+
r	−	−	−	?	?	−

The effects of a change in θ are ambiguous. The reason is that an increase in θ shifts both the *IS* curve and the *LM* curve to the right and hence that its effects on e and r depend on the relative magnitudes of the shifts in the two schedules. If the *IS* curve shifts out more (a large s_2 and a small $i_q q_r$) relative to the *LM* curve shift (a small m_4 and large m_2 and m_3), then e tends to rise and r tends to fall. If, on the other hand, the *LM* curve shift is greater relatively than that of the *IS* curve, the effects will be reversed. The ambiguities about the effects of a change in k arises from the ambiguity of its effect on the demand for money. However, if we assumed, as Tobin did, that $m_1 z_k + m_2 R_k$ [where $R(k)$ is now regarded as the current marginal product of capital] is negative, then we will have $\partial e/\partial k < 0$ and $\partial r/\partial k > 0$. Finally, the last column of the table shows the effects of open market operations.

So much for the temporary equilibrium of the model for given levels of the dynamic variables, $\bar{R}$, $\bar{e}$, k and v. To animate such "snap-shots" we must complete the model by specifying the behaviour of these dynamic variables. Stein proceeds in two steps. First, he permits only $\bar{e}$ and v to vary and terms the resulting dynamics short-run dynamics. It is assumed that $\bar{e}$ adjusts itself adaptively to the actual e,

$$D\bar{e} = \lambda_e(e - \bar{e}), \qquad \infty > \lambda_e > 0. \tag{12.32}$$

As for v, he assumes that the nominal money stock is increased at a given rate μ, so that

$$Dv = v(\mu - e), \tag{12.33}$$

where $D \equiv d/dt$. In these equations, e is taken to be a function of $\bar{e}$ and v. It turns out that this dynamic system may or may not have a stable equilibrium and that the stability of the short-run equilibrium is characterized by the condition

$$\lambda_e(e_{\bar{e}} - 1) < e_v v^*, \tag{12.34}$$

where all the derivatives are evaluated at the equilibrium of this dynamic system denoted by $(\bar{e}^*, v^*)$. From the above table, we know that both e_v and $e_{\bar{e}}$ are positive. Indeed $e_{\bar{e}}$ is greater than unity. The condition (12.34) states that in order for this short-run equilibrium to be stable, λ_e, the adjustment speed of inflationary expectation, should not be too large. The choice of v and $\bar{e}$ as variables in the "short-run" dynamics while still holding $\bar{R}$ and k fixed is somewhat arbitrary. But given the choice, the equilibrium of this dynamic system yields a different type of short-run equilibrium. If the previous equilibrium was Keynesian, this is closer to Radner-type temporary equilibrium in the sense that the markets are being cleared and that price expectations are fulfilled. A comparative statics analysis of this equilibrium produces the following results:

Change in

Effect on	$\bar{R}$	k	θ	μ
$\bar{e}^*$	0	0	0	1
v^*	$-$	(-1) sign e_k	(-1) sign e_θ	$-$

This table shows that the equilibrium rate of price change depends directly on the rate of monetary expansion μ and on nothing else. This does not mean, however, that μ has no effects on other variables. The real balances per unit of capital declines with an increase in μ or $\bar{R}$ for obvious reasons. An interesting question in this context is the effect of a change in μ on the rate r. From the above table, and denoting the equilibrium value of r by r^*, we have

$$r^*_\mu = r_{\bar{e}} + r_v \cdot v^*_\mu.$$

The first term is negative and so is r_v from the previous table, but v^*_μ is also negative. Hence the effect of a change in μ on r^* appears to be ambiguous. A little computation shows that

$$\text{sign } r^*_\mu = [+] \, \text{sign}(m_3 - m_2) + [+] \, \text{sign}[1 + \lambda_p i_q q_r (m_2/m_3)],$$

where $[+]$ denotes some positive magnitude. The last term in square brackets on the right is positive under the stability condition (12.31). Thus a sufficient condition that a faster monetary expansion *raises* the interest rate on bonds is that $m_3 \geq m_2$, namely that the demand for real balances be more sensitive to the bond yield than to the yield on physical capital. If indeed $r^*_\mu > 0$ and if changes in prices and interest rates are caused by μ, then e and r will be positively correlated. This gives rise to the phenomenon often referred to as the Gibson Paradox and for which there is substantial supporting evidence.[5] But according to Keynes (1930, vol. I, pp. 198–200), the proposition originally advanced by a Mr. A. H. Gibson was about a positive association between the price *level* and the *nominal* rate of interest, but *not* between the rate of change in the price level and the interest rate. Fisher attempted to explain the Paradox by means of his theory of *real* rate of interest. But his partial model did not serve the purpose (pp. 441–444). In order to explain the

---

[5]For an exposition of the Gibson Paradox, see, e.g., Keynes (1930, vol. II, pp. 198–208) and Fisher (1930, ch. 19). See also Stein (1971, pp. 144–156).

Paradox one needs a general equilibrium model which enables one to study interactions between the real and monetary factors. Keynes, in contrast, distinguished between the real and the monetary factors and attributed the Paradox to the real factors. In his account, the initiating cause was the natural rate of interest. When it begins to fall (rise), banks do not detect and respond to this quickly, so that there is a tendency for the market rate to lag behind and to fall (rise) less than it should if it is to maintain contact with the natural rate. Thus, "when the natural rate is falling, there is a long-period drag on the price level, and contrariwise" (p. 204). The Gibson Paradox reminds us once again of the importance of considering macroeconomic phenomena in an appropriate general equilibrium framework.

Finally, the long-run model is obtained by superimposing the dynamics of real resources and by identifying $\bar{R}$ with the marginal product of capital along its long-run path. In long-run equilibrium we will have prices changing at a rate equalling the difference between the rate of monetary expansion and the natural growth rate and furthermore $q^* = 1$. As Stein (1966) showed, this long-run model reproduces all the Tobin results sketched in the previous section.

(E)   The Keynes–Wicksell Models with Unemployment: As we saw above, the Keynes–Wicksell models stress the dynamics of market adjustments. These models are therefore better suited for short-run analyses than the neoclassical models which assume instantaneous marker clearance. But our model has so far been un-Keynesian in assuming continuous full employment of labour.

The purpose of this section is to extend the model to allow for the possibility of unemployment. For this purpose it is convenient to introduce the notion of money wage flexibility. Just like the price flexibility we introduced earlier, we define money wage flexibility as the percentage rate of change in money wages as a result of a one-percentage change in the excess demand for labour. Besides the excess demand for labour, we assume that inflationary expectations add to wage demands. So we write

$$\frac{DW}{W} = \bar{e}_p + \lambda w \left(\frac{L^d - L^s}{L^s} \right), \tag{12.35}$$

where $\bar{e}_p$ is the expected rate of inflation. In what follows we assume for simplicity that L^s, the supply of labour, is given constant (a "full employment" level of labour) and that the actual employment is always equal to its demand. Under these assumptions, (12.35) is simplified to

$$\frac{DW}{W} = \bar{e}_p + w \left(\frac{L - L^*}{L^*} \right). \tag{12.35a}$$

Equation (12.35a) may be interpreted as a Phillips curve relating the rate of increase in money wages to the rate of unemployment. While it is possible to provide micro-economic accounts of this relation, we shall not go into the details of such theories,[6] because our interest here is in the possibility of prolonged unemployment in the aggregate.

The question is whether an equation like (12.35a) is capable of explaining prolonged unemployment. Here again there is a disagreement between the monetarists and the Keynesions. According to the monetarists, full employment is the only sustainable state. The reasoning seems to be as follows:[7] Let L be on the classical labour demand curve which is a function of the real wage rate $w \equiv W/P$. When expectations have been given enough time to adjust themselves to the actual rate of price changes, $\bar{e}_p$ becomes equal to DW/W for, if not, the real wage would be changing. When DW/W becomes equal to $\bar{e}_p$, however, L must be equal to L^*. And this result is independent of whatever monetary

---

[6]See, e.g., the papers by Phelps and Holt in Phelps (1970).

[7]This is the logical implication of Friedman's view on unemployment. See, e.g., Friedman (1968).

policy is adopted. Monetary policy affects only the sustainable rate of wage–price inflation.

This reasoning raises two questions. First, the behaviour of real wages can only be determined when the behaviour of prices has been specified and appended to (12.35a). When such an equation is appended, will the system of equations generate an automatic force toward full employment? To answer this let us postulate a price adjustment equation of a form symmetric to (12.35),

$$\frac{DP}{P} = \bar{e}_w + \lambda_p \left(\frac{Y^d - Y^s}{Y^s} \right). \tag{12.36}$$

If we retain the assumption that the actual employment is always on a classical labour demand curve, Y^s, the supply of real goods and services, is a mirror image of such a volume of employment, namely, $Y^s = F(L(w))$, say. Y^d, on the other hand, may be assumed to depend on Y^s and the real rate of interest. Thus

$$\frac{DP}{P} = \bar{e}_w + \lambda_p \left(\frac{Y^d(Y^s(w), r - \bar{e}_p) - Y^s(w)}{Y^s(w)} \right). \tag{12.36a}$$

If we take the nominal interest rate r as given (by monetary policy), the right-hand side of (12.36a) is a function of the real wage rate. From (12.35a) and (12.36a) we get

$$\frac{Dw}{w} = (\bar{e}_p - \bar{e}_w) + \lambda_w \frac{L(w) - L^*}{L^*}$$
$$- \lambda_p \left(\frac{Y^d(w, r - \bar{e}_p) - Y^s(w)}{Y^s(w)} \right). \tag{12.37}$$

Equation (12.37) shows that the adjustment in the real wage rate is generally imperfect in the sense that the stationary value of w as implied by (12.37) need not be that which equates L to L^*. And this remains true even after price and wage expectations have worked themselves out. The sustainable level of employment depends crucially on the interest rate chosen. Equation (12.37) also has an important dynamic implication concerning stability. While the real wage rate is expected to exhibit a convergent behaviour with respect to itself (excepting possibly when the excess supply of goods and services is very large), addition of the adjustment equations for expectational variables can easily destabilize the system.

Secondly, from the Keynesian standpoint, the assumption that firms always operate on their classical demand for labour schedule is untenable, for this means that the firms perceive no quantity constraints even in the presence of a deficient demand for goods and services. When such quantity constraints are recognized, the demand curve for labour will be affected in a manner described in Chapter 11. We may express this fact as

$$L^d = F^{-1}[\min(Y^d, Y^s(w))], \tag{12.38}$$

rather than $F^{-1}(Y^s(w))$. In other words, actual Y can fall below $Y^s(w)$ and when it does, Y^d becomes dependent on the actual Y rather than $Y^s(w)$. In such a phase, the self-corrective mechanism of real wages becomes even weaker.

(F) We have presented above a class of dynamic aggregative models in some detail. These models are equipped with all the basic ingredients needed for a comprehensive dynamic analysis – wage and price flexibilities, endogenous expectations, unemployment, and in the long-run version, capital accumulation. The long-run model has suggested the possibility that money may affect real variables permanently in an economy like ours where it is prohibited to pay interest on money. The short-run model has shown the possibility of prolonged unemployment and its coexistence with inflation.

The reader must have noticed our rather loose usage of the term equilibrium. In our short-run models some markets are permitted not to clear. This has been our way of capturing the Keynesian notion of temporary equilibrium. Perhaps there is a more satisfactory way of formulating Keynesian temporary equilibrium models. Some interesting suggestions have appeared lately including Grossman (1974) and Tobin (1975). We hope that the current enthusiasm of the profession for temporary equilibrium studies will soon produce a more acceptable dynamic aggregative model to take the place of both the static *IS–LM* models of Keynesian origin and the all too implicit monetarist models.

References

Cass, C. and M. E. Yaari, "Individual saving, aggregate capital accumulation, and efficient growth", in: K. Shell, ed., *Essays on the theory of optimal economic growth* (Cambridge, Mass., 1967).

Fisher, I., *The theory of interest* (New York, 1930).

Friedman, M., "The role of monetary policy", *American Economic Review* (1968).

Grossman, H. I., "The nature of quantities in market disequilibrium", *American Economic Review* (1974).

Hahn, F. H., "On money and growth", *Journal of Money, Credit & Banking* (1969).

Hicks, J. R., *Value and capital* (Oxford, 1939, 1946).

Johnson, H. G., "Monetary theory and policy", *American Economic Review* (1962); also in his *Essays in monetary economics* (Chicago, Ill., 1967).

Keynes, J. M., *A treatise on money*, Vols. I and II (London, 1930).

Levhari, D. and D. Patinkin, "The role of money in a simple growth model", *American Economic Review* (1968).

Nagatani, K., "A note on Professor Tobin's *Money and economic growth*", *Econometrica* (1970).

Nagatani, K., "A monetary growth model with variable employment", *Journal of Money, Credit & Banking* (1969).

Phelps, E. S., ed., *Microfoundations of employment and inflation theory* (New York, 1970).

Samuelson, P. A., "An exact consumption – loan model of interest with or without the social contrivance of money", *Journal of Political Economy* (1958); also in his *Collected scientific papers*, Vol. 1.

Sidrauski, M., "Rational choice and patterns of growth in a monetary economy", *American Economic Review* (1967).

Stein, J. L., "Money and capacity growth", *Journal of Political Economy* (1966).

Stein, J. L., "Monetary growth theory in perspective", *American Economic Review* (1970).

Stein, J. L., *Money and capacity growth* (New York, 1971).

Stein, J. L. and K. Nagatani, "Stabilization policies in a growing economy", *Review of Economic Studies* (1969).

Tobin, J., "Money and economic growth", *Econometrica* (1965).

Tobin, J., "Keynesian models of recession and depression", *American Economic Review* (1975).

13

On the Theory of
Monetary Policy

(A)   Monetary theory was once regarded as the theory of
the determination of the absolute price level, no more and no
less. We have come a long way from that naive state of
understanding and have learned from experience, if not from
theory, that money has played a major role in the development of efficient and sophisticated economic systems such as
ours. But we have also learned that the efficiency of our
economic system is not only disrupted severely from time to
time by some shocks but is constantly exposed to fluctuations due to less obvious causes. What are the causes of
these recurring fluctuations and what can be done about
them? Is money contributing to these disturbances through
its own "misbehaviour", and if so, how? Further, is money a
proper instrument of stabilization policies designed to abate
or eliminate them and how does it compare with fiscal policy
in this regard? If money can be effective as a means of
stabilizing the economy, what will a desirable policy formula
look like? These are the fundamental questions to be answered by the theory of monetary policy. To answer them
would require a thorough understanding of the role money
plays in the economy both in theory and in practice. But
there is no broad agreement among economists about any
one of these questions. Despite the much publicized controversies between the monetarists and the Keynesians there

seems to be no clear sign of convergence to a more unified view on the relevant issues.

Given this state of affairs, the best we can do is to present a critical review of the controversies and indicate where to go from there. In Section B we first take up the monetarists' claims of the relative importance of monetary policy over fiscal policy and their supporting evidence. Section C looks at the Keynesians' stand on the same subject. Section D turns to the long-run aspect of monetary policy which became well known as a result of Friedman's optimum quantity thesis. Section E concludes the chapter with some remarks on the general subject of monetary policy and the prospects for the future.

(B) The quantity theory is a very simple theory. Written in the form of an equilibrium condition, it is summarized by the following equation:

$$Y = vM^s, \qquad\qquad (13.1)$$

where Y = the money income, v = the velocity of circulation of money, and M^s = the existing money stock. Because the theory is relatively simplistic, many issues are left implicit and hence it is capable of a wide variety of interpretations. It is mainly through the exploitation of these large degrees of freedom in interpretation that Friedman revitalized the quantity theory and has since made this seemingly innocuous equation a powerful weapon in a counter-attack on the Keynesian approach. In the rest of this section we shall study the monetarists' claims focussing on the following interrelated points: (1) the interest elasticity of the v function, (2) the relative efficiency of monetary policy over fiscal policy, and most importantly, (3) the causation from M^s to Y.

(1) First, the interest elasticity of the v function. In the old version of the quantity theory, velocity was largely an institutional constant and was not expected to depend on

interest rates. When Friedman restated the theory, v became a function of a variety of interest rates, including expected rates of inflation or deflation. Since Friedman's derivation of the demand for money function was based on a perfectly general model of asset choice, v will even include what Keynes called the marginal efficiency of capital. When v is made to depend on these interest rates, the causal relationship from M^s to Y (even if it existed) is unlikely to be very stable. The reader will recall that this was the reason Keynes abandoned the quantity theory. But Friedman did not. In Friedman's earlier view (1956, 1959), v was in fact almost completely interest-inelastic. Hence, despite the introduction of interest rates, they did not alter the theory's main conclusion. Since that time, however, Friedman seems to have changed his position. In his 1966 article, he said (p. 72):

> "I know no empirical student of the demand for money who denies that interest rates affect the real quantity of money demanded – though others have misinterpreted me as so asserting."

In what sense, then, does the quantity of money determine money or nominal income? On this point Friedman (p. 76, my emphasis) states:

> "If interest rates enter the demand function for money, it is clearly impossible to predict the level of nominal income or of prices solely from the nominal quantity of money. Knowledge of the interest rate, which is to say, indirectly of the real forces affecting the interest rate, is necessary to get a numerical value of velocity. However, *if interest rates are stable*, knowledge of interest rates is not necessary to predict changes in nominal income or in prices ..."

In his 1972 article, Friedman takes a stand that "the slope of the *LM* curve is not the key difference ..." (p. 906).

In short what Friedman is telling us is that barring

changes arising from the real sector, v remains quite stable and consequently, the relation between M^s and Y is also direct and predictable. If the historical record indicates a stable relationship between M^s and Y, it must then be the case that during the past century, there have been few significant changes due to real forces and that most of the observed changes have been due to monetary factors (provided one can establish the causal relation from M^s to Y). It is a short step from here to Friedman's well-known accusation of money's misbehaviour and his proposal for automatic rules. The question is: Are fluctuations in our economy caused by real forces or monetary forces? We note that this is where the most fundamental disagreement exists between monetarists and Keynesians. The latter, as we saw in Chapters 10 and 11, holds the view that fluctuations are typically due to real forces related to variations in expectations and the rate of return on physical capital required to clear the market for these existing capital goods. Thus the Great Depression in the 1930's becomes an important proof of real forces disturbing the economy from the Keynesians' point of view, whereas to the monetarists it is a rare exception.[1]

Two issues arise in this connection. First, how can we possibly separate disturbances due to real forces from those due to monetary forces? At the theoretical level no one has come up with a satisfactory answer although there have been some interesting attempts.[2] In the absence of guidance from theory the issue has become an empirical one, and Friedman claims to have presented conclusive proof of his position. The second issue therefore is whether he has established beyond doubt, on the basis of time series evidence, that fluctuations

[1] But Friedman and Schwartz devoted a large space of their *Monetary History* to the study of the Depression, as we saw in Chapter 10. It is strange that the Keynesians should not have done a detailed study comparable to theirs. See, however, Kindleberger (1973) and Temin (1976).

[2] See, e.g., Rose (1969). Rose defines "real" cycles as those which occur under Say's Identity, and "monetary" cycles as those which occur under Walras' Law but in the absence of Say's Identity.

have been primarily due to monetary disturbances. We shall come back to this issue in connection with the above-mentioned causation problem.

(2) Next, as for the relative effectiveness of monetary policy over fiscal policy, the monetarists adopt the position that pure fiscal policy, namely, an increase in government spending unaccompanied by an increase in money stock, will only have a negligible effect on money income, whereas monetary policy, namely, an increase in the money stock, will have a significant expansionary effect. The reason for the failure of pure fiscal policy is the so-called "crowding-out" effect; increased government spending will directly compete with private spending to yield a very small net increase in aggregate expenditure. In terms of the *IS–LM* model, this position may be described by the assumptions of a vertical *LM* curve (the interest insensitivity of the demand for money) and an almost horizontal *IS* curve (the high interest elasticity of the aggregate demand for goods and services), although the *IS* curve never plays an important role in the monetarists' analysis. But now that they have accepted the possibility of a positive interest elasticity of the demand for money, the slope of the *LM* curve can be of any size and the monetarists' claim will no longer be valid in the general case. Thus, in his 1972 commentary article, Friedman abandons the vertical *LM* argument completely and switches to the "second-round" effect through wealth changes. Let a once and for all bond-financed increase in government spending take place. This causes a rightward shift in the *IS* curve with the *LM* curve remaining constant. Call the increase in income due to such a shift in the *IS* curve the "first-round" effect of the fiscal policy action. This is the usual textbook answer on the effect of pure fiscal policy. But it is not the complete answer. The public now has a greater (nominal) amount of government bonds, and the amount of government bonds issued will increase until income has risen sufficiently so that the increased taxes (at fixed tax rates)

match the initial increase in government spending. The increase in the amount of government bonds issued is likely to depress their market price, and to that extent, the market value of government bonds will not keep pace with their nominal amount. Exactly what happens to the market value of government bonds as well as those of other assets is a matter to be decided in a general equilibrium framework of asset markets. In any case, however, some change will occur to the market value of assets or more simply the wealth held by the public. Let us suppose that private wealth increases as a result of the above-mentioned government action. An increase in wealth will probably induce the public: (1) to increase their current spending, and (2) to increase their demand for money *at given levels of interest rates and income.* This means that the *IS* curve shifts further out, while the *LM* curve shifts in or to the left. These shifts in the schedules induced by a wealth change give rise to the "second-round" effect. The direction of the second-round effect can be either expansionary or contractionary. Friedman now states (p. 922):

> "One way to characterize the Keynesian approach is that it gives almost exclusive importance to the first-round effect. This leads it to attach importance primarily to flows of spending rather than to stocks of assets. Similarly, one way to characterize the quantity theory approach is to say that it gives almost no importance to first-round effects.
>
> The empirical question is how important the first-round effects are compared to the ultimate effects."

Friedman's new view is therefore that the second-round effect almost offsets the first-round effects. For this result to hold, he would like the secondary (rightward) shift of the *IS* curve to be small, and the leftward shift of the *LM* curve to be large. While this is ultimately an empirical question, Friedman's assertion raises a number of questions at the theoretical level. First, the size of the second-round effect is not independent of the slopes of the two schedules. The flatter the *IS* curve, that is, the stronger the crowding-out effect, the smaller will be the effect on income of the second-round shift of the *IS* curve. Similarly, the steeper the *LM* curve, the stronger will be the contractionary effect on income of the leftward shift of the *LM* curve. So he cannot afford to ignore the slopes of these schedules. Second, Blinder and Solow (1973) have shown the possibility that a bond-financed government spending may be more expansionary in its ultimate effect than a similar government spending financed by money creation.

Turning now to the empirical evidence, we already described the major conclusion of the Friedman–Meiselman study. More recently, Andersen and Jordan (1968), two economists at the Federal Bank of St. Louis, have come up with an empirical study further supporting the monetarists' position. Using U.S. data for the sixties, Andersen and Jordan regressed quarterly changes in nominal *GNP* against both quarterly changes in the money stock and government deficits in the current and in the two preceding quarters. They found that many of the coefficients on money variables were both statistically significant and positive and large, while the coefficients on the fiscal variables were mostly insignificant and very small. Although the Andersen–Jordan results are at variance with those obtained by a number of large-scale econometric models (e.g., the Federal Reserve–MIT model, the Wharton School model, The Commerce Department model and the Michigan model), the results of both the Friedman–Meiselman and Andersen–Jordan studies seem to indicate that the monetarists' claim for the relative effectiveness of monetary policy may be correct. But is this the only possible interpretation of these empirical results? To answer this question we need to investigate the causality issue in some detail.

(3) In order for the monetarists' interpretation of these empirical results to be valid, M^s must cause Y, and not the other way round. Put another way, M^s, the supply of money, must be independent of demand. Strangely enough, monetarists have not given us a convincing argument on this crucial issue. We recall that Friedman made only a passing remark on this point in his *Restatement* (my emphasis):

> "The quantity theorist *holds* that there are important factors affecting the supply of money that do not affect the demand for money."

This is merely an assertion which calls for a proof. Friedman appears to have given us two answers. One is that M^s *can* change independently. But this is no proof that M^s has actually been changing autonomously. History indicates rather the opposite. The old "real-bills" doctrine implies a completely passive response of M^s to demand. The wartime period in which interest rates were pegged does not provide favorable evidence either. Indeed the Keynesian practice of controlling interest rates very much obscures the autonomy of M^s.

The other answer is an empirical one that changes in M^s have consistently preceded changes in Y over business cycles. But this seems only natural. Take an example of a firm which has just found a promising investment opportunity due to a new invention. Having laid out a detailed blueprint of the new investment project, the firm will first go to its bank for a loan to finance this project. Actual execution of the project will take place subsequent to, and conditional upon, the acquisition of such a loan. In other words, in this example, a monetary increase precedes spending. This is the fundamental feature of a monetary economy in which everyone is required to back his spending with cash. The fact that changes in M^s precede changes in Y is no evidence of the autonomy of M^s, nor is it meaningful, to interpret this fact as money being the determinant of Y. The only meaningful chain of causation in the above example is that from the invention or the consequent increase in the marginal efficiency of capital to changes in Y. And it is with exactly this type of causation that Keynesians are concerned. The point is that even when the initial change took place in the real side, a change in M^s can still precede a change in Y and the correlation between them can be quite high. We must therefore conclude that the monetarists have not really proved their case, at least using the type of arguments discussed above.

(C) Let us now turn to the Keynesians' arguments. Apart from differences in beliefs, perhaps the most important distinction between monetarists and Keynesians is in terms of their approaches to monetary issues. Whereas the former confine themselves to a single money equation, Keynesians insist on a general equilibrium framework including all other types of financial assets and physical capital. As the Tobin model we sketched in Chapter 11 illustrates, such an asset market general equilibrium model leads to a solution for a set of interest rates which are the crucial variables in terms of which any policy effects are to be assessed. The model refuses to adopt a short cut linking the money stock to income. Rather it forces us to spell out channels through which any particular policy works itself out. Another important feature of this type of model is that they recognize and incorporate factors representing sources of change due to real factors. In the Tobin model, these factors are the marginal efficiency of capital and the expected rate of inflation.

But faced with a vector of interest rates, how should one go about assessing the effects of monetary policy? For example, should we somehow average these rates and evaluate the policy effect on this average rate? Or, should we pick one rate which seems to be the most important? Keynesians have conventionally picked the "required" rate of return on real capital as the critical rate. Thus [Tobin and Brainard (1963, p. 387)]:

> "A monetary control can be considered expansionary if it lowers the rate of return on ownership of real capital, and deflationary if it raises that rate of return."

In terms of the Tobin model in Chapter 11, this means the following: Assume for simplicity that capital goods last forever. Let R be the marginal efficiency of capital relative to reproduction cost. Denote this cost by P. The market price of the existing capital goods, on the other hand, is Pq, which is the market-clearing price of these capital goods. Thus if an investor purchases one unit of these capital goods at the market price, the rate of return to him will be R/q. This is the required rate of return on real capital mentioned above. For a given level of R, this critical rate is inversely related to q. A monetary policy action is therefore expansionary if it raises q; it is deflationary if it lowers q. According to Tobin's comparative statics results,[3] an increase in the money stock, whether accompanied or unaccompanied by a matching reduction in government bonds outstanding, has an expansionary effect. But the results also show that a decrease in R depresses q. Thus when R is changing on its own, but behind the scenes, observed correlation between M^s and Y becomes unreliable and meaningless. Brainard and Tobin (1968) have constructed a dynamic model based on their previous general equilibrium models and have performed a simulation study of the manner in which the model adjusts to a number of cyclical variations in exogenous variables such as income, the marginal efficiency of capital, government spending and the capital stock. They have found that leads and lags do not provide information about causa-

---

[3]See Chapter 11 above. For a more detailed analysis in a multiple asset framework, see Brainard (1964).

tion and furthermore that the lead or the lag of any particular endogenous variable itself varies with the choice of the exogenous variable as the source of fluctuation. In the absence of a priori knowledge of the source of fluctuation, there is very little that one can conclude from examining the data.

The question therefore once again boils down to the identification of the fundamental causes of economic fluctuations. The single most important empirical study to date in this context is the Federal Reserve–MIT econometric model (1967) of the U.S. economy. This model was built with the specific purpose of investigating how monetary forces would affect the economy. In their analysis (1968, 1969) of the FR–MIT model, de Leeuw and Gramlich identify and evaluate the following three channels through which monetary policies operate:

(1) Cost of capital → Volume of investment (and consumption).
(2) Rates of return on bonds → Value of wealth → Volume of consumption.
(3) Credit rationing → Composition of investment.

The first channel is the one stressed by Tobin and other Keynesians. de Leeuw and Gramlich first obtain an empirical measure of the cost of capital and then examine its effects on various types of investment. The second channel is the well-known wealth effect. The third channel recognizes the sluggish response of interest rates and the incidence of disequilibrium in the loanable funds market on different types of investment. The model indicates that investment in housing is strongly affected through this third channel. On the basis of these preliminary investigations, de Leeuw and Gramlich first analyze the effects of a specific monetary policy (a billion dollar increase in unborrowed reserves starting in the 1st quarter of 1964 and maintained throughout). The results of de Leeuw and Gramlich (1969, p.

487) show: (1) that investment (including residential construction) is mainly affected through the first channel, (2) that personal consumption expenditures are primarily affected through the second channel, although they are also sensitive to the cost-of-capital factor, and (3) that in terms of the total *GNP*, the first two channels (and in that order) account for most of its variations, although the relative contributions of the three channels vary with the time period of assessment. The authors proceed to a similar analysis of a specific fiscal policy (a five billion dollar increase in the Federal government compensation of employees), which indicate that fiscal policy works more rapidly than monetary policy.

As these studies indicate, the Keynesians' story is very different from that told by the monetarists. This gap calls for an explanation. Whether or not those empirical issues can ever be conclusively resolved is an open question, but it is evident that a more dynamic, disaggregated approach is needed for further progress.

(D) In this section we by-pass short-run complications and focus our attention on the long-run equilibrium. In a long-run equilibrium where a dynamic system has settled on a stationary or a balanced growth path, we expect a fairly simple set of relations between the real and the monetary variables. In such a state, the position of equilibrium and the implied level of social welfare can be thought of as a function of a set of policy variables. In the simple growth models presented in Chapter 12, the long-run equilibrium of the economy depends on the policy parameter μ, the rate of monetary expansion. One can then ask the following comparative statics question: What value of μ maximizes the level of social welfare? This is the problem of what Friedman termed an optimum quantity of money. His analysis and conclusion, along with some criticisms, are sketched below.

Before we begin describing Friedman's paper (1969), it is perhaps best to ask why individual decisions should result in a "suboptimal" state. This would then help to clarify what he means by a monetary optimum.[4]

It should be recalled that when we studied the stationary state of a personal equilibrium, we arrived at the conditions (1.31):

$$P_k[f(k^*) - k^*] + Y - px^* = 0,$$

$$u_x^* - \lambda^* p = 0,$$

$$u_m^* - \frac{\delta}{1 + \delta} p_m \lambda^* = 0,$$

$$f'(k^*) - (1 + \delta) = 0.$$

Recall that δ was a positive rate of time preference held by an immortal individual. In his optimal stationary state, the amount of productive capital k^* is determined directly in terms of such δ (just as in the Sidrauski model). The amount of his consumption x^* is determined by this k^*, and the marginal utility of consumption, in turn, equals the shadow price of the stationary income. What is important for our purpose here is the second last equation, which states that the individual holds money up to the point where the marginal utility of money is equal to the shadow price of income multiplied by $p_m \cdot \delta/(1 + \delta)$, or in short, the marginal utility of money remains positive when δ is positive (we are of course assuming that the individual cannot be satiated with consumption and hence that λ^* is positive). As the last equation shows, the δ represents the net real interest in the stationary state. In other words, when there is a positive interest, the individual regards this as the cost of holding money. But what if the cost of changing the quantity of money was very low or free from the society's point of view? If so, the opportunity cost as viewed by the individual would be out of line with the social marginal cost of providing an additional unit of money. As Samuelson pointed out, this is the fun-

---

[4]For similar discussions, the reader is referred to the Feige–Parkin paper in Chapter 4 and Samuelson (1969). Clower (1968) expresses an entirely negative view on such an optimality concept.

damental nature of the suboptimality of laissez faire and the reason for studying the problem of monetary optimum. A monetary optimum is defined by a state where $u_m^* = SMC$ (social marginal cost of providing an additional unit of money). Given SMC, how can we induce individuals to hold money so as to satisfy the above equation? This, in brief, is the optimality problem as conceived by Friedman. For an interesting related study, see Bailey (1956). More recently, Barro (1972) has elaborated on the same issue.

Friedman considers a stationary society with a constant population with constant tastes and a given state of the arts. To justify the use of money, Friedman assumes that the society, though stationary, is not static in the sense that individuals are subject to uncertainty and change, while aggregates are constant. Even the aggregates may change in a stochastic manner around constant mean values. Individuals are assumed to be infinitely lived. The money in the society is all fiat money. In addition to money, there are two other types of assets, bonds (perpetuities) and real capital. Friedman distinguishes between real capital held by business enterprises and equities held by ultimate wealth owners. But since the distinction is inessential, we shall speak of real capital alone. The economy is also assumed to be perfectly competitive.

His first step is to distinguish between the two different kinds of returns each of these assets offers to the owner, i.e., (1) the values of non-pecuniary services, and (2) the (real) rate of pecuniary return. The non-pecuniary services of money consists mainly in reducing the number of trips to the bank and other stores, and in providing a feeling of security against possible contingencies. Additionally, the non-pecuniary services of money include "satisfaction from being wealthy". This last type of services is shared by all other forms of assets. Besides, Friedman assumes the productive services of money, but we shall ignore this return here. If we measure non-pecuniary services in dollar values, the two kinds of returns are made comparable. For each asset j ($j = m, b, k$, say), what matters is the sum of these two kinds of return, which may be written as $MNPS_j + r_j$, where *MNPS* stands for the marginal (dollar) value of non-pecuniary services, and r_j is the marginal real rate of return. If the three types of assets were to be held simultaneously in an individual's portfolio, it must be true that $MNPS_j + r_j$ are the same for all j. The real rate of return on money is by convention equal to $-DP/P$, the (anticipated) rate of deflation.

Consider a stationary state in which the immortal individuals have all settled into a stationary pattern of action. What would the common values ($MNPS_j + r_j$) be equal to in such a stationary state? They would be equal to the internal rate of discount at zero saving which he denotes $IRD(0)$.[5] In particular, for money,

$$(- DP/P)^* + MNPS_m = IRD(0). \tag{13.2}$$

Suppose $IRD(0)$ were known. What would be the condition for a monetary optimum if, in fact, changing the quantity of money is costless from the society's point of view? The condition would clearly be that

$$(- DP/P)^* = IRD(0), \qquad MNPS_m = 0, \tag{13.3}$$

i.e., the convenience yield of money at the margin, $MNPS_m$, be zero. At such a point the individual would be satiated with "liquidity". Thus the optimum is described by the rule that the value of money appreciate at the rate equalling the internal rate of discount prevailing in the stationary state. In order to ensure the existence of such a satiation point, Friedman makes a contrived effort. In particular, he assumes that while "money dominates bonds in the provision of non-pecuniary services" ($MNPS_m > MNPS_b$) when both yield positive services, there is a point, due to abundant

---

[5]Friedman thinks of the *IRD* as a function of saving. He also considers the possibility that the *IRD* is a function of the level of consumption and the wealth–income ratio, but makes little use of them.

holdings of both money and bonds, where they simultaneously become zero ($MNPS_m = MNPS_b = 0$) after which point, $0 > MNPS_b > MNPS_m$. His discussion in this context is least convincing.

Finally, Friedman attempts to calculate the magnitude of welfare gain that could be realized if the U.S. economy moved to such an optimum. To do so, he first specifies the demand for money function. Using the data for early 1968 he estimates the quantity of high-powered money to be about six weeks' personal disposable income, which provides a "minimum" estimate of the quantity of "money". When he allows for other non-interest-bearing money, he estimates it to be about ten weeks' personal disposable income (he added one half of demand deposits). This figure he uses as a "maximum" estimate. Note that these quantities of money demanded are conditioned by what people thought to be the anticipated rate of price inflation at that time. Friedman assumes that the anticipated rate of inflation was 2% per annum.

Now suppose that the internal rate of discount was 5%. This would mean that the optimum rate of deflation was 5% which implies a 7 percentage point decline in the cost of holding non-interest-bearing balances. By how much would the quantity demanded of money increase if we were to move to the optimum state?

He assumes a demand for money function of the Cagan–Bailey type,

$$\log M = a - 10(DP/P)^*. \tag{13.4}$$

According to this demand function, a 7 percentage point decline in $(DP/P)^*$ raises $\log M$ by 0.7. The antilog of 0.7 is about 2, meaning that money balances would slightly more than double. The money balances would have increases from 6 weeks' to 12 weeks' personal disposable income, if we use the "minimum" estimate. Assuming that the $MNPS_m$ was initially 7% but is zero in the optimum, and adopting a simple averaging device, the welfare gain per weeks' personal disposable income is calculated as

$$\frac{(0.007) - 0.00)}{2}(12 - 6) = 0.21.$$

Multiplying this by personal disposable income, the welfare gain corresponding to the assumption of 5% $IRD(0)$ and the "minimum" estimation of the quantity of money is calculated to be 2.3 billion dollars per year for the U.S. economy whose capitalized value (at 5% discount) is 46 billion dollars. The welfare again calculated in this manner increases with an increase in the money base and the internal rate of discount. For the "maximum" estimate of money and for the internal rate of discount of 33% (initially) and 17% (terminally), the flow welfare gain becomes 105 billion dollars per year, and its capitalized value (at the terminal discount rate of 17%) rises to 630 billion dollars.

Friedman's analysis is not convincing in a number of respects. Does such an optimum exist? Why does holding of real balances become more costly than holding bonds after a certain point? Is the demand function (13.4) valid when bonds and real capital are allowed for? What would happen to other rates of return when $(-DP/P)^*$ is changed? How can one estimate $IRD(0)$ especially when individuals are mortal? What sort of time path should we follow if we were to move to the proposed optimum from the present inflationary state? What would be the order of magnitude of such adjustment costs? In short, Friedman's analysis is peculiarly lacking in three important ingredients: (1) an explicit general equilibrium analysis, (2) an analysis of dynamics leading to and revolving around such an optimum, and (3) an analysis of risk and uncertainty. This is a remarkable feature, given the nature of his inquiry. The extent to which considerations of some of these neglected aspects, in particular (3), affect the conclusion can be seen from Tobin's discussion below on the same subject.

Tobin (1968), in contrast to Friedman, laid an emphasis on uncertainty and risk. Various forms of assets can only

promise uncertain returns to their owners. Part of such
uncertainty or risk is social in nature, e.g., uncertainty concerning technological changes, taste changes, changes in the
economic environment imposed by the rest of the world, etc.
But a large part of uncertainty or risk as perceived by
individuals is private in nature. Individuals naturally base
their decisions on the total risk, social and private. But from
the society's point of view, there is no reason why social
decisions should be influenced by private risks. Various
insurance schemes are the devices the market economy has
developed to cover or reallocate these private risks, but
informational and other difficulties prevent these private
insurance schemes from developing to the full. The problem
is how to induce individuals, who are subject to private risks
in addition to social risks, to behave in such a manner that
the social decisions arising out of their collective behaviour
reflect social risks but not the private ones.

The role of money in this context is one of providing these
individuals with an alternative, safe (or safer, we should say)
store of value. The introduction of such a safe asset
generally influences individuals' intertemporal allocation
decisions. But the most important effect is that such a safe
asset, when made sufficiently attractive to risk-averse individuals, is capable of shifting out the opportunity locus
subjectively perceived by such an individual toward the
social opportunity locus which is free from private risks. In
this sense the problem of monetary optimum is to determine
the extent to which the government or the monetary
authority should render the benefit of such social insurance
by using the "faith and credit" embodied in them. Tobin
provides a graphical illustration of his discussion using
Mean-Variance analysis. But the answer in this case is bound
to be complex. The major problem seems to be the general
indeterminancy of the discounted price of money. In
Arrow's terminology in Chapter 8, the present money is a
composite security promising to pay a certain number of
units of money for all outcomes. In the absence of complete

contingent markets, the discounted price of such a security is not uniquely determined. So even if there is no gap between private risks and social risks, there is a fundamental ambiguity about the optimal rate of return on money.

By manipulating such a composite security alone, the government will not be able to attain *the* social optimum. In order to attain it, the government would have to fill in a sufficient number of instruments, wherever the private markets fail to do, so that these instruments may cover all the contingencies. This would mean that the notion of monetary optimum becomes a much more complex problem requiring an extensive intervention of the government in the financial markets at large, and not just in the narrowly defined money market alone. Short of this ideal situation, one would be dealing with some constrained optima and a variety of corresponding optimal rules. Another problem concerning the notion of monetary optimum is the problem of stability. Given that a competitive system with multiple capital goods has inherent elements of instability, how can money be used to stabilize the system? As our model in Chapter 12 suggests, the policy of holding μ constant may be inappropriate in this regard. Looked at from these standpoints, we must conclude that the question of monetary optimum is bound to be a much more complex question even in the long-run than some answers in the literature suggest it to be.

(E) It is evident from what we have seen that despite decades of serious research, our knowledge of the role of money in economic activity is still far from complete. The monetarists' claim that money matters (in some overriding sense), which is based on observed high correlation between money stock and money income, leaves many fundamental questions unanswered. Is the stock of money really an independent variable causing changes in money income, or is money income affected primarily by real forces, with the money stock passively responding to changes in income?

Assuming that money is the principal causal factor, through what channels does money work out its effects? The monetarists' position is that the real part of our system is basically stable and that money is the cause of disturbances, whereas the Keynesians' position is just the reverse. The reader will notice that this has for long been the central issue in business cycle studies. The Monetarist–Keynesian controversy is essentially this same old issue in another guise. The productivity of the controversy has, however, been limited because of the reluctance on the part of monetarists to spell out their theory in sufficient detail so as to provide specific testable hypotheses capable of being confirmed or rejected by the data.

While wide margins of uncertainty about the role of money continue to exist, there is some evidence that monetarists are gaining popularity as regards the current practice of monetary policy. The Federal Reserve System (FRS) of the United States has changed the principles upon which it bases it's policy considerably in this direction in the past several years. The most important body responsible for the formation and execution of the System's policy is the Federal Open Market Committee (FOMC) headed by the Chairman of the Board of Governors of the FRS.[6] The FOMC meets every four weeks and issues a directive to a senior officer of the Federal Reserve Bank of New York called the Manager of the System Open Market Account. The directive consists of two paragraphs. The first paragraph contains statements about recent key economic and financial developments and also a general statement of current goals of the System. The second paragraph contains the FOMC's instructions to the Manager for guiding open market operations in the interval between FOMC meetings. Prior to 1966, the operating instructions made reference to various in-

---

[6]Other members consist of the six other members of the Board of Governors of the FRS, the president of the Federal Reserve Bank of New York, and four of the remaining eleven Reserve Bank presidents.

dicators of money market conditions such as member bank borrowings at the Federal Reserve discount window, the net reserve position of member banks, the interest rate on Federal Funds and the Treasury bill rate. Beginning in 1966, the FOMC supplemented the reference to money market conditions with a reference to certain monetary aggregates, such as bank credit, and later the money supply (typically M_1 and M_2). This reference was contained in a proviso clause until 1970. In 1970, when the present Chairman Aurthur Burns took office, the emphasis on monetary. aggregates increased sharply (the second paragraph of the directive issued on March 10, 1970; my emphasis):

> "To implement this policy, the Committee desires to see moderate growth in money and bank credit over the months ahead. System open market operations until the next meeting of the Committee shall be conducted *with a view fo maintaining money market conditions consistent with that objective.*"

In practice, the FOMC now sets target growth rates of monetary aggregates several times a year.[7] This means that its time horizon is about two to three months. Given such target rates, the new idea of the Federal Reserve System is to keep the actual rates within certain tolerance limits around the target rates leaving interest rates and liquidity conditions to conform to monetary aggregates. Actual growth rates of monetary aggregates are computed over two-month periods. Whenever the actual rates get out of the tolerance limits, vigorous market operations are conducted to bring them back in line.

While we are not in a position to fully evaluate the effects of the new policy rule of the Federal Reserve System on economic activity, two things are to be noted. First, short-

---

[7]For a concise summary of the recent history of open market policy, see *Federal Reserve Bulletin*, February 1971.

term interest rates have shown wide fluctuations in the past
five years. Whether these fluctuations are due to the new
policy or due to exogenous shocks is yet to be determined.
But these fluctuations may be an indication of the instability
in the demand for money function.[8] Second, despite explicit
specification of target rates, actual growth rates of money
stocks have shown wide variations in the same period.
During the year between March 1974 and March 1975, for
example, the two-month growth rates of M_1, translated into
annual rates, ranged from minus one percent to eleven
percent, whereas the target rate was in the 5–6 percent
range. The reason for this is again not clear. But this fact
may be an indication that the Federal Reserve System does
not have tight enough control over money stocks.

We must conclude that we need much further work before
we come to a better understanding of the role of money in
our economy. By the very pervasive nature of money, such
work will necessarily involve complex exercises in dynamic
general equilibrium models. Traditionally monetary
economics have had two biases. One is the bias toward
partial equilibrium methods in which the real part of the
system is treated as given or is very incompletely specified.
The other is the bias toward empirical methods of an
episodical kind which have very little to do with theory.
These biases may be attributable to the lack of an adequate
theory of a monetary economy. The recent rise in interest
among many competent economists in the problems of temporary equilibrium and money is encouraging in this regard.
We hope that a workable model of a monetary economy, as
sketched by Keynes (1936, pp. 193–194), will soon come out

---

[8]Indeed, there is now some evidence that the FRS is not entirely
satisfied with the policy of attempting to control the money stock only.
See, e.g., the recent revealing testimony of Burns to the Senate committee
on Banking, Housing and Urban Affairs (reprinted in *Federal Reserve
Bulletin*, March 1975), where Burns complains about the difficulty of the M_1
policy largely on Keynesian grounds.

of present research efforts which will then provide better guidance to empirical studies on this complex but important subject of money.

References

Andersen, L. and J. Jordan, "Monetary and fiscal actions: A test of their relative importance in economic stabilization", *Federal Reserve Bank of St. Louis Monthly Review* (Nov. 1968).

Bailey, M. J., "The welfare cost of inflationary finance", *Journal of Political Economy* (1956); also in: K. J. Arrow and T. Scitovsky, eds., *Readings in welfare economics* (Homewood, Ill., 1969).

Barro, R. J., "Inflationary finance and the welfare cost of inflation", *Journal of Political Economy* (1972).

Blinder, A. S. and R. M. Solow, "Does fiscal policy matter?", *Journal of Public Economics* (1973).

Brainard, W. C., "Financial intermediaries and a theory of monetary control", *Yale Economic Essays* (1964); also in: D. D. Hester and J. Tobin, eds., *Financial markets and economic activity* (New York, 1967).

Brainard, W. C. and J. Tobin, "Pitfalls in financial model building", *American Economic Review* (1968).

Clower, R. W., "Comment: The optimal growth rate of money", *Journal of Political Economy* (1968).

De Leeuw, F. and E. M. Gramlich, "The channels of monetary policy", *Federal Reserve Bulletin* (Jan. 1968 and June 1969).

Friedman, M., "The quantity theory of money: A restatement", in: M. Friedman, ed., *Studies in the quantity theory of money* (Chicago, Ill., 1956).

Friedman, M., "The demand for money: Some theoretical and empirical results", *Journal of Political Economy* (1959).

Friedman, M., "Interest rates and the demand for money", *Journal of Law and Economics* (1966).

Friedman, M., "The optimum quantity of money", in his *The optimum quantity of money and other essays* (Chicago, Ill., 1969).

Friedman, M., "Comments on the critics", *Journal of Political Economy* (1972).

Keynes, J. M., *The general theory of employment, interest and money* (London, 1936).

Kindleberger, C. P., *The world in depression 1929–39* (Berkeley, Calif., 1973).

Rose, H., "Real and monetary factors in the business cycle", *Journal of Money, Credit & Banking* (1969).

Samuelson, P. A., "Nonoptimality of money holding under laissez faire", *Canadian Journal of Economics* (1969).
Tobin, J., "Notes on optimal monetary growth", *Journal of Political Economy* (1968).
Tobin, J. and W. C. Brainard, "Financial intermediaries and the effectiveness of monetary control", *American Economic Review* (1963); also in: D. D. Hester and J. Tobin, eds., *Financial markets and economic activity* (New York, 1967).

Index of Names

Index of Subjects